DS

Kitchener's Men

Kitchener's Men

The King's Own Royal Lancasters on the Western Front 1915–1918

John Hutton

Pen & Sword
MILITARY

First published in Great Britain in 2008 by
Pen & Sword Military
an imprint of
Pen & Sword Books Ltd
47 Church Street
Barnsley
South Yorkshire
S70 2AS

ISBN 978 1 84415 721 1

Typeset in Ehrhardt 11/13pt by Phoenix Typesetting, Auldgirth,
Dumfriesshire.

Printed and bound in England by Biddles Ltd, King's Lynn

Pen & Sword Books Ltd incorporates the Imprints of Pen & Sword Aviation,
Pen & Sword Maritime, Pen & Sword Military, Wharncliffe Local History,
Pen & Sword Select, Pen & Sword Military Classics and Leo Cooper.

For a complete list of Pen & Sword titles please contact
PEN & SWORD BOOKS LIMITED
47 Church Street, Barnsley, South Yorkshire, S70 2AS, England
E-mail: enquiries@pen-and-sword.co.uk
Website: www.pen-and-sword.co.uk

Contents

List of Plates

4th Battalion, officers' group, 3 May 1915, just before the battalion left for France
4th Battalion men taking a break during a route march
4th Battalion arriving in Tonbridge, March 1915
A group of 4th Battalion men, autumn 1914
Brussels, January 1919, 4th Battalion led the march past the King of the Belgians
British troops advancing during the Battle of the Morval, September 1916
Arrow Head Cope, September 1916
B Company officers, 7th Battalion, King's Own, France, October 1916
7th Battalion in Clevedon in February 1915
Platoon of 7th Battalion men taken at Lucknow Barracks, Tidworth, June 1915
7th Battalion in France, summer 1917
7th Battalion in training at Clevedon, spring 1915
La Boisselle, 3 July 1916
7th Battalion, marching through Candas, band playing, late summer 1915
7th King's Own men with captured German prisoners after the attack on La Boisselle
Oblige Trench, captured by 7th King's Own, Battle of Messines, 7 June 1917
8th Battalion Sergeants' Mess, autumn 1914
Major Berry, CO of the 8th Battalion, interviewing a sergeant about demobilization
Troops of 76 Brigade travelling on light railway, Pilckem Ridge, 25 September 1917
Sergeant Tom Mayson VC
Longueval village, September 1916
Complete devastation, Delville Wood, September 1916
11th Battalion on parade, Blackdown Barracks, June 1916
11th Battalion officers, Blackdown, June 1916
11th Battalion Sergeants' Mess, Blackdown, June 1916
4 Platoon, A Company, 11th Battalion, Blackdown, June 1916
Looking north from the positions held by the 4th Battalion at Givenchy, April 1918
Looking back towards Trones Wood from Arrow Head Copse
Road leading north-east from La Boisselle
7th Battalion marched together for the last time down this road, 4 February 1918
Scene of the 7th Battalion advance towards the Intermediate Line, August 1916
8th Battalion retreated through the village of Neuville Vitasse in March 1918
The area around Avelette bridgehead defended by the 8th Battalion, April 1918
View from The Orchard at Delville Wood
Lonely Trench, south of Guillemont, attacked unsuccessfully by 8th Battalion
Infantry Hill looking north from Monchy Le Preux
Scene of the advance of 11th Battalion on 25 April 1917
Eastern edge of Bourlon Wood, attacked by 11th Battalion, 25 November 1917

Preface

This book is, first and foremost, the story of some truly extraordinary men. They came from the Furness area of north-west England and responded to the call to defend their country and its values at a critical moment in the nation's history. They endured incredible hardship, suffering and violence as a result.

These men served in every major theatre of land operations in the Great War of 1914–18, from the Western Front to Gallipoli, from Salonika to Mesopotamia. Many of their friends and comrades never returned to the community they belonged to. Many of those who survived were never to be the same again.

In the main, these men had a hard life even before they joined 'Kitchener's Army'. They worked in the local mines, in the steel works at Hindpool and Millom or in the shipyards at Barrow. Some earned a modest living as farm labourers or estate workers. Many more came from the wide range of heavy industries that were based in the Furness and surrounding areas. Many of these jobs were dangerous occupations to be employed in as accidents and fatalities were commonplace. Living standards were low. Most of them left school at an early age with minimal qualifications. They faced a lifetime of hard labour – punctuated by periods of unemployment as the fortunes of their employers ebbed and flowed. For some of them, joining the new armies being raised in the late summer of 1914 might have been both an adventure as well as an escape. But it would be men like these who were to form the bedrock of the New Armies that were established in the months after war was declared in August 1914. They were to become efficient and effective soldiers. The men from Furness were to be no exception. They were to take on and defeat the most powerful military force in the world – the German Army. And they were to feature in all of the major campaigns of the war.

Men from the Furness area joined every branch of the armed forces and served in just about every corps and regiment. All of these men served their country bravely. I hope some day their contributions can be recorded. This, however, is the story of those who joined the local infantry regiment, the King's Own (Royal Lancaster) Regiment. This story of the men from Furness has never been told before. Partial accounts do however exist. For example, there is an excellent history of the 1/4th Battalion – a territorial force – published in the 1930s by one of its former commanding officers. But the history of the Kitchener Battalions of the King's Own – the units formed immediately after war had been declared in August 1914 – has never been brought together in one volume.

In August 1914, the King's Own had two regular battalions, the 1st and 2nd and two territorial battalions, the 4th and 5th. The 1st was based in the UK and went out to France with the first troops of the British Expeditionary Force in August. It sustained heavy losses during the retreat from Mons. The battalion had pitched camp on the forward slope of a hill near Haucourt on the morning of 26 August. Unbeknown to them, they were under observation from concealed German infantry and artillery positions less than half a mile away. Almost as soon as they had started their breakfast they came under heavy machine gun fire from German infantry. There were over 200 casualties, including its commanding officer, Lieutenant-Colonel Dykes, who was killed. Dykes had served with the battalion for nearly twenty years and had fought with it at Spion Kop during the Boer War. In the first burst of fire 83 men were killed. The battalion went on to serve the rest of the war on the Western Front. It suffered heavy losses on the first day of fighting on the Somme on 1 July, when 9 officers and 400 men became casualties.

The 2nd was stationed in India at the outbreak of war in August 1914 and eventually reached France in December 1914. In May 1915, during the Second Battle of Ypres, the battalion was practically annihilated by enemy gunfire on the Frezenburg Ridge, losing 15 officers and 890 men, including its own commanding officer, Lieutenant-Colonel Martin. The battalion was reformed and then sent to serve in the British Expeditionary Force at Salonika, where it was to serve out the remainder of the war, fighting alongside one of its sister service battalions, the 9th.

There were many men from the Furness area serving with both the 1st and 2nd Battalions and their record of service and sacrifice was truly remarkable. Details of their deeds are described in the Official History of the Great War. They make impressive reading.

But the main focus of this account is the history of the so-called service battalions of the King's Own, raised from the Furness area, which served on the Western Front – namely the 7th, 8th, and 11th Battalions. The history of the 6th and 9th Battalions will be the subject of a second volume. The 6th Battalion, part of the 13th Division, served at Gallipoli and then in Mesopotamia, where it remained until the Armistice in November 1918. The 9th Battalion, in 65 Brigade of 22nd Division, served only six weeks in France before being ordered to Salonika, where it too remained throughout the whole period of the war.

All of these units were formed by the men who responded to Kitchener's call to join a new army that could fight and win the world war. Inevitably, as the war went on and the casualties mounted, the places of these original volunteers from the Furness area were taken up by an increasing number of men from other parts of the north-west and indeed, the rest of the UK. This process was speeded up by the introduction of conscription in January 1916. The connection between these service battalions of the King's Own and the Furness and North Lancashire area became diluted as a result. But the connection remained and wherever possible the replacement drafts for these battalions were made up of men from the local area.

I have also included in this narrative the service of the 4th Battalion. These were local territorials – all from the Furness area. Almost to a man, they all agreed to serve overseas for the duration of the war. They were under no obligation to do so as the battalion had been raised and formed primarily for the purpose of home defence. They volunteered to serve overseas as the casualties amongst the regular units of the British Expeditionary Force began to mount. Without their support, the British Army could not have held their part of the front line from the beginning of 1915 until the Kitchener battalions arrived later that year. I have included them in this story because they too were part of the local response to the outbreak of war. And the record of the 4th Battalion is a truly outstanding one. Three of its members were to go on and win VCs. It was to serve three and a half years on the Western Front.

The 5th Battalion was drawn largely from men from the Lancaster and Morecambe areas. For this reason I have decided not to include details of this famous battalion's exploits in this account. The 5th Battalion went to France early in 1915 and spent the next three and half years fully engaged in the hard fighting and trench warfare of the Western Front. For most of the war, it fought along-side its sister battalion, the 4th, in the same West Lancashire Division, the 55th. There are some references to the 5th Battalion in later parts of this narrative. The men of the 5th had much to be proud of. A second territorial battalion from the Morecambe area was also raised at the beginning of the war, the 2/5th Battalion. It too served on the Western Front for much of the war.

The 11th Battalion of the King's Own was a bantam outfit drawn largely from miners from the across the regiment's traditional recruiting areas. Bantam battalions were raised from men who would not have met the Army's minimum physical standards of height and strength.

My interest in telling this story goes back many years. I remember meeting some of the old soldiers in my constituency. They were very few in number, but the years had not diminished the searing memory of the time they spent in the trenches. On the doorstep and in their homes they would recount some of their own experiences, hoping that future generations would never have to go through what they had . The intensity of that experience was still with them, decades after the events themselves had long since faded from common memory. They remembered the horrors of trench warfare. But they also recalled the friendship and comradeship of their fellow soldiers. They remembered their mates who had died. They missed them. They had managed to survive themselves, but they too were undoubtedly victims. Many had been wounded – physically in some cases, psychologically in many others. They are all dead now. But their memory must be preserved for future generations to reflect on and ponder. They have left an extraordinary mark on the history of our country.

On many of my own trips to the battlefield areas of France, I would look out for and often locate the gravestones of the men from the Furness battalions of the King's Own. Sadly, they were all too easy to find, scattered as they were across all of the main battlefields from Ypres, Festubert, Givenchy, Loos, Arras and the Somme. Altogether, hundreds of men from the Furness area were killed and thousands wounded in the service of the King's Own in the Great War.

This book is therefore dedicated above all to their memory, to the men from towns like Barrow, Dalton, Ulverston, Grange and Millom. It was these men that won the war. They were the men who did the fighting and the dying in circumstances that are beyond the ability of any of us to imagine. So it is right and proper that their story should now be told, because it must never be forgotten. I hope I have told the account of their service and sacrifice fully and fairly. They deserve nothing less.

In writing this book I have also enjoyed the fantastic support of my wife and family. I could not have written this book without them. Over the years, they have had to listen to the endless stories and accounts that have come to light during my research. They have always been behind me. I am eternally grateful to them.

Gavin Birch helped me with much of the hard work in drawing together the historical data. Peter Donnelly at the King's Own Regimental Museum in Lancaster has also provided essential material. Anyone who is interested in the history of this famous regiment will find the Museum a fascinating place to visit.

Gavin Tomms and Jenny Simpson lent me the use of their beautiful home on Rhodes to begin writing this book, for which I will always be grateful. Ken Anderson took the photographs of the battlefields. I owe him a huge debt for his help and kindness.

And finally, I want to express my thanks to the staff of the National Archives, the British Library at Colindale and the Imperial War Museum who had to deal with my endless requests for help and assistance. They were brilliant.

John Hutton,
London, 2007

Chapter 1

The Summer of 1914
and the Outbreak of War

The crisis in Ulster and the possibility of civil war over Home Rule for Ireland loomed very large in the public consciousness for most of the summer of 1914. The legislation to provide for Irish Home Rule was about to complete its passage through Parliament after three years of intense political controversy. The Ulster Volunteers under Sir Edward Carson, armed and trained, were determined to resist any breaking of the ties that bound Ireland to the rest of Britain. The Liberal government under Herbert Asquith was equally determined to force the issue and defeat any challenge to its authority.

In July, the King had convened a special conference at Buckingham Palace to explore whether there was any possibility of a peaceful settlement between the Nationalists and the Ulster Unionists. The signs were not promising. In July 1914, it looked more probable that any imminent war would occur in Ireland than in Europe.

The assassination in Sarajevo of the Austrian Archduke Ferdinand at the hands of Serbian nationalists in June had obviously generated considerable concern. But the events that would eventually lead to war were concentrated in the immediate fortnight before 4 August. Up until those fatal days, for most people in Britain, the killing of the Austrian Crown Prince was a very European affair and of little immediate concern to them. If there were to be war it would probably be confined to the Balkans. Britain would not get entangled in it. The fuse that would eventually ignite into a worldwide conflagration would prove to be a very short one indeed. For much of the summer of 1914, it was life as normal.

This was certainly true in the Furness area of what was then north-west Lancashire. Alongside reporting the major national and international news stories, the local press was busy celebrating the golden wedding anniversary of Captain and Mrs Tyson of Ulverston and Mr and Mrs George Hosking of 50 South Row, Roose.

The shipyard of Messrs Vickers, the main employer in the area then and now, and on which the economic prospects for the region depended, looked set to win a further order of naval guns from the Admiralty, bringing new work into the area. In fact the yard was already full of orders, both naval and commercial. The expansion of the Royal Navy's Dreadnought class of battlecruisers had seen several contracts awarded to Vickers. And work was under way on a number of P&O vessels – passenger liners for the lucrative transatlantic market.

Across the district as a whole work was steady. The iron ore mines were busy, as were the iron and steel works at Hindpool and Millom.

There was a row over the salaries paid to senior officials of the Barrow Corporation. The Barrow Chamber of Trade had protested strongly that the salaries were too high and would represent an unfair tax burden on the trade's people of the district. The council nonetheless went ahead with the increases.

The state of the water supply in the Furness area was generating controversy with concerns being expressed about both purity and lack of pressure within the system. The water mains at Newton in Furness were also in a poor state.

James Clarkson had just retired as general manager of the Barrow Co-operative Society after thirty-five years of service, during which time the Society had grown rapidly and occupied a prominent place in the commercial life of the district, with thousands of members enjoying the benefit of the 'divvie'.

There was a steady stream of personal tragedies hitting the headlines. At the end of July, John Fallows, a tourist from Manchester staying at Kents Bank House near Grange, committed suicide by cutting his throat with a razor borrowed from another lodger. In the Barrow and Ulverston magistrates court a succession of cases involving fighting and using indecent language were dealt with firmly by the local justices.

The economic fortunes of the district were heavily dependent on the success of the shipyards. Most of the work in the yards, in turn, depended on the Royal Navy. But the Navy was not the only branch of the armed forces with a connection to the Furness area. The district had always enjoyed a long association with the Army. The King's Own Royal Lancaster Regiment, the local regiment to the area, was one of the oldest regiments in the Army, having been originally raised in the seventeenth century. The local territorial battalion of the King's Own in particular featured prominently in the life of the local community.

The 4th Battalion of the King's Own had been formed in 1908 as part of Lord Haldane's efforts to improve the professionalism and effectiveness of the British Army. As a Territorial unit, its main role was in home defence, allowing the regular battalions to serve abroad in defence of the Empire. It was made up of men from Millom, Grange over sands, Barrow, Dalton and Ulverston. It was an active, well-trained and well-led unit. Its activities always drew close press attention. It was, in every sense of the word, part of the fabric of local life. In the summer of 1914, its commanding officer was Lieutenant-Colonel Wadham from Ulverston.

On 18 and 19 July 1914, the battalion had taken part in its annual rifle-training weekend at Rougholme Range. About 200 men of all ranks attended. Many of the officers and men who were to feature so prominently in the life of the battalion over the next few years were there. They were all local men. Majors Thompson,

Pooley and Rutherford, Captains Barnes, Caddy, Barratt, and Pearson, Lieutenants Balfour, Mawson and Kennedy. Barnes, Caddy, Balfour and Thompson all went on to command the battalion in France. At the outbreak of the war, Lieutenant Balfour lived with his family at Chetwynde in Barrow. Lieutenant Kennedy was the eldest son of leading Ulverston dignitary Myles Kennedy of Stone Cross Ulverston.

Sergeants Page, Howarth, Booth, Hannigan and Waye all took part in the shooting competition. Sergeant Howarth, drawn from the Ulverston area, won the Colonel's Cup. Many of these men were not to survive the bloodbath of the Western Front. Some, like Company Sergeant-Major Page of Cavendish Street, Barrow, were to die within a few days of entering the front-line trenches without even firing a shot in anger at the enemy.

At the beginning of August, members of the 4th Battalion took part in a boxing competition in Dalton, with Private Corbett of Dalton winning the final bout.

During that first, fateful weekend in August 1914, the 4th Battalion of the King's Own were taking part in their annual training camp in the Lunesdale Valley in Westmorland. They formed part of the North Lancashire Brigade of the West Lancashire Territorial Division. The brigade, under the command of Colonel Stockwell, camped on Sunday 2 August at Devils Bridge near Kirkby Lonsdale. Serving in the brigade alongside the 4th were the 5th Battalion of the King's Own which recruited from the Lancaster and Morecambe area and the 4th and 5th Battalions of the Loyal North Lancashire Regiment from Bolton and Preston. In total, over 12,000 men had come together to train for war. And war lay just around the corner.

On 4 August, in dramatic scenes in London and across the country, Britain declared war on Germany after it had violated Belgium territorial sovereignty as part of its war plans for defeating France. The German forces were at the beginning of a massive encircling movement that was designed to see Paris captured from the north, and the huge French armies deployed along the German border cut off from behind. The declaration of war saw Britain swamped with a patriotic swell of emotion.

The training camp at Kirkby Lonsdale was cut dramatically short. Anticipating the likely course of events, the 4th were sent back to Barrow on the morning of 3 August with a warning to be ready to respond to the order to mobilize. Mobilization orders were issued on the 4th and men began reporting for active service on the morning of the 5th. They spent the next few nights billeted at Holker Street School, close to Barrow town centre.

The war had begun. It wasn't only British armed forces who were visible in Barrow in the early days of the war. On 6 August a contingent of Turkish sailors who had arrived a few days before left the town for Newcastle to catch a boat home. They had come to Barrow to crew the latest addition to the Turkish Navy, the battleship *Rashudieh*. On the outbreak of war, the Admiralty had however taken over the ship for use by the Royal Navy. The Turkish sailors cut a remarkable dash as they marched through the town on their way home, in naval dress – full navy bottom trousers, red borders on their 'dickeys' and with their heads covered by long red fez hats.

In early August 1914 the 4th Battalion was not at full strength. On 5 August 766 men reported for duty. Its full war strength was 979 men. For some time, the battalion had been behind in its recruitment. All this was soon to change. Its initial duties were to guard the shipyard and the docks at Barrow. Detachments were also sent out to mount a guard on the Leven and Kent railway viaducts that carried the Furness Railway line into Barrow.

In the mean time, recruiting offices were set up in the Strand and in Ramsden Square in Barrow and in Queen Street and the Drill Hall in Ulverston. Similar offices were established in Millom.

The sight of the newly mobilized territorials of the 4th King's Own on the streets of Barrow heightened the sense of national emergency. Barrow docks had been placed under the control of the military authorities. There was an air raid scare during the first few days of the war in Barrow, when it was thought that the town would come under attack from German Zeppelins. In fact no air raid attack was made against Barrow throughout the whole of the war.

Other equally visible signs of war were appearing. Recruiting meetings were being arranged across the Furness area in response to Lord Kitchener's appeal to raise new divisions for the army. Volunteers were coming forward in large numbers. Local municipal authorities began to organize fundraising committees. The middle-class ladies of Dalton in Furness formed a committee to supply comforts to the troops at the front. A large gathering in the immaculately tended gardens of Dowdales, the home of Mrs Kellet in Dalton, agreed to set up a sewing circle to supply shirts and socks and anything else they thought might be of use to the soldiers. They also agreed to mount a door-to-door collection in the town.

Vickers agreed to keep open the jobs of those who volunteered and to match any allowances paid by the government to their families left behind. The owners of the Hindpool steel works made a similar offer but by the middle of September, this offer was suddenly withdrawn, as the company was finding it hard to maintain production with so many workers having left to join the colours. The war had brought valuable new contracts to the steel mills of Barrow. Production – not recruitment – had become the company's and the country's number one priority. Vickers, too, was beginning to experience the same problematic loss of key workers, as the recruitment drive in the Furness area gathered pace. The company were eventually forced to modify their generous offer of an allowance to every man who joined the colours. From early September, this was restricted to those who were members of the Territorials and other reserve units.

Notwithstanding these hiccups, recruitment for the 4th Battalion was proving to be highly successful. By early September an additional 327 men had enlisted with the 4th Battalion – over half of these joining in the first week of September as the news filtered back to Britain of the retreat from Mons and the victory at the Battle of the Marne. The small British Expeditionary Force of just over 100,000 men that had left for France in early August had received heavy casualties in the first fortnight of fighting. The 1st Battalion, King's Own, had been in the thick of the fighting during the retreat from Mons. On 26 August it sustained very heavy casualties at Haucourt when it was caught in the open and subjected to heavy artillery and machine gun fire from hidden German units. Over 200 men had been killed in little over twenty minutes.

By the middle of September, the first casualties from the 1st Battalion, King's Own, had begun returning to the Furness area and were keen to tell their story of the fighting at Mons and during the retreat. One of these was Private George Kellet from Barrow. Private Kellet was to speak at a large recruiting meeting in Dalton. He had spoken powerfully of the hard fighting he had been part of and the need for more recruits to replace those like him who had fallen. 'The sights we have seen have made strong men weep', he told the packed meeting at the Co-operative Hall. The majority of these first new recruits for the King's Own came from Barrow. All of these men had volunteered for service abroad.

Typical of these early recruiting meetings was the one held in Ulverston Drill Hall on Monday 7 September. The Drill Hall was packed. Councillor Dilworth, chairman of Ulverston District Council, presided. On the platform with him was Lady Moyra Cavendish, wife of Lord Richard Cavendish. The Cavendish family owned a great deal of land in the Furness area and had been instrumental in the enormous industrial development that had taken place in Barrow since the middle of the nineteenth century. As well as being the honorary colonel of the 4th, he also commanded the 5th Battalion of the King's Own, which recruited from other parts of north Lancashire. The local Conservative MP for Ulverston, George Haddock, the former Liberal MP for the constituency John Bliss JP, Major Pooley from the 4th Battalion and the duchess of St Albans were also present.

In a highly charged and emotional speech, Mr Haddock claimed that it was clear to all that the Germans were determined on war and had tried to induce Britain to watch France brought to her knees. Referring to Britain's guarantee of Belgium sovereignty, he said the Germans wanted to tear up 'that scrap of paper' which represented 'the integrity of Belgium and the honour of the British, French, Russian and German nations'.

'I never saw an assembly of men more earnestly determined to resist such a proposal than the House of Commons on the 3rd August', he said. Germany had been

caught napping this time. She had been advised by her Ministers and spies that in Britain we were too occupied with our internal affairs and would not dare venture into the (European) arena. As the Foreign Secretary Sir Edward Grey had pointed out had this country stood aside, we would have suffered all the hardships of the war and then would have had to meet alone the great forces of Germany later on. We are fighting a ruthless, relentless and barbarous foe who made war not only on soldiers and sailors but on women and children and if they won in the fight what would we in this country expect? It is the duty of every man to prepare himself against the eventuality of our shores being invaded.

Mr Bliss followed with a different argument. For him, the Great War was to be a war against militarism and a defence of European freedom and liberty.

It was frequently said that there was no calamity greater than war. I do not agree. A dishonourable peace is a greater calamity. That peace this country might have purchased six weeks ago – at a price – was a price we were not prepared to pay. It would have meant the breaking of our solemn word to the smaller nations. History tells us that nearly all the battles for freedom had been fought by the smaller nations, England included. We could not betray and leave our allies France and Belgium in the lurch at their time of desperate need.

I am proud our Government chose war, with all its horrors, rather than an infamous and degrading peace.

Those who came forward now to pay their 'debt of honour to the country would, by their own endeavours and example ensure that liberty was assured and maintained in Europe and that the demons of militarism would be swept away from the earth'.

Lady Moyra read out a message from her husband. He earnestly appealed to every able-bodied man in the Ulverston district to enlist in some branch of HM Forces, preferably the King's Own. A thousand recruits had come forward on the other side of Morecambe Bay to form an additional territorial battalion of the King's Own and she felt sure the response from the Furness area would be equally positive. She would prove to be right.

A similar meeting was also held in Allithwaite on 2 September. Sixty people had packed in to the Allithwaite Institute to hear the local vicar, the Revd J W Gilbertson declare the war to be a 'righteous War' in defence of a weaker nation. This theme was picked up by Mr Bliss, the other speaker, who had, by this time, addressed numerous recruiting meetings across the district.

Remember, we are fighting in the first instance the battle of the smaller nations against the great brutalising forces of militarism. We are fighting for the liberty for the people against the militarism which has crushed the German people for so long. I believe we shall do away with that spirit of militarism. We are fighting this war for the sake of democracy and against the despots who rule; we are fighting for the sake of the children who shall come after us. I believe that when this war is over peace will reign in Europe as it has never reigned before and there will be no more war amongst civilised nations.

Bliss's rallying call succeeded in winning more new recruits for Britain's rapidly expanding armed forces. How many men responded to his eloquent denunciation of German militarism, and how many were simply caught up in the patriotic mood of the times is impossible to tell.

In the first three weeks after the declaration of war, over 600 men from Barrow had joined the armed forces, mostly the King's Own, other Lancashire regiments and the Royal Engineers. Hundreds more had joined at Ulverston and Millom.

On 9 August, a crowd of 200 volunteers had assembled outside the new fire station in Abbey Road, Barrow, in response to an appeal from Colonel Huthwaite, a retired officer of the 4th Battalion. Huthwaite owned a stock-broking business in Duke Street Barrow and his son, a young lieutenant in the 4th Battalion, was to go on and serve the battalion with great distinction throughout the war. The men were presented with regimental badges and marched to Vickers shipyard to be presented to the commanding officer as new recruits to the battalion.

Recruiting meetings were held regularly throughout the district in August, September and October. Meetings were held at the Market Place and in the Picture Palace in Ulverston, at Cartmel Fell, Grizebeck, Kirkby, Grange, Flookburgh and Haverthwaite, as well as Barrow, Dalton and Askam. There was a particularly large open-air meeting in Tudor Square, Dalton, in October. Speakers from all the main political parties, the King's Own and national organizations made the case for men to enlist in the new army that was needed if Britain was to win the world war. As a result of the Tudor Square meeting, four brothers from Dalton all enlisted with the King's Own. George, Harold, Richard and Thomas Lytham left shortly afterwards to begin their training at the Lancaster depot as new recruits in the 7th Battalion.

On 10 September a large crowd gathered at Askam Railway station to bid farewell to the latest batch of young men to enlist in service battalions of the King's Own: 27 young lads, all footballers signed up with Askam Football club, left to join the King's Own Regiment at the depot in Lancaster, and were played out by the Town Band. More were said to be waiting for the opportunity to join the King's Own.

As part of the call by Lord Kitchener to raise a further six divisions for the army, a new battalion of the King's Own was immediately formed. The 6th Battalion was recruited by the end of August. The 7th, 8th and 9th Battalions were recruited during September as part of the second and third waves of recruitment to the New Armies. Kitchener had always recognized that the war would not be over quickly and that it might in fact last for several years. The British Army would have to be significantly larger than at any previous time in its history if it was both to match the fighting strength of the German Army and to emerge victoriously from the conflict. Kitchener had a poor opinion of the territorials.

Although they were needed to fill the gaps created in the regular army because of the heavy fighting in France, he decided not to base his expansion of the Army on the Territorial model. Instead, he had decided to recruit, in effect, an entirely new branch of the regulars, based on the existing regimental system and consisting of fit young men who would sign up for the duration of the war. Further second-line battalions of the Territorials were recruited – largely for home defence – but Kitchener's Army was not to be an army of Territorials.

All of the new battalions of the King's Own were initially manned entirely from its traditional recruiting areas in north-west Lancashire. The response from the Furness area had been loud and clear.

Chapter 2

The Fourth Battalion, King's Own Royal Lancaster Regiment, 1914–1919

Autumn 1914: the first days of the war

According to Lieutenant-Colonel Wadham, the commanding officer of the battalion,

> Little of any importance or worthy of note occurred during the time the battalion was stationed in Barrow. An air raid scare, involving the standing to arms of all ranks for several hours in the middle of a very cold night, forming the only excitement.
>
> The time was chiefly devoted to obtaining mobilisation stores, ammunition and equipment (not forgetting transport, which in those early stages of the war was a most heterogeneous selection, varying from a milk float to a motor lorry with water carts commandeered from the local authorities).

The battalion had been expecting to be moved to Ireland, and an advance party was sent to Liverpool on 8 August to prepare for the battalion's arrival. The orders were cancelled later that day.

On 10 August, the 4th Battalion was relieved of its duties in Barrow and the next day it marched to Ulverston, where the men were billeted in the Dale Street School and at the Victoria Grammar School. While based in Ulverston, the battalion continued to draw on equipment and mobilization stores, practised drill and completed a number of route marches to get the men as fit as possible. The 4th Battalion left Ulverston for Slough on 15 August in two trains early in the morning. The Town Band and many local residents and dignitaries were there to wave them goodbye. Behind the smiles and the tears lay the hidden fears of many parents, wives, children and friends that these young soldiers would never see Ulverston and the Furness District again. It was to be an eventful journey. En route to Slough, one of the carriages carrying the horses fell to pieces at Crewe, injuring several of the animals and delaying the train for many hours.

The battalion, as part of the North Lancashire Brigade, had been posted for guard duties on the Great Western railway line. They were found billets in the town at first, but as they were deployed along the railway line, the men bivouacked at the various railway stations along the section of the line they were responsible for, between Paddington and Maidenhead. They slept in the waiting rooms, without any bedding or material comforts of any kind. They were to perform these duties for the next three months. The Millom detachment, guarding the line at Langley Park, improvised a field kitchen from local supplies and erected a lean-to shelter from discarded advertising billboards and some newly acquired wagon sheets. The new recruits to the battalion stayed at Slough where they underwent an intensive course in infantry training.

These were duties the men had not been trained for. Few of them appreciated the dangers of the permanent way. Sadly, some of them were to become casualties before they were to set foot in France. One such casualty was a young sergeant from Ulverston, John Tindall. John was the eldest son of the inspector of police in Ulverston and worked in Barrow. He was 22. On his very first day on guard duty, John was hit by a train and died almost immediately. He was buried with full military honours at Ulverston parish church on Thursday 20 August. John was the first man from the 4th Battalion to die on active service in the Great War.

But it wasn't the trains alone that presented the greatest danger. Those on guard duties took their responsibilities extremely seriously. Sentries were given daily passwords to use if they were challenged. Failure to respond could bring tragic consequences for those involved. On 31 August, another sentry, Private Fred Benson, on guard duty between Burnham Beeches and Slough, shot Lance-Corporal Thomas Ward of Grange over Sands when he failed to respond when challenged. At the inquest in Slough two days later, Private Benson said he had heard someone approaching along the track. He challenged the person three times to identify himself. When no response was made he fired a single shot and fatally wounded Lance-Corporal Ward. Ward was in fact coming to relieve Private Benson. Two civilian witnesses said they heard the challenges being made. They also heard Private Benson cry out 'Oh Tommy, dear Tommy, have I shot you?'

In Thomas's tunic pocket there was a letter from his sister and it described the recent shooting of a motorcyclist by a sentry. She begged her brother to be careful. 'I have worried about you ever since', she wrote. A verdict of justifiable homicide was returned, and Thomas too was buried a few days later in Grange with full military honours.

Guard duties on the Great Western line continued uneventfully for several more weeks. The weather was glorious. The men could enjoy leave in Reading and London. The officers were made honorary members of the golf club at Stoke Park. But they all wanted to get out to France as soon as possible. They had several early opportunities to do so, but only if they were prepared to leave the North Lancashire Brigade and form part of other formations en route to the front. The battalion's commanding officer, Lieutenant-Colonel Wadham, took the very strong view that they should stay part of the North Lancashire Brigade, and serve with the other battalions from their own part of the country – men they had trained with for many years in peacetime. In wartime, their natural desire was to stick together.

On 26 November, the battalion moved to Sevenoaks to continue its training and preparations. The men were to spend several weeks in the St Johns end of the town, largely billeted in empty buildings and houses. Over the next few weeks the battalion would be moved around the south-east several times to facilitate the arrival of other territorial units for training and equipping. Many of these were being concentrated in the south-east. Tens of thousands of soldiers were on the move. They were being housed in makeshift camps, in public buildings, schools, village halls and in peoples' homes.

It wasn't an easy time for the 4th. The needs of Vickers still loomed large in the life of the battalion. Many of its recruits had left their jobs in the shipyard when the battalion had been mobilized, leaving the company short of valuable skills. Now Vickers wanted them back, as orders from both the War Office and Admiralty began to stack up. Over 300 men were called back to Barrow in the early spring to serve in the shipyard, causing havoc with the battalion's preparations for war service. Replacements had to be found and then trained up. It meant further delays in the battalion being ready to join the other Territorials in France.

In response to the loss of so many men from the battalion, a new recruitment drive was initiated. This time the focus would be on other parts of Lancashire, which were not likely to be affected by the needs of the defence industries for key workers. On Easter Monday, a recruiting team was sent to Blackpool. Recruiting teams were also sent to Lancaster, Chorley and Preston, with two recruiting sergeants in charge of each office, to drum up men to replace those who had returned to the Barrow shipyards. By the end of the week a further 100 recruits had been enlisted. At Preston, the recruiting team had the help of the Volunteer Training Corps drum and fife band as well as the St Vincent school band. In Chorley, the Town Silver Band helped them draw in the crowds. The recruiting team travelled to Bamber Bridge, Wheelton, Whittle-le-Woods, Garstang, Coppel and Addlington.

But the battalion's traditional recruiting grounds as a territorial unit were not being entirely ignored. A team under Captain Hibbert and Lieutenant Goodwin was sent to the Millom, Broughton and Bootle district. Gradually, the numbers recruited began to bring the battalion back up to its wartime strength.

Despite the loss of the 300 men and the problems this caused to the battalion, preparations for departure to France continued apace. They were issued at around this time with the famous short magazine Lee Enfield rifle – one of the iconic symbols of the Great War.

Sadly, however, the men were not able to enjoy Christmas or New Year at home. No home leave was granted. Instead, Christmas was spent in Sevenoaks. Plum puddings were provided, courtesy of the readers of the local newspaper, the *North Western Daily Mail*. On 22 February, the battalion was moved briefly to Margate for a week. It returned to Sevenoaks for a couple of days before being ordered to Tonbridge. On 14 April, the battalion received the news it had been waiting for. It was to proceed to France as soon as possible. The battalion was to form part of the 51st Division. Most of the territorial divisions had by now already left for overseas service. The last of the territorial units to leave for France would be the 51st Division. This was a Scottish Territorial Division. But the division was short of one brigade. The North Lancashire Brigade was to take up its place. The 4th Battalion became officially part of 154 Brigade.

The order to move

The division began concentrating at Bedford in April 1915. On 1 May, an advance party of 3 officers and 100 men left for Southampton with the battalion's horses and vehicles. The rest of the battalion left for France on 3 May. They caught trains in the afternoon to Folkestone, arriving at 19.40. They immediately embarked on the troop carrier and by 23.00 they had arrived in Boulogne. The 4th Battalion had joined the war.

The next day they marched to Pont de Brique station and got on the train for Berguette. On arrival they marched to Ham, where they spent two days cleaning up, preparing and checking their equipment. On 6 May they were marched to Calonnes, arriving early the following morning. They spent the next week there on training and induction. For most of the time they were there, the men were under orders to be ready to move up to the trenches at short notice.

By the time the battalion arrived in France, the Western Front had reached something of a stalemate. The trench lines extended from the Vosges mountains on the Franco–Swiss border to the port of Nieuport on the Belgian coast. A continuous line of fortifications stretched some 300 miles, sometimes no more than 20 or 30 metres apart. The initial German offensive through Belgium, designed to outflank the main French forces concentrated in the Alsace/Lorraine region in the centre by a giant encircling movement, had been successfully halted by the victory at the Battle of the Marne. The British had defended the town of Ypres with heroic tenacity, holding on to a symbolically important part of Belgium, despite facing overwhelmingly superior numbers. In doing so they had sustained horrendous casualties. And crucially, the retreat of the British and French armies in the north, which had put in jeopardy the entire military campaign of the Allies, had been reversed by the victory on the Marne in early September. Since then, and with winter approaching, both sides had been content to remain on the defensive, to regroup and wait for the spring to arrive.

On the British section of the Western Front, from around Ypres in the north to Loos in the French coalfields, the BEF at the beginning of 1915 was moving from the defensive to the offensive. This was largely a response to developments on the Eastern Front. The success of the Central Powers during the winter of 1914/15 against the Russian armies in the east had seen the Germans move their military strategy away from conducting major offensive operations against French and British forces. During March and April, eight German divisions had been withdrawn from France and sent to the Eastern Front to help in a new offensive designed to inflict a defeat of such strategic importance that Russia might be forced to pull out of the war altogether. But the switching of emphasis and resources away from the west to the east gave the British and French their own opportunity to try and turn the tide of advantage in their favour.

The first British offensive battle of the war was therefore initiated, at Neuve Chapelle in March. It was not a huge success. The initial opportunity created by an early breach of the lightly fortified German front line by British troops had petered out into tactical stalemate. The British commander in chief, Sir John French, was anxious for the initiative to be maintained. He wanted maximum pressure to be exerted on the German positions in the surrounding area, notwithstanding the shortages of men, equipment and ammunition that still dogged the British war effort.

In early May, the Battles of Aubers Ridge which began on 9 May and Festubert on 15 May had concluded with very heavy losses being incurred by the British for little territorial or tactical advantage whatsoever. The fighting at Aubers Ridge had been particularly unsuccessful. In fact it could only be described as slaughter. One brigade involved in the battle, the Bareilly Brigade of the Indian Corps, had lost over a thousand men in a few minutes.

At Festubert, the outcome was a little more promising. The front line had moved a few hundred yards forward, but no breach in the German positions had been secured. Even if it had, it is doubtful whether the British forces had the resources to exploit such a breach to any real effect. But with limited supplies of both men and ammunition at their disposal, the British had forced the Germans out of their heavily entrenched positions to a hurriedly improvised new line. The success was due entirely to the fighting spirit of the infantry. Once again, as had happened at Neuve Chapelle, the British – largely due to the lack of available resources – had been unable to exploit the opportunity that presented itself to them. Although these battles had been closed down by the end of May, the 4th Battalion was at real risk of being pushed into the front line to support these faltering attacks.

The general commanding the 55th Division, Major-General Richard Bannatyne Allanson, had already met Sir Douglas Haig, who was in command of the First Army, to express his concerns over the threatened deployment of his newly arrived troops. On the morning of 19 May, he had gone to see Haig at his headquarters. He did not make a good impression. In his diaries, Haig described Bannatyne Allanson as 'anxious'. This unfavourable impression was again confirmed the following day when Haig and Bannatyne Allanson had a major altercation about the need for an offensive spirit amongst the newly arriving troops. Bannatyne Allanson felt that the 55th Division was not yet fully trained, a view that caused Haig to explode with fury. 'What he wanted was grit and determination', he wrote later. Soon afterwards, Bannatyne Allanson was relieved of his command and sent home to England.

None of these rows filtered down to the 4th Battalion and fortunately for them the moment of danger had passed – though not for long. Sir John French and Sir Douglas Haig remained determined to find fresh ways for the BEF to maintain the impetus against the Germans. Their focus would now move onto smaller, more limited advances where the risk of large-scale casualties could be minimized at the same time as holding German troops in their current positions. The French Army was heavily engaged with the Germans in an effort to capture the Vimy Ridge in the Artois region further south, a crucial area of high ground which dominated the battlefield area – north and south – for many miles in each direction. Britain had to show its support for its ally by mounting attacks of its own to support the French operations. But it too was suffering from the serious loss of personnel and equipment, which the battles of March and now May had accentuated.

As the immediate pressure on the 4th had been lifted, they could spend time preparing for trench warfare and the ordeals that were to lie ahead of them. On 20 May, under the supervision of a battalion of the Leicestershire Regiment, the battalion had its first experiences of trench duties in the reserve lines. It was exposed to the rigour and routine of trench discipline by an experienced battalion that had been out since August. The men became familiar with the routine of 'Stand To' at dawn and dusk as they prepared for possible infantry assault. Dawn and dusk were the most likely times for any such attack. The men would have been taught the essential lessons in how to survive a tour of duty in the front line. Familiarity with signalling arrangements was important too. Officers became familiar with the requirements of trench inspection duties and ensuring the welfare of their men.

On 25 May, it was time for the real thing. The battalion marched to Le Touret, south of Armentieres, near the Neuve Chapelle battlefield and relieved the 7th Gordon Highlanders in the front line. The first full day in the trenches on 26 May was spent quietly. There was little enemy activity to report. In the evening they had their first exposure to heavy artillery fire. The first casualties occurred the following day. A heavy enemy barrage had killed three men and wounded ten others by midday. In the early evening the men 'stood to' to resist an anticipated enemy infantry assault. It failed to materialize. At no time did they fire their own weapons. As was to prove so often the case, they were simply the targets for enemy gunners.

In a letter home to his friends in Barrow, Major N E Barnes, the battalion second in command and a solicitor in the Barrow law firm of Poole & Son and Barnes, revealed that the dead soldiers were Sergeant Atkinson, and Privates George Tyer and Edward Fisher. Another wounded private, A Leviston from Urswick near Ulverston, died a day later from his injuries. In his letter, Major Barnes said:

We have had three days and nights in the fire trenches with no one between us and the enemy. We have now commenced three days supporting the rear. We have been wonderfully lucky . . . there were lots of cases of bullet holes through caps etc. The men have been wonderfully cool and good.

The 28 May was also a quiet day. By 2 am on 29 May their first tour of trench duty was over. They were relieved by the 8th King's Liverpool Regiment and marched back half a mile to the reserve trenches. The following day they came under renewed artillery fire. Shrapnel killed Company Sergeant-Major Page during this attack. Sergeant Page lived with his parents in Cavendish Street in Barrow. He had been an active member of the Territorials and the Reserves for twenty years. He had been employed as a draughtsman at Vickers. He was 37 years old and left behind him a widow and infant son – a child that had been born after Sergeant Page had been mobilized. He had only spent forty-eight hours with his baby son before his death at the Le Touret redoubt. That evening the men marched back to safer billets in the village of Le Touret itself, although they were still at risk from long-range enemy artillery fire. For the next three days the men provided working parties to the front-line positions. There was one further fatality. On 31 May, the battalion marched back to Hinges in the support lines, out of reach of enemy gunfire. They had undergone their first baptism of fire.

The overall health of the men was reported in the daily battalion war diary as 'good'. There had been a minor outbreak of measles, but apart from this, the men were being well fed and looked after. They had received their first mail from home, including presents of food and clothing.

The first few days of June were spent resting and cleaning up. On 6 June the battalion was back in the front-line trenches at Le Touret. One company was positioned in the firing line, two in reserve and one in close support. The next day there was little enemy activity. However 8 June was to prove anything but peaceful. A heavy enemy barrage landed directly on the firing line and lasted for several hours. Ten men were killed in D Company and one in C Company. Twelve other men were wounded. The battalion was relieved on 10 June and Lieutenant-Colonel Wadham returned to England on sick leave. He would not join the battalion in France again. His place was taken by Major Thompson. The battalion would soon find itself in the thick of it.

Sir Douglas Haig, in command of the First Army to which the 51st Division was attached, had been planning further action after the ending of the Battle of Festubert on 25 May. Sir John French had left to Haig the choice of target and the timing of any further action. Haig had decided to launch an action against the German lines near Givenchy, scene of bitter fighting during the battle of Festubert. On 30 May Haig had issued orders for the preparation of a limited attack against the line Chapelle St Roche–Rue d'Ouvert, involving an advance of around 250 yards. The attack was to involve all three divisions of IV Corps; the

51st, 7th and Canadian Divisions. The attack of the 51st Division was to be of brigade strength: 154 Brigade was designated to mount the attack.

On the night of 15 June the battalion was back in the reserve lines at Le Touret. Its job was to act as support for the main attack, which was to be launched by the 4th Loyal North Lancashire Regiment, another territorial unit from Preston, and the 6th Scottish Rifles. The 4th King's Own and the 4th Loyal North Lancs were to fight together in the same brigade for the whole duration of the campaign on the Western Front. Once the main attack had started, the 4th King's Own were to come up in support and push through to the final objective – the third line of German trenches at Rue d'Ouvert – and consolidate the ground won.

The attack started at 18.00 with a short bombardment of the enemy front line and the blowing of a mine opposite the Duck's Bill, a salient in the enemy trench line further to the south. The mine was blown as a diversion but failed to divert anyone. The barrage too, was largely ineffective and in fact only served to give notice to the Germans that an attack was imminent. When the men of the 4th Loyal North Lancs started their dash towards the enemy front line, the Germans were ready for them. The defending infantry were observed to stand up above their parapet in order to engage the advancing men from Preston with heavy rifle and machine gun fire. There were many casualties. Despite these heavy losses, they had managed to penetrate the German lines in several places.

At 20.00 it was the turn of the King's Own to press home the attack and to capture the brigade's final objectives. B, C and A Companies made the advance over the open and flat countryside between the British and German front lines. The land provided absolutely no protection or cover of any kind. The men were exposed to enfilade fire from murderous machine guns on their right and left flanks. It was difficult ground to move over. The area was covered in shell craters from previous fighting during the Battle of Festubert, which made rapid movement very difficult. They managed to get into the third German line of trenches, having passed through a heavy enemy artillery and machine gun barrage. Bitter hand-to-hand fighting ensued, the bayonet being used on both sides. There, however, the forward companies became effectively cut off from the rest of the battalion and the brigade. Telephone communications with battalion and brigade HQs were severed almost as soon as the first attack had started. Lieutenant Gardner was put in charge of relaying messages by runner, but these too came under heavy enemy fire. The conduct of the battle, like so many in the years to come, had now become one where the actions of individual company and platoon commanders and NCOs were to prove decisive. But there was little going in their favour.

Enemy machine gun and artillery fire made it practically impossible and suicidal for any one to cross no man's land with fresh supplies of ammunition or water. It wasn't enemy fire alone that was the problem. As the position of the 4th King's Own was far from clear to brigade or battalion HQ, British artillery fire

The scene of the battalion's first engagement on the Western Front. The battalion advanced behind the first wave led by the Scottish Rifles and the Loyal North Lancashire's.

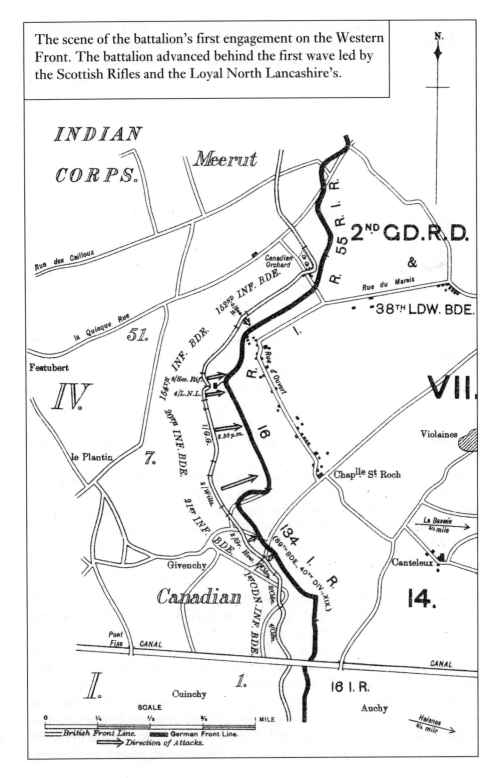

designed to provide them with a measure of supportive cover against German counter-attacks began landing short, inflicting further casualties on the men at a critical moment in the fighting. The position of the battalion was becoming increasingly desperate.

By midnight it was clear that the advance position held by the 4th King's Own was rapidly becoming untenable. The forward posts were running out of ammunition and bombs with which to resist counter-attacking forces. The Germans had mounted a series of counter-attacks, which had succeeded in driving in the line of trenches held. The men had lost contact with the battalion on the right and their left was in the air. It was a hopeless position. There was only one course of action open to them if they were to avoid pointless further casualties. They would have to retire. Orders were therefore given for a fighting retreat.

The battalion finally reassembled back at Le Touret at 10.00 the following morning, having had to retreat through yet another heavy enemy artillery barrage. In total, 5 officers and 147 seven men had become casualties. Many more were missing. Amongst the missing was Captain Pearson, of Spennithorne, son of the official receiver of the Barrow district, and Lieutenant Walker, the son of the manager of the Barrow branch of the Liverpool and Manchester Bank in Ramsden Square. Lieutenant Walker worked for the Furness Railway Company in Barrow. His body was never recovered. Amongst the officers killed was Lieutenant George Bigland of Bigland Hall Haverthwaite, who had joined the 4th Battalion shortly after war had been declared. He was killed in the fire trench before the advance had even commenced. Captain Pearson would eventually return to Barrow early in 1916. He had been ill for some time during his spell in captivity and had returned home as a medical evacuee. He was to take no further part in the war.

Private George Ryland from Ulverston was also amongst the dead. He was only 19 years old and was a member of the battalion band. He had been serving as an orderly for Major Barnes during the attack and was killed by a sniper. Sergeant Frank Postlethwaite, and Privates 'Big Tom' Blake and Ernest Curwen from Dalton were also killed.

Tommy Blake was one of the battalion cooks and before the war lived in lodgings in Market Street Dalton. Tommy was an enormous man, well over six feet tall. He was renowned throughout the battalion for his famous roly-poly puddings which he used to make in an army sock. He had worked in the local iron ore mines and had seen Army service in the Royal Engineers before joining the King's Own when he moved to the Furness area. Private Steve Williams from Duke Street in Askam was reported missing, feared dead. He was never seen again. The same fate befell Private Robert Horne who was 21 when he went missing on 15 June. His body was never found. In August 1914 he had been working as a barman in the Crows Nest Hotel on Barrow Island. His parents lived in Rawlinson Street. He was one of the first of the Kitchener recruits to join the battalion. Private Richard Newsham's body had also disappeared. He had been in the Territorials before the war and lived in Cartmel with his parents. Privates Isaac Harrison of Stainton and Phillip Roberts of Devonshire Street, Dalton, suffered a similar fate. Fred Williams, an 18-year-old private from Canal Head, Ulverston, would also never make it home to see his friends and family. He was a labourer at the North Lonsdale Iron Works and had been one of the first to join up in August 1914. Private Jack Logan, a 26-year-old single man from Ulverston, was another fatality. He had worked in the Swarthmoor and Ulverston Co-op. Private Jacob Cubitt had joined the battalion in the heady days of August 1914. He was only 17 and lived with his parents in Egerton Buildings on Barrow Island. He went missing on 15 June and his body was never seen again.

Private John Henry Evans wrote home to his mother at Skelgate, Dalton, a few days after the attack.

> My Division made an attack on Tuesday evening (16th) and took two lines of German trenches and we went up to re-inforce them under a murderous shellfire. We reached the position and had just commenced to dig ourselves in under cover when my entrenching tool was knocked out of my left hand and I felt a sharp pain in my right elbow. I was dressed by our medical officer in the reserve trenches and then made my way to the dressing station. It is a bullet wound in the right arm, just under the elbow. It is not a serious wound. There was a lot of wounded men that night.

Sergeant William Farish of Ulverston was another of the wounded. He was a member of a bombing party under the command of Lieutenant Taylor. Taylor was killed. Only four out of the twenty members of Lieutenant Taylor's party were to make it back to the British lines. Fairish reached the third German lines with the remnants of his platoon. There he was wounded in the buttock and was only discovered two days later in no man's land by a party from one of the Guards regiments that had by that time relieved the King's Own in the front line. He was incredibly lucky to have survived at all. He was discharged from the Army in December that year. In January 1916 he was awarded the DCM, along with Corporal Alfred Graves and Private John Carrick, both from Barrow.

The battalion had suffered a heavy blow. It had made a valiant contribution to the action at Givenchy but at a massive price to its combat efficiency as an effective fighting force, which would take time and effort to recreate. The action itself had changed very little, either at the particular section of the front line that had been attacked or more widely as far as the overall conduct of military operations against the Germans were concerned. The front lines remained as they were prior to the attack. There had been no territorial gains on either side. The British attack had been easily dealt with by the Germans without the need to call on any of their reserves being held elsewhere along the front. The operations had produced no local, tactical or strategic gains for the British at all. The attack had however served one useful purpose. It had maintained the new offensive campaign against the German lines initiated at Neuve Chapelle and continued the need to exert pressure on the enemy. After all, to remove the occupiers from France and Belgium, the Allies had no option other than the military one.

The battalion itself had only been at the front for just over six weeks. It had, however, now acquired real battle experience and a reputation for gallantry that would stay with it for the rest of the war. Sergeant William Bell from Ulverston was awarded the Military Cross for bravery during the action at Rue d'Ouvert. He returned again and again to no man's land – which was being continuously raked with machine gun fire – to recover the wounded men of his battalion. The MC was usually only awarded to commissioned officers. Bell had won a rare distinction in being one of the very few NCOs to win this decoration during the entire course of the war.

The battalion now enjoyed a few well-earned days of rest and recuperation. On the 27 June it was back in the front line at nearby Laventie, having taken over again from the 8th Liverpools. The trench strength of the battalion was now just under 400 – a third less than the month before.

Its exploits at the front line were being faithfully and fully reported back home in Furness. As a result, on 24 June the men received a gift of 300 pairs of socks from Miss Dora Wadham, the daughter of the battalion's former CO. In a letter to the editor of the *North Western Daily Mail*, Lieutenant-Colonel Thompson wrote:

> May I through the columns of your paper, thank the children attending the local schools, members of the various working parties, and others who have contributed these kind gifts and assure them that the socks are very much appreciated by the non-commissioned officers and men who have received them.

Officers were clearly expected to provide their own socks.

July was a quiet month for the battalion. They were in and out of the trenches in the Laventie sector for most of that period, receiving only slight casualties. The battalion was gradually reinforced by new drafts of men from the Lancaster training depot.

In August the battalion moved further south, to the Somme front, where it was to enjoy a period of well-earned rest over the next few months from the kind of military action at Givenchy. These trenches had recently been taken over from the French and were considered less dangerous in comparison to the area the battalion had just left. There had been little action here since the early months of the war. All of this was to change dramatically the following July when the Battle of the Somme began.

The battalion was billeted at Henancourt for most of the time it was not in the front-line trenches. In August the battalion received its first issue of Lewis guns, the new light machine gun that was to add considerably to the battalion's fire-power in the trenches. Early in September, the battalion also received another important piece of equipment – the gift of a new melodeon for the band from Mr Hearne of Victoria Avenue, Barrow. This brought the number of melodeons in the band to two, the earlier one being the gift of the Dalton Town Band, when the battalion when left the Furness district in August 1914.

The section of front-line trenches held by the 4th during the next few months were in the Aveluy and Authuille area just north of Albert. Casualties were few and far between. However, on 13 October Lieutenant-Colonel Thompson was wounded by shrapnel and was temporarily replaced by Major Barnes. Confirming how quiet this sector of the front line was at this time, virtually all of the casual-ties in the battalion in December were accidentally sustained. A grenade being demonstrated in training exploded prematurely, killing Lieutenant Ward and wounding thirteen other men. One man would later die from his injuries. He was Private James McQuade of Devonshire Buildings, Barrow.

The men were heavily engaged in strengthening the trenches and dugouts in the front line for most of this period, which were in a poor condition after their recent occupation by French troops.

The needs of the local Furness economy continued to haunt the battalion, even though it was now heavily engaged in front-line activity. On 28 October, one NCO and seven other men were sent home to work in the Hodbarrow mines. Not-withstanding these losses, the battalion continued to receive a steady stream of new recruits from the regimental base. During this period, for example, nineteen new NCOs joined the battalion. In December, the battalion was strengthened by the arrival of a further forty men, twelve of whom were rejoining after spells in hospital. On 18 December, Sergeant William Kirkby of Cobden Street, Dalton, was blinded after shrapnel removed one eye completely and severely damaged the other. He was discharged on medical grounds in March 1916.

The battalion's first Christmas of the war was spent in the front line at Authuille, under enemy artillery fire. In seven months at the front line, the battalion had so far been engaged in one major action. The next year, 1916, was to be an altogether different experience for the men from Furness.

1916: a new division and a new onslaught

In January the battalion was moved out of the Somme area in preparation for joining a new division. The old West Lancashire Territorial Division was to be reformed as a new fighting unit on the Western Front. The battalion marched in stages via Montigny, Coisy and La Chausee to Longpre-Les Corps-Saint near Abbeville to join the new 55th Division, under the command of Major-General Jeudwine. The battalion now formed part of 164 Brigade. During January over 100 new drafts joined the battalion from base – the largest reinforcement since they landed in France.

The British Army in France was gearing up for a major new offensive operation on a much bigger scale than even the battles of 1915 at Neuve Chapelle, Festubert and Loos. At a conference of the Allied Powers at Chantilly in December it had been resolved that all four would open new offensives against the Central Powers in 1916. The British and French would act side by side in a major operation either side of the River Somme in Picardy. The French would take up the larger part of the operations, but the British would make a major contribution. The British effort would be the biggest operation it had been involved in since the start of the war. Given the length of time that would be needed to assemble the necessary troops, ammunition and equipment for such a huge undertaking, it would be the spring at least before military operations could begin.

Haig, who had by now replaced Sir John French as commander in chief of the BEF, would have preferred a different offensive, further north around Ypres aimed at driving the German lines back towards the northern Belgian coast. Joffre, commanding the French armies had lobbied hard for a joint Anglo–French operation on a wide front on the Somme. Haig, in an effort to show solidarity with the French, had agreed to it. There was only one part of Joffre's plans to which Haig did not accept. Joffre was planning a series of subsidiary attacks along the German front in the run-up to the main offensive on the Somme. These attacks would, he argued, have sapped the strength of the German armies and prepared the ground for a decisive breakthrough in the spring, when the main offensive would be launched. Given the huge losses already sustained by the French Army since the start of the war, Joffre argued that these attacks should be led by the British forces now arriving in France in such large numbers.

Haig rightly did not want to see the strength of the BEF drained away in a series of speculative actions that would have been difficult to mount and which might ultimately have served only to pave the way for a largely French triumph on the Somme. Joffre and Haig eventually agreed that the proposed preliminary engagements would be undertaken by both armies in a shorter period immediately preceding the main battle.

Matters were, however, effectively taken out of the hands of either Joffre or Haig. In February 1916, the Germans launched a huge attack against the French lines at Verdun. The entire focus of French military operations and planning necessarily became focused on defending the fortress of Verdun. The battle assumed epic significance for both sides. The death toll reached enormous proportions, sapping the strength of both armies. This titanic struggle would last several months.

It was also to have significant implications for the agreements reached at Chantilly. The French were now unable to mount an operation on the scale envisaged because of the losses they were sustaining at Verdun. Britain would have to assume the main responsibility for the conduct of the Somme battle. The length of front to be attacked would also have to be considerably reduced. And it would be Haig, not Joffre, who would be making the final judgements about tactics and strategy for the battle itself. The eventual front for the attack was to run from Gommecourt in the north to Maricourt in the south – a front of some 15 miles. The original objectives for the first day of the battle were for an advance of over a mile and a half. The British would deploy a force of twenty-six divisions and precede the advance with the biggest artillery barrage of the war, designed to destroy the German front and support lines. The attack would be a walk over and herald the rolling up of the entire German position on the Somme and possibly the end of the war itself. The 'Big Push' was on. It was into this eventual cauldron that the 4th Battalion would be plunged.

By the end of January, with the concentration of the new 55th Division now completed, the battalion marched from Longpre to Bertencourt and then on to billets at Candas. For the first two weeks of February the battalion was engaged in the construction of a railway line from Candas to Puchevillers. This line was needed in order to improve the movement of supplies and ammunition required for the forthcoming Battle of the Somme. The weather during this time was terrible, with heavy falls of snow and bitter frosts at night. On 16 February the battalion marched through blizzard conditions to Sombrin. Training in close order drill and in dealing with gas attacks took up most of their time. Major Barnes, who had been in temporary command of the battalion, left for specialist training and Captain Caddy took over his duties as commanding officer. On 25 February the battalion left Sombrin for Monchiet, again in terrible weather conditions in preparation for resuming front-line trench duties. The next day they relieved the 10th King's Liverpool Regiment (Liverpool Scottish) in the front line at Bretencourt. It was still snowing hard and trench conditions were desperately poor. The battalion was effectively engaged in a battle with the elements rather than the Germans. The Germans were fighting the same forces too. As a result, there was very little hostile action on either side until the battalion was relieved on 2 March. During their tour of duty in the front line, they had a visit from Major-General Jeudwine, the GOC of 55th Division. Jeudwine was not an invisible commander, safe and secure in the rear echelons. He was very much a hands-on leader who liked to get up to the front line with his troops to see at first hand the conditions in which they were being asked to fight and die. He was renowned amongst the men of the division for his concern over their welfare – so much so that he earned the not entirely flattering nickname of 'Judy'.

The next week back in billets at Monchiet were spent either on making up working parties or in training. The men were put to work improving the road from Govy to Beaumetz, part of the essential logistical infrastructure for the operations due to start sometime in the summer. On 8 March they were back in the front line again at Bretencourt. Conditions in the front line were again generally fairly quiet. On the first day in the trenches, Company Sergeant-Major Harold Gendle from Barrow died of wounds received after he was shot by a sniper.

On their relief by the 8th Liverpools on 15 March, the battalion marched back into the reserve lines at Bretencourt where Lieutenant-Colonel Carleton assumed command of the battalion. During the next few days in reserve, the battalion was reinforced by four new subalterns and forty-three other ranks from the base depot. The battalion spent one further very quiet spell of front-line trench duty at Bretencourt and on 28 March went into Divisional Reserve at Monchiet, where it spent the next few days in training.

A similar pattern of duties was repeated the following month. The battalion continued to receive reinforcements, building up its trench fighting strength. During April the battalion served two tours of duty lasting eight days in the front lines. There were no reported casualties in the battalion. The rest of the month was spent furnishing working parties and in further training exercises.

In May a further draft of sixty-six soldiers joined the battalion, as well as five new junior officers. One of these new arrivals was Private John Sloane from Preston. He deserted the battalion two weeks later while they were in the trenches at Wailly and was eventually executed in July. John Sloane was the only soldier in the battalion to face the firing squad during its three and a half years of service on the Western Front. The battalion completed two further periods of front-line duty at Bretencourt. On 16 May, Private William Postlethwaite from Barrow, who had been with the battalion since its arrival in France, was killed by shell-fire. He lived in Smeaton Street and had worked in the shipyard at Barrow before the war. When the battalion was out of the line, the men were engaged in working parties and fatigues. The Artists Rifles, a battalion of the London Regiment, became attached to the battalion for induction into trench warfare.

In early June, the battalion marched to Simencourt in the rear area for further training. Lieutenant-Colonel Carleton was promoted to command 98 Infantry Brigade and Major Balfour, a Barrow man and one of the original officers who mobilized with the 4th Battalion in August 1914, assumed temporary command. The men were initially engaged in building gun emplacements on the Doullens–Arras road. These would be used in the preliminary bombardment leading up to the opening of the Somme Battle. A further draft of sixty-eight men joined the battalion. Towards the end of June the battalion was once again occupying the front line, this time at Agny where it sustained a few minor casualties as the result of enemy artillery and trench mortar fire. Command of the battalion passed to Major Swainson on 16 June.

A raiding party under the command of Lieutenant Johnson came under friendly fire from sentries manning one of the battalion's outposts, wounding Lieutenant Johnson and three of his men. The remaining fateful days of June 1916 were spent by the battalion in the front line at Agny, a safe distance away from the start of the one of the most significant and eventually decisive encounters of the world war

All through the early months of 1916, the British high command had been refining the details of their forthcoming campaign on the Somme. The area that had been identified for the attack was a beautiful region of gentle, rolling countryside of fields and woods, largely untouched by the heavy fighting that had characterized other parts of the British line. The area had seen little conflict since the early days of the war. After the victory at the Marne, Von Kluck's Second Army had fallen back to the Somme. Static trench lines were established which had remained largely unchanged ever since.

The campaign in the Somme would be far from straight forward. The Germans had spent the time since September 1914 creating a formidable system of defensive lines. The original single trench line had been replaced with a complex front system of three lines of trenches approximately 200 yards apart. The front-line trenches were protected by strong belts of barbed wire 15–30 feet deep in places. The higher ground was strongly fortified. Strong points and redoubts were established at all of the critical points. The villages on the front line, such as Beaumont Hamel, Thiepval, Ovilliers, La Boiselle, Fricourt and Mametz, had been made into virtual fortresses.

Deep beneath the trenches, the Germans had created dugouts 20–30 feet below ground and large enough to provide effective protection for their front-line garrisons from British artillery fire. Not content with these defensive measures, the German defenders had created a second and had started on a third line of defence. The second line was around 2,000–4,000 yards behind the front line. It was not as formidable as the first line. But there were a number of very strong fortifications such as the Schawben Redoubt and the Nordwerk. Much of these defences were out of range of the British field artillery. Most of it was also out of observation as well, but a section of it had been placed on the highest ground around Mouquet Farm and Pozieres.

All in all, it amounted to a very strongly held position indeed. Winston Churchill, in his war memoirs, later described the German defences at the Somme as 'undoubtedly the strongest and most perfectly defended position in the world'. The assault on it would prove to be possibly the hardest single job undertaken by the British Army in the war to date.

Having come to a decision to attack on the Somme at Chantilly, the British commanders were divided about the scale and objectives for the forthcoming operations. Haig was known to favour a major operation with ambitious objectives for a significant advance. Although the German positions were acknowledged as being strong, the front line was in fact located on the forward slopes of the gentle hillsides, making it vulnerable to British artillery fire. Rawlinson, the army commander in charge of planning the Somme campaign, was aware that his own corps commanders favoured a more modest assault with strictly limited objectives.

The original plan he submitted to Haig for approval in early April was therefore for a more limited attack by ten divisions. It was effectively a 'bite and hold' operation whose objective was simply to kill as many German soldiers as possible with as few casualties to the British as possible. It envisaged limited territorial gains and limited penetration of the German defensive lines. The first stage was to consist of a series of attacks on the German front line. The second move forward would be undertaken as and when preparations could be made. The attack would be preceded by an intensive artillery bombardment of between two and three days designed to cut the enemy barbed wire defences.

Rawlinson knew this plan would not meet with Haig's approval. He was right. On 14 April, Haig set out his comments on Rawlinson's plan in a note to the Fourth Army commander. The planned artillery bombardment meant the loss of any surprise; the plan was too cautious overall and limited in its objectives; there was no role for the cavalry to exploit any opening and take the enemy from the rear and flank; and because of its strictly limited objectives, the plan failed to offer the beleaguered French forces fighting at Verdun any prospect of relief. Haig had an altogether different operation in mind. He wanted to capture the German first and second lines in a single advance, ignoring the real difficulties of providing effective artillery support for such a mission, particularly in relation to the second line.

Haig's preference was not for an unlimited offensive, but for a much more ambitious battle of manoeuvre that would seriously hamper the German action at Verdun and take much of the immediate pressure off the hard-pressed French Army. And having made what he hoped would be a decisive breakthrough on a broad enough front, then to exploit the breach with a rapid advance into the German rear areas, cutting off the remaining front-line positions held by the German forces.

The arguments between Haig and Rawlinson over the exact scale and nature of the campaign continued throughout April and May. By the end of May the plan was clear. It would involve an attack by eleven divisions on a 24,000 yard front from Serre in the north to Montauban in the south. The first objective was to overrun the German second line from Serre to the Pozieres–Albert road. To the south of this line, the attack would be more limited. It would include taking the villages of Contalmaison and Montauban. The depth of the advance was ambitious. In the northern half of the attacked area it would range from between 3,000 and 4,000 yards. South of the Albert Road it was to be between 2,000 and 3,000 yards. The attack would be preceded by an artillery bombardment of five days duration involving over 200 heavy guns and 2,000 field guns. When all of these objectives had been secured, the focus of the attack would switch to the south-east, to secure the left flank of the French advance. Gains of this magnitude would represent the biggest single advance on such a broad front since the war started.

However, the scale of the fighting at Verdun had a dramatic effect on the ability of the French Army to contribute to the attack on the Somme. The original plans had envisaged an attack by thirty-nine French divisions. By the beginning of June it was clear that the French Sixth Army and its twelve divisions would be all that might be available for the flanking assault south of the Somme. This reduction in the expected contribution of the French forces to the battle had the effect of switching the focus of the advance due east rather than south-east. Haig even had it in mind, if the breakthrough did occur, to aim for an advance towards Monchy, some 40 miles to the north. Intelligence reports coming in to GHQ also seemed to indicate that the Germans had little by way of available reserves to strengthen the Somme position in the event of a large-scale attack. This opened up in Haig's mind the possibility of even more dramatic advances, possibly even to Douai, 70 miles to the east of the Somme battlefield.

With the overall plan of attack now agreed, the preliminary bombardment was begun on 24 June. The infantry attack itself was scheduled to begin on 30 June. The bombardment was absolutely central to the success of the campaign. The initial bombardment was concentrated on destroying the barbed wire in front of the German trenches. On 26 June the full bombardment started, with heavy guns firing on the German front and second lines, gun batteries, communication routes and supply dumps. Just as the heavy bombardment began, the weather deteriorated sharply, hampering observation by the RFC spotter aircraft. The infantry attack was postponed for two days to allow the artillery to effect more damage on the positions to be attacked. Zero hour was now to be 07.30 on Saturday 1 July.

The bombardment, although the largest and heaviest mounted by the British so far in the war, turned out to be largely ineffective. There were not enough guns, particularly heavy calibre guns, to affect the necessary damage on such a long frontage. The wire was not sufficiently broken up to allow the infantry un-impeded passage on a large enough scale. Shrapnel had been used for much of the wire cutting. This had simply failed to damage the fixed barbed wire forti-fications. The heavy artillery had also failed to damage the deep dugouts into which the front-line German infantry had retreated at the start of the barrage on 24 June. A lot of the shells also failed to explode on impact because of problems with the fuses. The effectiveness of the counter-battery fire was also less than had been expected. Few of the German guns had been put out of action by the time the assault was launched on that beautiful sunny Saturday morning.

Except in the south, the infantry attack was a complete failure. At Serre, the soldiers who 'went over the top' barely advanced at all before they were cut down by machine gun fire from the German trenches. At Beaumont Hamel, a huge mine planted under the Hawthorne Ridge Redoubt was detonated ten minutes before the infantry advanced, giving the defenders precious minutes to escape from their dugouts and man the front lines. The attacking infantry were slaughtered. No British soldiers entered the village of Beaumont Hamel that day, or would do so for another four months. At Thiepval, the Irishmen of the 36th Division fought bravely and advanced deep into the German positions, even entering the Schwaben Redoubt. They were eventually forced back, by the ferocity of German counter-attacks, to their own starting lines later on in the evening. At Ovillers and La Boiselle a similar pattern repeated itself. Whole battalions were simply wiped out under a murderous barrage of artillery and machine gun fire as they tried to make their way forward.

The only significant advance took place at the southern end of the battlefield, where British infantry took Montauban and all of their first-day objectives. The British were advancing alongside the French. Here the artillery barrage had been much more effective, supported as it was by the impressive gun fire of the famous quick-firing French '75s'.

The 4th Battalion was spared from the fighting on the first day of the Battle of the Somme. It remained in the line further to the north. On 1 July the British Army suffered its heaviest casualties on any day of fighting in its history: 20,000 men were killed and another 40,000 were wounded, the equivalent of four of the eleven divisions involved in the assault.

The 4th Battalion was still deployed in the front-line trenches at Agny. It was to remain blissfully quiet for the next three days, although the sound and fury of the battle would have been obvious to all of the men. For the rest of the month, the battalion continued to enjoy a peaceful tour of duty, both in reserve and in the front line. It sustained some casualties however. During this time Private William Barrow from Broughton was wounded. He subsequently died in a casualty clearing station on 5 July. On 16 July the battalion entered the trenches at Blaireville. For most of the month the battalion was being prepared for its eventual engagement in the Somme campaign and spent the next few days training. It also began its move south to join the battle. On the night of 25 July, the battalion marched to Candas and then went by train to Mericourt. It then marched to Meaulte into a heavily overcrowded camp site. As a precursor to its involvement in the forthcoming attack, the 55th Division now became attached to XIII Corps of Fourth Army. On 26 July it marched up to Happy Valley and underwent further training and re-equipping. On the night of 30/31 July it was moved into the front-line trenches on a line running north and south between Trones Wood and the village of Guillemont. The battalion had arrived at the apex of the British advance on the Somme.

The main focus of the whole Somme battle had been switched to its southern flank following the gains made on 1 July. Slowly, in a succession of smaller scale operations, the British had moved up through Mametz Wood and through the German second position on the Bazentin Ridge. In each of these battles, its sister battalions, the 7th and the 8th, would eventually be engaged. The advancing British forces were now coming up against some very strongly entrenched German positions. At Longueval, Delville Wood and High Wood further to the north, ferocious fighting would take place for several weeks before the British were to succeed in taking their objectives.

The village of Guillemont lay directly in the path of the advance. It was just to the south and below the higher ground of Delville Wood. In front of the village, the British front line lay on the edge of Trones Wood, a mere 200m from the village. For the British and the Germans, the village occupied a position of strategic importance. The German line turned towards the north–east at this point. If the British were to take the village and press on behind it, the whole

German position on the Somme could be turned. Several attacks had already been made on the village without success. The defenders were deep underground and were covered by protecting arcs of machine gun fire and the massed ranks of the German artillery behind them. In front of the village the ground was open and largely flat. These innocuous fields became the graves of thousands of British soldiers, amongst them many of the men of the 4th King's Own.

The whole of the front line was under constant and extremely heavy German artillery fire. The fighting in Trones Wood had been particularly hard, with the wood changing hands several times in July. The scenes of carnage and slaughter were abundant. Body parts littered the ground and even the branches of the few surviving trees above. The bodies of dead soldiers lay unburied in no man's land for days. In the hot weather the stench became overpowering. Enemy artillery fire in no man's land frequently had the effect of flinging the bodies of these unburied soldiers into the air, dismembering their remains, again and again, sometimes depositing these grim remnants into the front-line trenches on both sides. Shell craters dominated the landscape, churning up the ground repeatedly so that it became completely devoid of any recognizable features. It was a scene of indescribable carnage and horror.

On 31 July, the front line was heavily shelled, killing Lieutenant Lincey and four other men. Twelve men were wounded and evacuated form the firing line. The same pattern repeated itself the following day. Numerous casualties were inflicted on the battalion by the murderous shellfire from German guns.

At 8.30 in the evening of 2 August, a platoon from B Company attacked a German machine gun emplacement but were forced to retire. They could not get through the barbed wire and the highly accurate and effective artillery fire made it impossible for them to advance. After twenty minutes a second platoon from B Company went forward under Lieutenant Brockman who had joined the battalion at the end of May and succeeded in capturing the position, largely as the result of fire brought to bear on it from the battalion's Stokes Mortar team. Two of the men to lose their lives in the early hours of 3 August were Lance-Corporal Percy Smith and Private George Simpson. Both men came from Barrow. Neither body was ever found and both men are recorded on the Thiepval Memorial. Private Harry Parker from Barrow also died during this attack. Early in the morning of 3 August, the men were relieved by the 4th Loyal North Lancs and moved into reserve at Dublin and Casement trenches two miles to the rear. The men were not out of harm's way. Private James Hems, from Ambleside, was killed by a sniper as he left the trenches that night. On 4 August, Private J Whittam was wounded by long-range shellfire and died later that day. He was 35 years old and had joined the battalion in May the previous year. He had worked before the war at the Low Mill Tannery in Ulverston.

For the next four days the battalion enjoyed a quiet time. They played sports, bathed and rested. The division had been asked to prepare a fresh attack on Guillemont. The 4th was chosen to execute it. On the evening of 7 August the battalion was sent up the line again, this time to a position at Arrow Head Copse, south-east of the village. They relieved the 4th Loyal North Lancs and completed the relief by 1.00 am. At 04.00 the attacking soldiers crawled out of the firing line and took up their attack positions about 50 yards ahead of them. There they waited until the protective artillery barrage descended on the German positions. At 04.20 the attack began. The 8th Liverpools were on the left, the 2/5th Lancs Fusiliers on the right. The plan for the advance was for the 4th to attack to the south of the sunken road joining Guillement to Trones Wood.

The 4th King's Own was one of four battalions attacking the village that morning. These battalions were attacking on their own, with no supporting action being taken by the British to the north or the French to the south. The attack failed to take the village, although some ground to the south was captured. As soon as the men began to advance they were met by terrific machine gun fire and a flurry of grenades. The men were forced to retire and started to dig in 50 yards in front of their start lines. For all of this time they were under enemy gun fire, which took a heavy toll of men. The British guns, unsure of the exact position of the 4th King's Own, were firing short, inflicting even further casualties and adding considerably to the horrendous conditions the men had to endure. None of the attackers managed to enter the German front-line positions.

For most of the day the men tried to hold out, fully exposed as they were to enemy observation and fire. Early in the morning of 9 August, they were relieved by the 10th Liverpools and marched back to bivouacs at Carnoy where the roll call was taken by platoons. Seven officers had been killed, including the young Lieutenant Brockman who only a few days before had gallantly led the attack on the German strong point. His body was never recovered. In total, 256 men had become casualties , of which 46 were confirmed dead, and 56 were missing; 154 men had been wounded. Well over half the battalion had been taken out of action in the attack.

Lance-Corporal William Smith took part in the second wave of the attack.

> We had orders to go over the top as supports to number 9 platoon and at the same time to keep in touch with the 8th Liverpools. When we received orders to fix bayonets and go over we couldn't see anything of the Liverpools on our left – who should have joined with us on the Sunken Road in front of Trones Wood. So we extended further to our left, crossing over the Sunken Road at about 6 paces intervals which took us about 15 yards over on the left of the Sunken Road. We didn't get in touch with the Liverpools. So we advanced towards the German line. But when we had advanced about 100 yards from Arrow Head Copse we were stopped by the German barbed wire which was very thick and had not been touched by our artillery. By what I saw, the Germans had retired out of their front line and into the support line and from there they kept throwing bombs and trench mortars at us. When the smoke cleared I saw

the Germans with half their bodies stuck over the parapet of their trench, blazing away at us. It was then that the Lancashire Fusiliers came up to us and the next second the order came for us to retire.

Lance-Corporal Shaw of C Company who also took part in the second wave of the advance provided a similar account of the chaotic fighting.

My platoon, 11 platoon, went over as supports to 9 platoon in front of Arrow Head Copse. Drifted rather too much to the left until part of the platoon was on the left of the Sunken Road and the rest on the right of this road. Ordered to keep in touch with the 8 Liverpools but could not find them. We advanced as far as German front line, about 100 yards but could not get through the wire. This wire was plain concertina wire with one or two rows of barbed wire laced through it. It was unbroken – 5 yards in depth. It was immediately in front of the German trench. We commenced digging a new trench between 35–40 yards off the German wire but were bombed out and also fired on by machine guns shortly after we had commenced digging. The machine gun was in the German second line, which was no great distance from their first line – about 20 yards. The machine gun was directly opposite to Arrow Head Copse and was firing directly to its front. The German front line was about 5 feet deep and was strongly held all day.

Sergeant Jackson of C Company was also in the second wave of the attack on the right. When he was about 80 yards in front of the firing line he met one of the officers who ordered him to bring up his platoon as, according to the officer, he was in contact with the enemy. When his platoon got up into the first wave they all charged together but were met by a very heavy shower of bombs and machine gun fire. They then fell back and tried to take whatever cover they could find. He could not remember how long they stayed there. Once the smoke had cleared he saw barbed wire on screw pickets along the enemy's front, which was barely damaged. There were two rows of wire and they were well put up. There was a mound directly in front from which an enemy machine gun was firing. The distance between the mound and Arrow Head Copse was 150 yards. After the advance was checked he endeavoured to dig in close up to the German wire but the enemy machine gun fire prevented this. Sergeant Jackson also confirmed that the British guns were firing short amongst the men in front of him and that, as direct result, they were forced to retire. He finally came in at around 7.30 in the evening.

Sergeant Jackson and Lance-Corporal Shaw both believed that there were bombs attached to the German wire, which exploded as soon as the wire was touched.

Major Balfour, who lived at Chetwynde House in Barrow, assumed command after the injuries to Lieutenant-Colonel Swainson, becoming the only officer from Barrow to command a battalion of the King's Own during the war. He gave this account of the operations.

At 20.15 on the 7th August, the battalion proceeded to the trenches and relieved a portion of the 9th battalion of the King's Liverpool Regiment occupying the sector south of Trones–Guillemont Road.

At 03.45 am the first line, consisting of two platoons of each company crept out in advance of the front trench, at the same time as the remainder of the battalion occupied the advanced trench. At 04.10 am, the first advanced a short way and waited 4 minutes, the second line left the trench and took up a position 20 yards in the rear of the first line. The second line was closely followed by 2 platoons of the 4th Loyal North Lancs as a carrying party.

At 04.15, the enemy placed a very violent barrage of artillery fire (shrapnel) on the fire trench. The first and second lines crept closer to our own barrage to escape the enemy fire.

At 04.20 am, the battalion went forward again and the first line immediately came under heavy bomb fire. This was absolutely unexpected and caused heavy casualties and the attack was arrested. The enemy then opened very heavy rifle and machine gun fire, which caught the second line as it came up to re-inforce the first. Further advance being impossible owing to uncut wire the battalion retired out of bombing distance from the German trench and started to dig in 50 yards in front of our original trench. These operations occupied 20 minutes. The enemy maintained a very heavy barrage of shrapnel on the sunken road during the whole of this time.

The only means of communication during this time, with the exception of one company to which the telephone wire was intact, was by runner. Communication with the battalion on the left was completely lost.

It was ascertained that the battalion on the left was reported to be in the village of Guillemont and it was intended to make an attempt to get into touch with the right of this battalion. Stokes mortars were brought up and were ordered to destroy the barricade on the Sunken Road leading to Guillemont with the idea of attacking and taking this point, which would have enabled an advance on the left to be covered. There was a great deal of delay in bringing up the mortar ammunition and the difficulties of communication were great, which made it extremely hard for orders to reach their destination. This delay gave the enemy a long period of rest, which was unfavourable to the success of any further enterprise.

The Stokes Mortars bombarded this barricade but were not successful in damaging it. It was intended for a bombing party to assault at noon, but the situation was seen to be quite hopeless for the success of such an enterprise.

Our artillery in the meantime kept up an intermittent bombardment. For a long period they were shooting very short and our front line had to be cleared. It was with the greatest difficulty that the artillery were informed of this, during which time the battalion had suffered casualties from this fire. It was decided that any further attack was impracticable, and it was then decided to improve the present position as far as possible, and to render it easily defensible in the event of any hostile offensive.

The battalion was by this time greatly reduced in numbers, and was also fatigued by the strain of the heavy fighting. It was not known what had happened to the battalion on the left, and although all effort was made to ascertain their position, no information could be obtained. It was impossible to obtain accurate information of the situation, which made the situation worse.

There was a shortage of officers.

After dark it was intended to dig out a fresh trench running from our barricade, held by a party of bombers on the Sunken Road, to join up with a sap which had been driven forward. This was interfered with by the enemy who were reported to have a patrol out in front, and also bombing parties established in shell holes close to the proposed trench. A party was sent out to clear these parties, which was done. The remainder of the night was spent in trying to collect the wounded, improve our original position and clear the battlefield. At 03.55 am on the 9th, the battalion was relieved by the 10th Liverpools.

Amongst those who lost their lives on that fateful day was Sergeant Richard Usher, aged 23. Before the war, Richard had worked in the office of his father's building firm in Coniston. He had also been a prominent local scout. He had joined the battalion in the early days of August 1914. His cousin, Sergeant William Jackson from Haverigg, was seriously wounded, having been buried by an exploding shell. Other men from Coniston were also to die on 8 August. They included Lance-Corporal Sol Robinson, aged 34. He had joined later in the war, at the end of 1915. He was a quarryman by trade.

Private William Cowper, aged 26, who lived with his mother in Egerton Buildings, Barrow Island, simply disappeared without trace. His body was never recovered. The same fate befell Private Nelson Athersmith who lived in Swan Street, Ulverston. He had worked before the war in Dickinson's newsagents in Market Street, Ulverston. The youngest soldier to die following this action at Guillemont was Private Charles Gregory. Charles had worked at the Barrow steel mills before the war and lived with his parents in Melbourne Street, Barrow. He was 19. He had only been with the Battalion in France since May. He had left England the day after his nineteenth birthday. He died of his wounds three days later. Private John Parsons was another soldier killed during the fight for Guillemont. He was 29 and worked in the Vickers shipyard prior to the war. His parents lived at Kendal. Private Edgar Woodburn's body was never recovered. He born in Lindale and had been a farm labourer. Many other young men from Barrow died in this abortive attack. Amongst them were Sergeant George Robinson, Corporal Norman Hill, Lance-Corporal William Haythorn and Privates Frank Rigg, Neil Jamieson, Walter Glover, Charles Frearson, Thomas Sharp and John Lockhead. Others were to die later from their wounds, including Privates Samuel Myerscough from Barrow Island and Thomas Corlett and Thomas Smith from Barrow. Thomas Corlett died on 12 August at the casualty clearing station at Corbie. He was 20 years old. Before the war he had lived with his parents at Silverdale Street.

Two brothers from Fell Croft, Dalton, died together in action on 8 August. Privates Edward Nicholson had joined the battalion a few years before the war. His brother William joined in November 1914. He was only 20 years old. Amongst the wounded were four pals from Backbarrow, Privates John Backhouse, James Marshall, Hugh Edmondson and George Woodward. Two soldiers from Rusland were also wounded on this day: Privates Stephen Jackson and John Steele.

In fact the attack was almost doomed to fail right from the beginning. It was a predictable and anticipated movement by the British. Zero hour for the attack was fixed at exactly the same time as previous attacks on Guillemont. The heavy guns had lifted from the German front line fifteen minutes before the infantry attacked, giving plenty of time for the Germans to man their parapet. This is confirmed by the accounts of both Shaw and Smith. The opening barrage had completely failed to destroy the barbed wire protecting the enemy front line. The artillery barrage had also moved ahead of the advancing men from the King's Own too quickly, giving them inadequate protection as the attack was being pressed home. The failure of the troops on the left in particular to advance simultaneously had caused some loss of direction in the attack, as the men began drifting to the left. Command and control suffered as a result. The unexpected bomb attack from the Germans as the first men advanced must have come from enemy soldiers occupying shell craters in no man's land, and once the first advance had faltered, there was no prospect of any real success, as the Germans were fully alert to the fact they were under attack. The failure of this attack was typical of the conduct of the Somme battle in August. The men of the 4th Battalion paid a huge price for the tactical failures and lack of imagination of the high command.

It was not through any lack of courage on the part of the 4th Battalion that the attack had failed. For most of the day they had attempted to move forward. When this had become impossible, they had stuck to their positions even under intense fire and under the most difficult and hazardous conditions it is possible to imagine. They were fully exposed to the German defenders and to artillery fire.

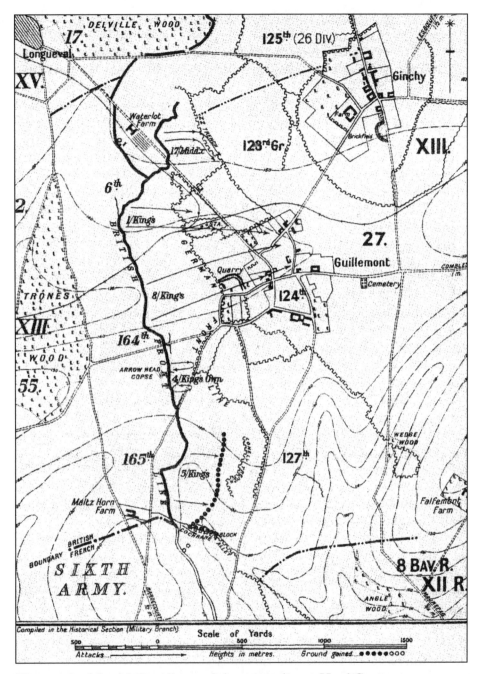

The attack of the 4th Battalion on 8 August at Arrow Head Copse.

Shell craters provided some cover. Anything else they had to dig for themselves. Command and control during the attack also came under very great pressure. The CO, Lieutenant-Colonel Swainson, had been severely wounded early on in the attack as he moved forward with the initial advance. Undoubtedly, this officer was leading by example and he had paid a terrible price for his impressive display of authority. He was eventually brought back to the British trenches under heavy machine gun fire by Lieutenant Coury, a young lieutenant with the 4th South Lancs, a pioneer battalion tasked with the job of helping the King's Own dig a communication trench from the old firing line to the newly held ground. This young man was to do more than rescue Colonel Swainson. He helped rally the men under fire and led them forward to try and press home the faltering attack. This act of incredible gallantry on behalf of Lieutenant Coury was to result in the award of the Victoria Cross. Colonel Swainson died a few minutes after he was brought back to the British trenches. Lieutenant Coury was to survive the fight. Major Balfour took over command of the battalion again.

Colonel Swainson had been born in 1877 and lived at Stonecross, Kendal. Educated at Shrewsbury School and King's College Cambridge, Swainson was a veteran of the Boer War, where he had fought with the Lancashire Fusiliers. He had gone out to France with another Kitchener battalion, the 6th Duke of Cornwall's Light Infantry.

On 10 August, Major-General Jeudwine visited the few who had survived the attack to pass on his compliments. But they were not to be allowed any rest just yet. On 11 and 12 August large working parties of seventy men were found for the duties in the front and reserve lines.

On 14 August the men marched back to Maricourt, arriving in billets early in the evening. The casualties had been so severe that the battalion was reorganized into one single company. The next few days were spent relaxing and resting. On 26 August, 100 new men were sent to reinforce the battalion. These men all came from the 10th Manchesters. This new draft significantly affected the composition of the battalion. Most of these men were from Lancashire but not from its traditional recruiting grounds. Its ties to the regiment's traditional recruiting areas were beginning to weaken. The same was to be true for many other battalions involved in the fighting on the Somme. The large influx of new recruits allowed the battalion to be arranged into two companies. It was to stay in this position for several weeks.

Early on 19 August, the battalion left by train for Abbeville and then proceeded by route march to Lambercourt, a delightful village where the men were given a very warm reception by the local residents. Here they stayed until 29 August. During these peaceful days, a further forty new recruits arrived to bolster the strength of the battalion. Major General Jeudwine made two further visits to bring the men up to date with recent operations on the Somme. They refitted and prepared themselves once again for further front-line action.

On 29 August they left their rural idyll and marched to Pont Remy where they caught trains to Maricourt. The battalion then marched to Dernancourt where they set up their camp in a cornfield. The following day ten new junior officers arrived to take the places of those who had recently become casualties. On 31 August they marched to support trenches in the area of the Albert–Corbie road.

August had not been a successful month for the British on the Somme. Little real progress had been made against objectives like High Wood and Delville Wood. Guillemont remained in German hands. The smaller scale, more localized engagements which had come to characterize the offensive had neither stemmed the flow of casualties nor achieved the wearing down of the German defences that had been hoped for. September would bring better results, but not for the 4th King's Own.

For the next few days the battalion underwent extensive training and helped in the construction of a number of strong points. On 6 September they were moved to Becordel. On 8 September they relieved the 1st South Staffordshires in Montauban Alley in brigade reserve lines.

Rawlinson and Haig had been planning another major onslaught on the German positions for September after the frustrations of August. This time they would have the use of their secret weapon – the tank. It was hoped that between sixty and seventy of these new weapons might be available to support a fresh infantry attack which would seize the German third line, capture large numbers of German guns and so open up the way for the cavalry to break through into the rear, heralding a new phase of open warfare. The tank was in fact at an early stage of its technical evolution. The early models were prone to mechanical breakdown, and were very slow-moving. Few of the infantry battalions had worked out how to fight alongside them effectively. Their crews were new and only partially trained. The 4th Battalion, like many others, had never even seen one. It would prove to be a highly risky strategy to plan a major attack around this new secret weapon.

The German third line had by now become a formidable obstacle, with deep dugouts, heavy barbed wire and now the fortified strong points of Martinpuich, Flers, Geudecourt, Lesboeufs and Morval added to it. Rawlinson did not believe these positions could be taken together in one advance. He foresaw no circumstances where soldiers on horses were likely to be more successful than those on foot in overcoming machine guns and artillery. He again favoured a more cautious attack involving six divisions, which would aim to capture all of the first-line positions and some of the main tactical points behind it, such as Flers and Martinpuich, with the aid of the new tanks. He would then mount further operations against the third-line positions when the troops and materials were ready, possibly within forty-eight hours of the capture of the key tactical points.

Haig had a different analysis. He wanted a much stronger attack, which would take the troops as far forward as possible. He felt there was evidence of collapsing morale amongst the Germans, which Rawlinson should be exploiting with a much more aggressive and ambitious plan.

The commander in chief naturally prevailed in this discussion. A stronger attack was now agreed involving four corps and eleven infantry divisions, attacking along a broad 12,000 yard front. The first objective was to finally capture and secure all of the German front line – an objective originally set for the initial attack on 1 July. Secondly, the infantry was to capture the village of Flers, and then move forward to capture the ground east and west of it. The final objective was the capture of Geudecourt, Morval and Lesboeufs, establishing a defensive flank for the cavalry to break through to Bauman and possibly beyond. The tanks would operate in small groups, reaching each line of enemy trenches ahead of the attacking infantry. Gaps of 100 yards would be left in the artillery barrage around the attacking tanks. The battle would start on 15 September.

In the mean time, a series of limited attacks continued all along the Somme front. Guillemont was finally captured on 3 September.

On the morning of 9 September, the 4th King's Own received fresh orders to take part in another infantry attack, this time on German trenches known as Hop Alley on the eastern side of Delville Wood. The battalion was to mount a second attack on these enemy trenches after an earlier attempt on the 9th had failed to make any progress.

The battalion duly attacked as planned on 11 September. The attack was to be a surprise and was not accompanied by any artillery barrage on the enemy trenches. The battalion attacked Hop and Ale Alley at 05.15 am. D company was on the left, A and B in the centre and C on the right. The attack failed almost as soon as it started. The war diary of the battalion records the fact that the men were 'very tired and there was no dash in the attack which failed directly'. As soon as the men left their trenches, the Germans opened up with rifle and machine gun fire. The men immediately took cover and made no further attempt to move forward. For good reason. Any forward movement in these conditions would have meant instant death or injury. Fortunately, the casualties were light, although two junior officers, Lieutenants Glenie and Spearing were both reported missing after the action. Their bodies were later recovered from the battlefield. Once again, the men had been asked to do something no troops, however brave and battle hardened, could succeed in achieving. It was impossible for any soldiers to make headway against positions which were held as strongly as these and where the defenders had ample time to bring down accurate and deadly fire over the ground that had to be crossed. The men had no covering fire of any kind to protect them as they made their attack. It was actions such as these that gave rise to the accusation that strategic command of the battle was ineffectual and was helping to add unnecessarily to the casualties being sustained. Private William Rimmer from Barrow, one of the original pre-war Territorials, died in this attack. His body was never found. Another casualty was Sergeant Robert Robinson, originally from Carlisle but who had been mobilized with the battalion in Barrow at the beginning of the war.

The misery was not over yet. On 12 September, the battalion still occupying the front lines near Delville Wood suffered heavy casualties during a massive German artillery barrage on their positions. The men had little protection from gun fire. They had no deep dugouts in their hastily improvised defences. William Philip from Barrow, one of the original Territorials, died on this day in the trenches. They were relieved that night by the 8th King's Royal Rifle Corps and returned to bivouacs at Becourt in a pretty miserable condition. The next day the battalion moved to Ribemont and sheltered under canvas tents. Four new junior officers, including Captain Gardner, joined the battalion.

The next few days were spent bathing, resting and in training duties. The battalion was not engaged in the major battle launched on 15 September. Instead on that day a large detachment of 120 men from the 4th Battalion was sent to a prison camp to guard German prisoners captured in the opening phase of the fighting. On the 17 September the battalion moved again to Becordel. The next day the battalion moved forward to take up positions near the front line at York Trench and was issued with extra supplies of bombs and small arms ammunition. The prisoner detachment returned to the battalion. No action took place and they marched back down to Becordel again and pitched their bivouacs in drenching rain near the Mametz prisoner camp. Major Balfour who had been in temporary command left for hospital treatment.

The battle that began on 15 September produced some significant successes. The villages of Martinpuich and Flers together with large sections of the German second-line positions were captured. The tanks had played an important role in these operations, particularly at Flers, where the arrival of these huge lumbering beasts was to prove altogether too much for the defenders to deal with.

High Wood, which had resisted repeated attacks from the middle of July, finally fell to 47th Division. However, the German third line had not been substantially penetrated. Although the British had secured a major advance, particularly when compared to the disappointments of August, they were still confronted by strong opposing forces that showed no real sign of a collapse in morale. Every yard of ground was still being strongly contested. The fighting was far from over.

After the initial advance, the next few days saw a series of sporadic engagements designed to capture individual strong points in the line.

The battalion, although out of the front line, was still heavily employed. Large parties of officers and men were sent up to the front line over the next few days as working parties, in the Longueval area, helping to improve the trenches and to carry up supplies.

On 24 September they were ordered to take up reserve positions in front of Delville Wood. They were lightly shelled on the way up.

Another major assault on the German positions took place on the following morning, in which the 55th Division was to be heavily employed. This action resulted in further progress being made. A section of the German third line from

Martinpuich to Combles had been captured. The villages of Geudecourt, Lesboeufs and Morval were all secured.

On 26 September, the sporadic enemy shelling of the previous couple of days got much heavier. Major Balfour returned from treatment in hospital. The battalion, ominously, was ordered forward to support an attack launched from Gird and Gird Support trenches by the 8th Liverpools, east of the village of Flers, which had just been captured from the Germans in the fighting that had begun on 15 September.

At 02.00 am on 28 September, the battalion took over the captured Gird and Gird Support trenches from the 8th Liverpools. Their positions were heavily shelled all day by the German guns. Three battle patrols were sent out during the day, with Lewis gun teams attached, to try and locate the enemy positions and to harass enemy working parties engaged in strengthening the German line, which was now being gradually pushed further and further back. During one of these patrols, Private Fred Fittes went missing. He was reported to have been killed, but his body was never found. Fred was 32 years old and lived with his young family at 9 Harrogate Street in Barrow.

The following day they were relieved by the Royal West Surreys and marched back to Mametz. Later that afternoon they were in billets at Dernancourt. This action would prove to be the last contribution the men of the 4th Battalion would make to the Battle of the Somme. The battle itself would continue until the middle of November. Over 600,000 British soldiers became casualties during the four and a half months of fighting. Many of the Kitchener battalions had been practically wiped out in their first major period of combat. And no breakthrough was achieved. The cavalry never fanned out into the open countryside behind the front line to harry the German trenches north and south. But the German losses were equally horrendous. They had been forced out of some of the most strongly held positions on the entire Western Front. And the French had hung on at Verdun.

For the 4th Battalion, King's Own, the Somme had been a gruelling two months. They had sustained hundreds of casualties. They had enjoyed a relatively quiet time since their first introduction to the horrors of trench warfare in June 1915. Now they had endured some its worst tribulations: days spent under constant gun fire; the anxiety of being under a continuous state of readiness to return to the front line at short notice, where the prospects of death or serious injury were real and imminent. On top of all this were the heavy fatigue duties and working parties that continued day and night, even when they were out of the immediate danger zone. The battalion had been ravaged by heavy casualties. But they had come through it.

On 1 October, the battalion moved back even further from the front line to Longpre. The battalion was being redeployed from the Somme theatre. Its next destination was to be the Ypres salient.

On 3 October the battalion reached camp at Poperinghe, west of Ypres, where it spent the next eleven days training and re-equipping. On 14 October the battalion went by train from Brandhoek to Ypres. Later that evening the men went into billets in the ramparts of that famous walled city.

The Ypres salient had seen two vicious battles in the first nine months of the war. In May 1915, the Germans had used poison gas for the first time during the second battle of Ypres. Since then, however, there had been no major engagements between the opposing forces at Ypres. It remained a deadly place to serve as the British positions were all overlooked by the high ground occupied by the Germans. The Gravenstafel, Frezenberg, Pilkem, Gheluvelt and Passchendael Ridges all provided perfect observation points from which artillery fire could be directed onto everything that moved in or up to the British lines. Its very name was to send a shiver down the spine of all those who were to serve on the Western Front. Now it was the turn of the 4th Battalion to serve in the salient. They were, as events turned out, to spend the next twelve months at Ypres.

For much of the time between October 1916 and July 1917 the battalion was engaged in holding the front line, and carrying out support duties when it was in reserve. There was little heavy infantry fighting around Ypres in these months.

Haig had, however, long favoured a major British offensive at Ypres, designed to secure a rupture in the German lines and a possible movement towards the Belgian coast. In November 1916, shortly after the arrival at Ypres of the 4th Battalion, he had asked Sir Herbert Plumer, commander of the Second Army, to prepare offensive operations against the German positions at Ypres. But there was disagreement between the politicians and military over exactly what Britain's military tactics in 1917 should be.

The new British Prime Minister, David Lloyd George, deeply concerned by the huge casualties on the Somme, favoured a switch away from the Western Front altogether. He wanted to offer instead support to an Italian offensive against the Austrians and was reluctant to sanction any major new offensive on the Western Front at all. He did not have huge confidence in the ability of Haig and the other generals to conduct successful operations with minimal loss of life to the troops. He was willing for British guns to move to the Italian front, but not for more squandering of men and material on the Western Front.

Lloyd George had however also fallen under the spell of the new French commander, Robert Nivelle, who had replaced Joffre at the end of 1916. Nivelle proposed a dramatic plan to breach the German lines with a large scale French infantry assault on the Chemin des Dames above the River Aisne. Lloyd George gave his backing to the new French commander's plans, and came down in favour of Haig providing British support to the French operation. This was done with some effect. The Canadians had stormed and taken the Vimy Ridge in April 1917 in one of the most dramatic coups de main of the war. But the Battle of Arras, launched in the same month, had largely descended in to the same sort of grindingly slow and hugely costly battle of attrition as on the Somme the previous summer, with little appreciable gain to show for it. More significantly, the French attack under Nivelle was a complete failure that resulted in massive casualties to the French and a consequent large-scale act of mutiny on the part of its army, rendering it incapable for the moment of any offensive action. The initiative therefore swung back to Haig and his plans for an attack in Flanders. Over the next few months these plans would come to a fearful fruition.

Their first tour of duty in the firing line during this period of time began on 15 October 1916 in positions along the Menin Road. It was an uneventful time and after four days they were relieved without any serious casualties. Twelve new officers arrived to join the battalion, which was now formed back into the original four companies, with Captain Gardner taking command of A Company, Captain Slater B Company, Captain Huthwaite C Company and Captain Williamson D Company. The whole battalion was engaged in working parties when they were out of the line.

On 23 October they were back into the front line again, where they found the trenches in a very poor state of repair. A and B companies were in the firing line, pumping out the water that was flowing into it, revetting the trenches and putting up rolls of barbed wire in front of them. C company was in reserve and D in the support lines. The weather at this time was beginning to get steadily worse as winter approached. The men were fully engaged in trying to make their trenches fit for purpose, and were busy deepening and draining them. On 25 October, they were all wearing rubber wading boots in an effort to keep their feet reasonably dry, as the water was over the duckboards in many places. They sustained five casualties from enemy gun fire – one soldier being seriously wounded. On the night of 27 October they were relieved, with no further losses.

For the next two nights the men were in billets in the ramparts at Ypres again, performing fatigue duties. On 30 October they marched to Elverdinghe where they were to spend the next few days in billets near the Chateau, performing a mixture of drills, training and working parties.

On 7 November they returned to Ypres. In the evening of 8 November, they relieved the 6th Liverpools in the front line, much of which was now a series of manned shell craters rather than joined-up trenches. One platoon occupied shell holes, which formed the outpost line in front of the rest of the battalion.

Early in the morning of 9 November they were subjected to light enemy shelling from field guns. Later in the morning the whole front line was bombarded by gun fire and trench mortars. About fifty of the trench mortar rounds landed in the trenches occupied by the 4th Battalion, but miraculously there were no casualties, although some damage was done to the parapet in the front line. The next day was spent repairing the damage. On the afternoon of 11 November, another enemy barrage landed on the battalion, this time it was *minenwerfer* and light trench mortars. Once again there were no casualties. Scouting patrols were sent out in the early morning of 12 November and these reported enemy working parties out with flashlights. There was no firing. The following day they were relieved by the 4th Loyals and moved back once again to Ypres.

On 13 November, Lieutenant-Colonel Balfour went back to London on leave and Captain Slater took over temporary command. Virtually the whole battalion was involved in working parties for the next few days until the men went back into the front line on 18 November. On their way to the front line the battalion marched through the famous Menin Gate. Major Brocklebank assumed command of the battalion.

The trenches were again in a state of poor repair and further extensive work was done on them. On 19 November, Sergeant Edmondson from Barrow was killed by a sniper, a constant danger in this sector of the line. On 24 November Captain Slater, who had only recently been in command of the battalion, was badly bruised during an enemy trench mortar barrage and was sent to hospital to recover. The next day they were relieved again by the 4th Loyals and went returned to billets at Ypres. That day they sent up 206 men on working parties to the front line.

On 26 November the battalion was replaced in the reserve lines by the 5th Loyals and went by train to Brandhoek where they marched into camp. For the next few days the battalion was engaged in various training and drill routines. On 30 November they had the luxury of taking baths at Poperinghe. A similar regime prevailed for the first week of December.

On 8 December, the Lewis gun teams travelled by road to Ypres. The battalion followed by train from Brandhoek to Ypres, back into billets in the ramparts where it spent the next few days in training. On 14 December, they relieved the 4th Loyals in the Railway Wood sector. Owing to the heavy rain, parts of the front line had collapsed. Making good the damage caused by the terrible weather occupied the whole battalion for the next few days in the line. Over this period the enemy fired a heavy barrage onto Ypres, at Hell Fire Corner – an important crossroads just outside the town which was a crucial link between the front and reserve lines – and on the area around the Menin Gate. The British guns retaliated equally strongly on the German lines.

On 15 December, the battalion working parties put up a total of sixty-three coils of barbed wire – concertina as well as apron wire in the ground in front of the firing line. The heavy gun fire continued all day long. Two of the officers' servants were wounded when one of the shells exploded near the cookhouse of HQ Company. At 4.30 in the afternoon, a red rocket was fired from the opposing front lines, and the battalion prepared for a possible enemy attack. The British guns opened rapid fire on the German front line for an hour. Two men were wounded in the exchange of gun fire and one man was sent down the line suffering from shell shock. The trenches occupied by the 4th Battalion were severely damaged, but no enemy infantry assault was launched against them. The next day was spent trying to repair the damage.

During the morning of 17 December, the Germans exploded a small mine underneath one of the shell craters being manned as part of the 4th's outpost line. Underground tunnelling and the planting of mines had been a feature of trench warfare since almost its beginning. This was the first time the 4th Battalion had been its victims. They were lucky. This time there were no casualties, as the mine was only a small one, perhaps no bigger than a large minenwerfer. The trench leading up to the shell hole had been destroyed as had 20 yards of trench immediately behind, burying one of the Lewis gun teams temporarily.

On 18 December the men were employed in fixing the damaged trenches and in strengthening the wire in front of the new crater caused by the German mine. On the night of 18/19 December, the men were relieved by the 5th Liverpools and went into reserve positions at Ypres. An officer, Lieutenant Holdsworth, and one other man were wounded on patrol that evening.

During this time, the battalion was asked to mount a major raid on the German lines at St Julien, in the north-east sector of the salient. The purpose of the raid was to gain information on the German front-line position, to enter the trench and cause as much damage as possible, and finally, to capture prisoners for intelligence purposes. A party of 200 men under Captain Clarke was briefed and trained for the mission, which was due to take place on 23 December.

The Intelligence Report of VIII Corps gave the following account of the raid,

> At 5.25 under a very effective barrage, a raiding party of 200 men entered the enemy trenches between south of Oder House and Cameroon Trench and penetrated to the support line. Trenches badly knocked about – no identification obtained. First men arrived back in our lines about 6.45. Hot baths, clean uniforms and hot breakfasts were ready for them.

The raid, judged by its mission and purpose, was not a brilliant success. No prisoners had been taken as the front line had been evacuated by the Germans as soon as the British barrage fell on it. No identifications or intelligence were gathered. The gun fire had also caused considerable damage to the trenches, probably more than the men were capable of inflicting themselves.

The raid was over within an hour and twenty minutes. Lieutenants Hartley and Smith were wounded. Two men were killed, and thirty were wounded. Three men were reported missing. One of those to die during the raid was Private John Halligan of Fay Street, Barrow. He was 20 years old. Private James Millington, also from Barrow, died in this action.

The next day the battalion relieved the 4th Loyals in the front line, in the area around Wieltje, to be relieved themselves on the night of 28/29 December. A second Christmas had been spent in France. A second one in the front line. This one too was quiet, with no enemy activity reported and no further casualties. They travelled by train to Brandhoek where they were to spend the New Year and enjoy ten days out of the front line.

1917: Ypres and Cambrai

On the night of 12/13 January 1917, the battalion was once again back in the front line at Railway Wood. One company of the 4th Loyals, who they had just relieved, remained with the King's Own men in the front line to provide additional support. Over the next few days, the enemy shelled Mud Lane Trench sporadically, but the situation remained generally quiet overall. On 16 January they were themselves relieved by a battalion of the Sussex Regiment and returned to positions at Ypres. The next day they moved back to Poperinghe where they spent the next week in training, drill and company inspections.

On 23 January, A and B Companies moved to billets on the canal bank at Ypres to act as reserve to the left brigade of 38th Division. The rest of the battalion remained at Poperinghe where they continued their training exercises. On 3 February, C and D Companies moved by train to Bollezeele. A and B Companies joined them there the next day. They were put on alert to be ready to move at short notice, as the enemy had mounted an attack along the whole Corps frontage. At 2.30 in the afternoon, the whole brigade set off in full marching order to Esquielbeck. Shortly afterwards, they received the order to about turn – the whole exercise was simply an emergency drill. There had been no German attack.

In February 1917, the Germans had in fact begun a strategic withdrawal back to the Hindenburg Line, abandoning many of the positions that had been so strongly contested during the Battle of the Somme. The Germans were moving onto a defensive posture along the whole front as they concentrated their resources instead on the fighting in the east in an attempt to knock Russia out of the war. The main focus of their operations against Britain would, in the mean time, be the submarine blockade, being conducted from the ports along the Belgian coast.

On 27 February, the battalion relieved the 13th Welch Regiment on the front line at Wieltje. There they remained until 4 March when they were relieved by the 4th Loyal North Lancs. It had been another remarkably quiet tour of duty, spent improving the trenches. There were no reports any hostile enemy action at all.

The next few days were spent in billets on the Canal Bank. On 8 March they relieved the 4th Loyals in the front lines at Cross Roads Farm. The next few days were devoted to continuing the work on improving the trenches. On 14 March they were sent back to the Canal Bank for a rest, en route to Poperinghe again, where they were to spend the next ten days – and the battalion played football matches against the Honourable Artillery Company and the 8th Liverpools. On 27 March they were back in billets along the Canal Bank and relieved their sister battalion the 5th King's Own. On 28 March they were back in the front line, replacing the 5th South Lancs at Cross Roads Farm. They held these positions until 2 April, when they themselves were relieved by the 4th Loyal North Lancs

There were no reports of any hostile enemy action during this period of front-line trench duty. This pattern was to repeat itself through April and May.

Front-line trench duties were generally very quiet. The battalion provided working parties for the front line when it was in reserve. At the end of April and the beginning of May the battalion spent several days training for open warfare, an obvious clue that offensive military operations were being planned again. On 11 May the battalion suffered a few casualties at Potijze from heavy enemy shelling in retaliation for successful trench raids mounted by battalions on their flank. One of those to die was Private William Postlethwaite of Smeaton Street, Barrow. On 13 May, a patrol in no man's land had stumbled across an enemy working party and dispersed them with rifle fire. At the end of May and into early June, the battalion was employed in building a new reserve trench at Potijze called Cambridge Road. No one doubted now that moves were under way for some kind of offensive along the Ypres front.

On 7 June, huge mines were exploded underneath the German lines on the Messines Ridge, just south of Ypres. In a major success for the British, the whole ridge, which had been in German hands since the early days of the war, was captured. The ridge was regarded as an important strategic position over-looking the southern sector of the salient, which would need to be in Allied hands if there was to be any prospect of a successful advance. The Battle of the Messines Ridge was the precursor to the opening of the Third Battle of Ypres seven weeks later.

On 9 June, the battalion carried out a trench raid against Ibex Trench, the German trench opposite their front, capturing six prisoners and killing three others. No casualties were sustained by the raiding party. Two of its members, Lance-Corporal Charles Cooper and Private James McAlarney were both to receive Military Medals for their part in the raid.

From the middle of June onwards, the battalion was at Petit Difques, well away from the front line, and engaged in training for the operations that lay ahead of it. On the evening of 18 June, the Brigadier-General had come to brief them. In May, Haig had announced at an Army Commanders Conference at Doullens that the main focus of British efforts on the Western Front would now centre on the Ypres salient, with the ultimate objective of securing the Belgian coast, ending the submarine blockade and ultimately pushing the Germans out of Belgium altogether. Operations would be divided into two distinct phases. First, the Messines Ridge would be captured. It would be followed by attacks on the whole front of the salient aimed at capturing the high ground and then breaking out towards the coast.

The German positions at Ypres were strongly defended and well constructed. Three lines of trenches lay in front of the British. Between these lines ran the Steenbeeke, which had long since burst its banks under the weight of persistent shelling and had created swamp-like conditions in the middle of the battlefield. But unlike the conditions prevailing on the Somme, the water table was too high to permit the construction of deep underground bunkers. The Germans had instead constructed hundreds of reinforced concrete pillboxes housing machine guns and field artillery. The Germans had rightly concluded that the attack at Messines probably meant that an attack at Ypres was not far away and had immediately begun strengthening their positions in the salient. By the end of July, the British would face not three lines of trenches but five.

If they were to attack, the British would face determined defenders, committed to holding every inch of ground. Behind the forward lines of breastworks lay strongly defended positions, with the carefully sited pillboxes designed to hold up the attack and drain the power of any forward advance. The third line was the main battle line, where any attackers would be met by the fresh troops of the reserve formations, backed up by the counter-attack regiments held back specifically for this purpose.

General Gough, who had been given command of the battle, planned to make an advance along the whole line of the salient of between 4,000 and 5,000 yards, in four jumps, spread over several hours of the first day, which would capture most of main battle area, including the third German line. Although not a complete breakthrough, this would represent a massive achievement for a single day's fighting in the conditions that prevailed in the salient in July. For Haig, this plan represented the least he would consider as acceptable.

The 55th Division was allotted a major operational role right in the centre of the planned attack, towards the southern end of the Pilkem Ridge: 164 Brigade and the 4th Battalion, King's Own, were to be in the front line of the attack. The attack itself would eventually begin on 31 July, after a heavy artillery bombardment of the enemy lines during which 4.3 million shells were fired.

On 2 July, the battalion broke off from its training to take up positions in the front line at Wieltje. They spent the time consolidating the line, constructing dumps, repairing the wire and conducting patrols into no man's land, trying to gather any new intelligence they could about the Germans in front of them. They were relieved on the 9 July and for the next ten days the whole battalion – nearly 520 men – provided working parties for the forward areas.

The preliminary bombardment started on 16 July. On 19 July the battalion was sent back to the reserve areas to prepare for the attack. They spent this time familiarizing themselves with every detail of their battle plans, aided by extensive aerial photographs of the ground they were to attack. Their operational orders contained one rather noticeable instruction:

> Operational Order No.44, 24/7/17.
> There will be on no account a promiscuous hunting for souvenirs. Company and platoon commanders and NCOs will take a special care that this order is obeyed as disastrous consequences have ensued in the past when troops have been allowed to indulge in this pastime.

On 29 July, the 'B List' men, who would serve to provide the core around which the battalion would be rebuilt after the attack, were sent off to the transport lines, even further behind the front. On the evening of 30 July, the rest of the battalion, about 400 strong, marched into Congreve Walk, their start line for the attack. There they waited for zero hour, 3.50 am on the morning of 31 July.

All around and above them was the fearful sound of the intensive British artillery barrage. Few if any of the men would have got any sleep at all that night. The artillery barrage on the left and in the centre of the British line of attack was hugely effective. Around the first and second line of German trenches, the barbed wire had been destroyed, most of the trenches obliterated and many of the pill-boxes put out of action.

The attack was launched by 165 and 166 Brigades and was supported by twenty tanks of 16 Company who provided valuable support to the attacking troops. The task of 164 Brigade and the 4th Battalion King's Own was to press the attack on to the final objective for the day, the Green Line. At 8.20 am, the battalion, under the acting command of Major Robathan, passed through the Black Line – the initial objective for the advance – that had been secured by the initial assault. They successfully captured all of the strong points in their path and reached the Green Line about three hours later. In the process, they captured 500 prisoners and four machine guns. The outpost line in front of the advance was established at around 12.15 pm. They could not, however, establish any contact with the battalion on their left, something which would bring dire consequences later in the day. This was to mark the limit of the advance on the first day of Third Ypres, and the men of the 4th King's Own were once again at the sharp end of it, with no one between them and the enemy.

At 3.00 pm the enemy counter-attacks began. The situation began to deteriorate quickly. The men at the outpost line made a desperate plea for more ammunition half an hour later. There were problems getting it up to them as by this time the enemy artillery had begun to lay down an effective fire on the captured ground behind them. The battalion sought help from the tanks. None were in action or available to offer any assistance. There were problems in arranging protective artillery covering fire, as their exact position was not known to the gunners. Their advance had, in any case, taken them to the extreme limits of the range of British field guns and the covering fire they were able to provide was sporadic and patchy. When they needed the support of the guns the most, it was not to be available to them.

At this point, the 4th King's Own and the 4th Loyal North Lancs, who had advanced with them, formed one composite battalion because of the heavy casualties each had sustained. Lieutenant-Colonel Withey of the 4th Loyal North Lancs took over command. They turned to form a defensive flank to their right to meet the weight of the German counter-attacks. Their left flank was however in the air and liable to attack as the battalion that was supposed to advance with them had not been able to get up alongside. This is now exactly what happened. Their position became completely untenable. To stay on would have meant certain death or capture. By 20.30, men from the composite battalion began

Lance Sergeant Tom Mayson, of C Company,
from Silecroft near Millom. wrote:

On the morning of 31st July we left Congreve Walk at 08.30 am. We followed behind No.4 platoon of the 4th Loyal North Lancs commanded by Lieutenant Ordish. We were detailed to mop up Somme Farm and its surrounding defences. We went over in artillery formation, the boys being in fine fettle. The enemy was putting up a barrage between Congreve Walk and his old front line, but we got through quite well with the loss of only one man. We went on without further losses to the Black Line, where we came under heavy machine gun fire from the left flank, but this gun was put out of action by troops on the left.

The 165th Brigade was consolidating the Black Line. We left the Black Line in extended order under heavy fire from a machine gun and an anti tank gun, which did not fire until the tank came up. We got about 50 yards from the machine gun when a tank came up and put it out of action. Another gun opened fire half left so I crawled to a flank for about 150 yards and got behind a mound and then found cover in a ditch. I approached to within 20 yards on the gun when I threw a bomb, putting the gun out of action and wounded 4 of the team. The remainder of the gun team belted into a dug out nearby. I went into the dug out after them, but only found three of them there whom I slew with the bayonet. My platoon then came up and pushed on with me. For a time there was some mixed fighting in shell holes. Then we came across some dugouts near the Weiltje Road, which we cleared, capturing 16 prisoners. Next we went across to Pond Farm, which we were not supposed to touch, but there was no one else at hand, where we captured from 100–150 prisoners. We were literally surrounded by them, and not one of them resisted. In the meantime, the platoon for which we were mopping up had gone ahead. I then reconnoitred Somme Farm, where I found the Brigade forward station. Finally my platoon started to dig in near the Wieltje Road. The enemy then began his counter attack in front and on both flanks. If we had had more SAA and if the troops on the flanks had not gone back we could have held out easily. Then we got to the Black Line, which was defended by outposts. We held the Black Line all right, at times under heavy shellfire. At 11.30 am next morning we received orders to withdraw to our original front line, which we did with the loss of one man wounded.

We had plenty of bombs, including German ones, but we were very short of SAA. Our Lewis guns were never used at all in the mopping up. My rations were plentiful and I was glad to have two water bottles.

arriving back in the Black Line. By this time, there were about 150 men of the King's Own still on the battlefield.

At 01.30 am on 1 August, the battalion received orders to retire to the Frezenberg Line. The new front line they occupied was from the top of St John Street to Warwick Farm. Fifty stragglers were also sent up to the front line having been collected from the rear. They held these positions all night, expecting a further counter-attack. None came. They were eventually relieved in the early hours of 2 August. The battalion reached Vlamertinghe by 5 pm. The men were given a ration of rum, hot food, clean underwear and baths. Colonel Balfour, the battalion commanding officer who had stayed behind with the B List men, now had the job of rebuilding the shattered remnants of his battalion. In the evening the battalion was moved by London omnibuses to Watou, via Brandhoek and Poperinghe, reaching their new camp at 01.00 on the morning of 3 August. Heavy rain had made the camp a quagmire, as the whole of the Ypres battlefield was soon to become.

In total, 15 officers of the battalion and over 200 men were either dead, wounded or missing. Of these 145 were wounded and 46 were reported missing, most of whose bodies were never recovered from the battlefield. Lieutenants Ford, Johnstone and Bradley were known to have died. Lieutenant John Douglas Johnstone was a young officer from Barrow. Other Barrovians were to share his fate; Privates Thomas Bowron, Robinson Shone and Albert Billingham all died on that day. Robinson was only 19. He lived with his parents at 307e Duke Street. On 4 August, in rest camps behind the lines, the survivors were asked to write their own narratives of what had taken place.

Sergeant Mayson was to win the Victoria Cross for his actions that day, the first of three to be awarded to men of the 4th King's Own in the war. It was he who led the assault on the dugouts referred to in his account of the day's actions, clearing the way for the battalion to continue its advance. His actions saved the lives of many of his fellow soldiers. Mayson would survive the war, return to the Furness peninsula and live out the rest of a long life, dying in 1958 in Barrow. He was an extraordinarily brave and modest soldier.

He would return on special leave to his home village in December when he was, quite literally, given a hero's welcome by the local community. He was also given £169 in War Bonds in recognition of his brave deeds. The citation for his VC in the *London Gazette* read:

> For most persistent bravery and devotion to duty. When, with the leading wave of the attack, his platoon was held up by machine gun fire from a flank, without waiting for orders, he at once made for the gun which he put out of action with bombs, wounding four of the team. The remaining three fled, pursued by Sergeant Mayson to a dug out into which he followed them and disposed of them with his bayonet. Later, when clearing up a strong point, this NCO again tackled a machine gun

single handedly, killing six of the team. Finally, during an enemy counter attack, he took charge of an isolated post and successfully held it until ordered to withdraw as his ammunition was exhausted. He displayed throughout most remarkable valour and initiative.

Sergeant Hewartson, in 7 Platoon, B Company, had a different experience:

Our advance from the Congreve Walk to the Black Line was uneventful. We had no casualties and met with practically no artillery fire. We advanced without any halt up to the Green Line. We started to dig in with the North Lancs until told that we were not required, and Captain Brocklebank ordered the company to return to the Gallipoli Somme Farm area, which we did and commenced to consolidate there. We remained there until we received orders to advance and support the North Lancs as the enemy were massing for a counter attack on the right. We got up to the North Lancs who were then withdrawing. We continued to withdraw back to the Gallipoli Ridge where we took up a defensive position, finally withdrawing to the Black Line. Second Lieutenant Warbrick got wounded in the first advance near Gallipoli. Up to that time he led us with great bravery. In fact his action was an example to all the men, not only of our own battalion but to men of other battalions.

Corporal Baines, of 2 Platoon, A Company, drew attention to the problems caused by the shortage of ammunition:

We advanced in artillery formation from Congreve Walk about 08.30 am and proceeded to advance to the Black Line, this was held by the 165th Brigade and met a machine gun barrage. Passing through the barrage we arrived at Gallipoli and there commenced consolidating. Word came from the 4th North Lancs that their left flank was open owing to the Battalion on their left failing to keep touch. We then moved over to the North Lancs left and dug in. In the Green Line during these operations we lost about 6 men wounded with machine gun and rifle fire. Word then came down for us to pull back as the enemy were seen to be pushing past both flanks. We dropped back as far as Hill 37. Here we remained until all our ammunition was exhausted. There came an order to fall back still further. This time we went back to Hill 35. We had been salvaging what SAA we could and used it all here. We then fell back on the Black Line. During the move from Gallipoli up to the North Lancs, Lieutenant McGIll was wounded. Corporal Cox took charge of the platoon. Corporal Cox was wounded during the move from the Green Line to Hill 37 and I took over the command of the platoon.

Second Lieutenant Gribble was in command of a platoon in B Company and described graphically the terms in which the fighting was conducted:

> The advance was commenced from Congreve Walk in Artillery formation in single file and at that time the enemy was intermittently shelling our own front line and had placed a feeble barrage on his own support line opposite Wieltje. The casualties were very few until the Black Line was reached. Many of the party leaving the Black line were hit by enfilade machine gun fire from the left. Enemy aeroplanes swooped and fired at us. Gallipoli was established as Company headquarters and then the men proceeded to consolidate, Lewis guns at this time being brought into play. Lieutenant Walker and myself with about 30 men constructed a small section of trench to the left front of Gallipoli overlooking the hollow ground and the crest beyond. An enemy machine gun constantly played over the high ground, which we then occupied. At this time two enemy aeroplanes flew over our position and machine guns were fired on them and later one of our own returned with information. I was able to observe the movements of the enemy from left to right by means of field glasses. Several bodies of enemy appeared over the crest line, but the attack was broken up by our own shrapnel fire and they then disappeared behind the crest. It was just shortly after this that the main enemy counter attack delivered on the Camerons to our right and that they withdrew. At this stage there was no artillery fire and the struggle was reduced to an open infantry fire fight, the supply of ammunition being a great difficulty. The men used their rifles well, adjusted their sights and fired intelligently. The power of this weapon must have been clearly impressed upon them by the good results they obtained, and one man near me gave some very good fire orders. On withdrawing to the Black Line myself and a party of about 15 men remained there during the night and the following day received orders to occupy the original front line to the right of Wieltje.

Lieutenant Walker was one of the officers wounded in the fighting.

Sergeant Walker, acting company sergeant major with B Company, offered a concise view of the day's events:

> I was with company headquarters and accompanied Captain Brocklebank to the Green Line. When nearing the Green Line we came across a snipers post on our left. Second Lieutenant Alexander, myself and 5 men went forward in front of the first wave of the North Lancs and tackled this post and put it out of action with rifle grenades which we found of great use. Lieutenant Alexander was wounded here. We returned to Gallipoli where company headquarters was established and

remained here until about one and a half hours later. We saw the enemy counter attacking . . . we took up a defensive position and withdrew to the Black Line when we had expended all of our ammunition.

Captain Brocklebank himself was wounded during the fighting and was reported missing at the end of the day. His body was never discovered.

Sergeant Brown of 12 Platoon, C Company felt that the men had been fully prepared for the tasks they had been allotted:

> This is the third battle in which I have participated at Ypres and I wish to say that on no previous occasion had I such clear instructions. The most dense man in the platoon had a perfectly clear idea of what to do. The aeroplane photographs were an excellent help and by studying them I was able to recognise my objective as soon as I got in the neighbourhood.

The area around Somme and Gallipoli Farms, so easily but only briefly held by the 4th King's Own on 31 July, would now take several more weeks of bloody fighting to recover. The first day of what would prove to be another four-month battle had been a modest success. Gains had been made by the French in the north and by the British on the left and centre of their advance. But no gains had been

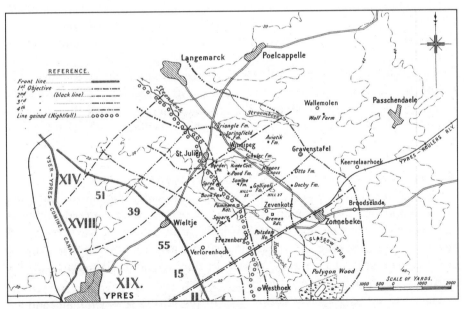

The advance of the 4th Battalion on 31 July, showing the direction of attack and objectives. It was during this attack that Sergeant Tom Mayson won the Victoria Cross.

made on the right flank of the attack around Gheluvelt, where many of the German batteries were located. The failure to make any appreciable gains here exposed the British to dangerous enfilade gun fire as they pushed further and further into an even more pronounced salient.

For their bravery that day, fifteen men were awarded the Military Medal and Sergeants James Cross and James Topham the Distinguished Conduct Medal.

On 5 August, whilst the bloody battle at Ypres continued in the most appalling conditions caused by incessant rainfall, the 4th King's Own were withdrawn well behind the front line to regroup and reform themselves into a fighting unit. They travelled by train via Hazebrouk and St Omer to Audruicq, then by motor lorries down the valley of the Hem to Bonningues Les Ardres, into excellent billets. The 8th Liverpools, which had undergone an even worse experience on the opening day of Third Ypres, were in billets in the same village.

They stayed there until the end of the month. Five officers and 120 men were sent up as reinforcements to boost the strength of the battalion. The men were granted a twenty-four-hour leave pass to Calais while the officers enjoyed a forty-eight-hour pass to the seaside at the mouth of the River Somme.

The men continued to train. They practised storming and taking pillboxes, strong points and machine gun positions. They did so over ground that had been prepared to match exactly the ground over which their attack would be launched. Their contribution to Third Ypres was far from over yet.

On 14 September they were moved by lorries and train to Goldfish Chateau, north of Ypres. Their camp was bombed the following day by enemy aircraft, killing one man and wounding three others. They were bombed again the next day too, this time three men were killed and five were wounded. On the night of 17/18 September, the battalion began their move up the front line. They were heavily shelled, with six men killed and seven wounded. On the evening of 19 September they took up positions near Hindu Cott and Somme farm, close to the scenes of the fighting on 31 July, ready to launch their attack the following morning, 20 September, with zero hour fixed at 05.40 am. The Battle of the Menin Road was to begin.

The battle had not gone well in August or in the first couple of weeks of September. Torrential downpours throughout August had caused havoc on the battlefield. Troop movements were extremely difficult. Moving the guns was almost impossible. Rapid infantry assaults across the shell-cratered terrain in these conditions was beyond the ability of the tiring soldiers in the front line. A series of repeat attacks against the all-important Gheluvelt positions had made no significant progress at all and only modest further advances had been made in the north and on the left centre of the front of attack.

Haig had effectively lost confidence in the ability of Gough to conduct successful operations in these conditions, and called in the services of General Plumer to deal the decisive blow on the right against Gheluvelt which would allow the resumption of a broader advance towards Passchendael and beyond. Plumer was to propose another of his by now famous 'bite and hold' operations against Gheluvelt, which would involve limited advances over ground that had been subjected to an enormous preliminary artillery bombardment that would target not only the immediate front, reserve and support lines that were to be attacked, but enemy batteries as well. And in front of the advancing British infantry would be a protective artillery barrage 1,000 yards deep, helping the infantry to consolidate their newly won positions before any counter-attack could be launched. The British were to enjoy a crushing superiority in guns over the Germans – maybe as high as four to one. For Plumer, any advance had to be within the limits of the artillery's ability to provide a protective curtain of fire. Gough would still command operations in the centre and on the left flank.

During the night of 19 September, men from eighteen assaulting infantry brigades got into position to launch the attack. At midnight it started to pour with rain again, making the ground over which the advance was to be made a sea of mud.

The 4th Battalion advanced at zero hour as planned and secured their first line of objectives, despite coming under heavy machine gun fire from Aisne Farm. The fire from German pillboxes was so heavy that the men began to lose the protection of the advancing creeping barrage. B and D Companies were aiming for the Red Line, an intermediate objective, A and C for the more distant Yellow Line. The men in these two companies suffered very heavily indeed from enfilade fire from their right. The battalion was being supported this time by the 4th Loyal North Lancs who pushed on ahead of the King's Own to capture the Green Line, the third line of objectives. Both battalions ended up defending the newly acquired front line around Schuller galleries under heavy and intense enemy gun fire. Here at least the British barrage had failed to put out of action the German batteries firing on them from Gheluvelt and Passchendael.

On 21 September, the 8th Liverpools and 5th Lancs Fusiliers took the attack forward under continuing enemy artillery fire. The 4th pushed on in turn to prepare for an expected counter-attack on 22 September. That day, the men continued to suffer from heavy enemy gun fire but managed to disperse a small counter-attacking force by their own machine gun fire and with artillery support. The evening of 23 September saw another particularly heavy enemy barrage. The battalion was eventually relieved in the early hours of 24 September. They went by train to Vlamertinghe and eventually reached Watou later that night.

The total casualties exceeded those for the first day of Third Ypres. This time ten officers were either dead, wounded or missing, as were 233 other ranks: 37 men were dead, 155 wounded and 25 were missing. There were six cases of severe shell shock. The battalion had suffered a 60 per cent casualty rate. The battle had however seen modest progress all along the front line attacked. The ground that had been won this time by the 4th King's Own was successfully defended against counter-attacking forces.

One of the soldiers killed on 20 September was Private John Smith of Duke

Street, Barrow. He was shot through the head by a sniper. He was 19 years of age. Before the war he had been serving an apprenticeship as a driller in the Vickers shipyard. He had only been in France for three months. Private Edwin Hamblett of Brooks Cottages, Ulverston, was reported missing after the battle. His body would never be seen again. Another young man killed on the same day was Private Andrew Morrow of Ramsden Dock Road, Barrow. He was just 20 years old. Private David Leech from Barrow also died on this day.

The Battle of Third Ypres would drag on for another seven appalling weeks of slaughter and suffering, gradually pushing the Germans back to the Passchendael Ridge which would be captured by the Canadians in November. No break-through was achieved and the Belgian coastal ports remained firmly in German hands right up to the end of the war. Most of the ground that had been won at such fearful cost in human life on both sides would be given up the following spring as the Germans made their last desperate gamble to win the war on the Western Front.

This encounter was to mark the end of the battalion's service at Ypres. On 25 September they marched to Hopoutre and then by train, travelled south to Bapaume. On 26 September they endured a long and tiring march to Vallulart Wood, north of Bapaume, in the Cambrai sector where they were to spend the next few days resting and re-equipping. On 2 October the battalion marched to Longavesnes.

For most of October the battalion served in the front line in a very quiet section near St Emilie. Fifteen new officers and forty-eight other ranks joined the battalion, whose trench strength was less than 350. Only one soldier, Lance-Corporal Masters, was reported as being killed on active service. The battalion was being allowed time to recover its fighting strength again.

After the failure of the Battle of Third Ypres to bring about the decisive break-through, Haig had been planning one more attack before the end of 1917. With the exit of Russia from the war after the Bolshevik Revolution in October, Haig was rightly determined to find a way of bringing about a decisive victory on the Western Front before the Germans were able to switch their forces from the east and mount their own powerful attack against the Allies. Although the United States had entered the war against Germany in April, they had still not deployed a significant force on the Western Front and were not in any position yet to offer material support. The only army capable of launching a further major offensive on the Western Front would be the British.

Haig had always believed in the potential of the new tanks to engineer a major breach in the enemy lines and thus bring about a return to conditions of open warfare where Britain and its Allies might be able to win a major tactical victory. The previously quiet stretch of the line at Cambrai was chosen as the perfect location for the first large-scale deployment of tanks in an effort to breach the enemy lines. The ground had not been subjected to heavy artillery fire so there were few shell craters as obstacles. It offered good prospects for a tank advance.

Hundreds of tanks would attack simultaneously under an enormous artillery barrage, to be followed up by the infantry and eventually the cavalry. The proposal for an attack upon the Cambrai front had been initially discussed between the French and British commanders in April 1917. On 25 April, Haig had asked Gough and Rawlinson to prepare plans for an attack between Banteux and Havrincourt.

Although the ground might have been favourable for a tank attack, the positions to be attacked were extremely formidable. They formed part of the Hindenburg Line to which the Germans had withdrawn in the early months of 1917. It consisted of several layers of defensive positions, heavily wired by zones that were 100 yards deep in places, fortified villages and incorporated key features such as the unfinished Canal du Nord which was about 60 feet wide and a serious obstacle for both troops and tanks. The front trenches were particularly well constructed. The average width of the fire trench was 10 feet and more at the top and over a yard wide at the bottom. The trenches had therefore been clearly designed partly to deal with the threat of the new tanks. They were also over 7 feet deep. Many of the German batteries were in close support behind the Hindenburg Line. In total, the depth of the defended position was between 6,000 and 8,000 yards. But if the British were ever to make a decisive breakthrough, they would have to breach the Hindenburg Line. There was no escape from this obvious if unpalatable fact.

Despite the strengths of these positions, the section between Banteux and Havrincourt was identified as the obvious part of the line to be attacked. If the front and support lines could be broken here, a short advance northwards would threaten the whole German forward line, where it bulged forward to the west and north-west. A bigger movement towards Cambrai and beyond would threaten the enemy's positions both to the north and south.

A few days after the 4th arrived in the Cambrai sector, Haig asked General Byng, commanding the Third Army, which had recently taken over this section of the line, to prepare the final plans for the attack at Cambrai. The plan would see hundreds of tanks employed in the initial assault. Advances in artillery methods, such as sound ranging, flash spotting and map shooting had been developed which meant that the traditional preliminary bombardment could be dispensed with. So too were the tried and tested methods of ranging and registering the guns onto their targets, which could easily be identified by the enemy as heralding a British attack. Maintaining the potent weapon of surprise in these ways, the tanks would be used instead to cut the wire and help the infantry into the enemy's trenches. The artillery would provide a hurricane bombardment at zero hour, focused on the front lines, enemy batteries and support positions.

The objectives for the battle had been decided. They were first to break the German positions by a coup de main with the help of the massed tank formations. Secondly, the important positions at Bourlon Wood, Cambrai and the crossings of the Sensee River were to be seized, cutting off the German troops between the river and the Canal du Nord, and then getting the cavalry through the breach, and to advance north-eastwards, rolling up the German lines from the south.

The attack would be launched on a 10,000 yard frontage from the Bonavis Ridge in the north to the Canal du Nord in the south. The main attack would be in the centre of the front. Minor attacks, demonstrations and heavy artillery fire would be used as diversions to confuse the enemy as to the real intentions of the attackers. Having played a major role at Third Ypres, 164 Brigade and the 4th King's Own were now to play an important role in one of these diversionary attacks in the Battle of Cambrai, which, after a series of delays, would start on 20 November.

On 2 November, the battalion moved out of brigade support and moved into Divisional Reserve at Longavesnes. For the next three weeks it would be immersed in training for the forthcoming battle.

On the evening of 19 November it moved up to the front line east of St Emile at Gillemont Farm. The battalion attacked the German front line at Gillemont Farm at 6.20 am on the 20 November under a heavy machine gun and trench mortar barrage. The enemy wire was found to be thick and unbroken. On the right flank of their assault, A Company and one platoon of D Company made good progress and achieved their final objective. In the centre, however, the men came under very strong machine gun fire. When they reached the enemy support lines they came under a shower of rifle grenades and bombs. The enemy was resisting strongly. B Company and one platoon of D were heavily outnumbered, suffered a large number of casualties and were eventually held up short of their objectives. On the left, C Company and one supporting platoon of D met uncut wire and were able to make some progress until, running low on bombs and meeting stronger and stronger resistance, they were finally stopped short of their final objectives.

By 11.15 am the battalion had succeeded in holding 500 yards of the front line and some 200 yards of a communication trench. Their position was, however, always a precarious one. In front of the farm lay a steep slope behind which the enemy forces could gather for their counter-attack unseen either by the men of the artillery acting in support of them.

They were eventually forced to retire as, to make matters worse, the attack of the battalion on their left had failed to make any progress. B Company were also ejected from their positions by strong counter-attacks from the enemy. Towards noon, C Company and their supports from D had been forced back to the enemy front line. B Company was in danger of being cut off from the company on their right, so two platoons of 5th Liverpools were sent to reinforce the centre at around 12.45.

By 13.00 the position in the centre had become impossible to hold because of the sheer weight of the attackers and the men were finally pushed back to their original start lines. A Company now found both of its flanks in the air and also moved back, under fire, to their start lines as well. The war diary described the fighting as 'severe' all morning. They were eventually relieved that night by the 4th Loyal North Lancs. Their total casualties were 11 confirmed dead, 120 wounded and 80 missing, a total of 211. The losses of the brigade amounted to 34 officers and 569 other ranks. The battalion had taken another heavy battering. Amongst those who lost their lives that day were Sergeant Samuel Eagers, who was originally from Egremont and Lance-Corporal Fred Wenham from Barrow. Four Lieutenants, Procter, Powell, Latham and Taylor, were awarded the Military Cross for their actions that day. Sixteen Military Medals and one DCM were awarded to men of the 4th King's Own for their actions on 20 November. Many of the 80 missing men had been taken prisoner by the Germans during their counter-attacks, including Private George Cole who came from St Helens. In an account of the fighting that day, written after his return to the UK in March 1919, Cole described the scepticism of the men in the days leading up to the attack.

> We had practised the attack every day during the preceding fortnight, but the opinion of the majority of the men was, that we had a position to take, which we were numerically not strong enough to manage. Consequently, the spirit of the men generally speaking was certainly not one of over confidence. Beside the actual taking of the farm, it was necessary to push forward and establish outposts to protect what was to be our new front line. As events proved, the taking of the position was comparatively easy, but also the prediction of the men that we were not strong enough to hold it proved to be only too true.

Their role had however, only been designed to mount a diversion from the main attack that was going in further to the north of them. The task of 164 Brigade was to secure the enemy's front and support lines for a distance of 1,600 yards. The holding or defending of any captured ground, in fact, was never the mission objective. The fact that no territorial or tactical gain had been secured by the 4th was not the point. They had made their contribution to the overall success of the first day of Battle of Cambrai.

The British forces, in this case the Third Army, led by the massed ranks of nearly 400 tanks, had enjoyed their biggest success of the war so far. A wide breach had been made in the German lines and the troops had penetrated the German positions on a front of six miles and up to a depth of four miles. Over 4,000 prisoners had been captured, along with 100 artillery pieces. For the first time since the war had started, victory bells pealed in every parish church across the country, as Britain celebrated a great victory. But the German lines were far from fractured, and heavy reinforcements were sent urgently to halt the British advance and to recover the ground that had been lost. And the attack had fallen well short of the objectives that had been set for it. The successful initial attack was not followed by a powerful driving force to carry on the advance. The British had little in the way of reserves to throw in to the battle and to exploit the success of the first day. The attack exhausted itself and quickly came to an effective standstill.

In particular, the attack on 20 November had not managed to capture the crucial high ground at Bourlon Wood, on which Haig had placed such a heavy emphasis. Subsequent attacks on 21 and 22 November were similar failures. The 11th King's Own, the bantam unit raised in 1915 and now a part of 40th Division, was to play an important role in the fighting for this key feature of the Cambrai battlefield the following day.

By 27 November, the reserves of the British Third Army were effectively exhausted and the attack ground to a halt. The positions gained were to be consolidated, a defensive front along the Flesquieres Ridge established and a protective line thrown around Graincourt on the northern flank of the battlefield. The tank brigades were withdrawn as they began their move to winter quarters. The British were waiting for the inevitable counter-thrust from the Germans, and were left defending a far from ideal forward line.

Signs of an impending German attack began to be picked up on 28/29 November. On the evening of the 29th the following message was sent out from battalion headquarters to all companies of the 5th South Lancs of 166 Brigade, 55th Division, which held about 2,000 yards of the southern section of the front line at Cambrai:

> In the event of an attack you will hold the line at all costs. There is to be no retirement to any second line. Warn all ranks to be specially alert.

The main thrust of the German counter-stroke in the southern sector of the Cambrai front was about to land against the 55th Division.

The enemy attack was preceded by a gradual bombardment that built in intensity, with gas and high explosive shells. It cut all rear communications. In the forward line, machine guns and Lewis guns and their teams were either blown up or buried by the fire of very heavy trench mortars. The weather conditions favoured the attackers too. It was a dark morning with a heavy mist which hid the build-up of the counter-attacking infantry from British observation. In this sector of the line, the fire was directed principally on the 55th Division, whose defences on the forward slopes of the spurs running eastward from the high ground about Ronssoy–Lempire and Epehy–Peiziere commanded the valleys between.

The main blow landed on 166 Brigade and some battalions were forced to retire. The 5th King's Own put up a particularly stout resistance in Kildare, Meath and Limerick Posts. They were forced to relinquish Kildare Post after a fierce fight. Meath held out until the afternoon. At Limerick a mixed force including some of the 5th King's Own repulsed every attack made against it that day. It was on the extreme left of the divisional front that the enemy made his most dangerous incursion, at the Banteux Ravine near Villers Guislan. The 5th South Lancs were deployed in scattered outposts backed up by only two weak platoons of the 5th King's Own. The whole battalion was rapidly overrun and hardly a man of the South Lancashire survived. The whole position of the 55th Division began to look extremely vulnerable.

It would be essential in these circumstances for the division to maintain its hold on the high ground at Ronssoy–Lempire and Epehy–Peiziere. The 164 Brigade,

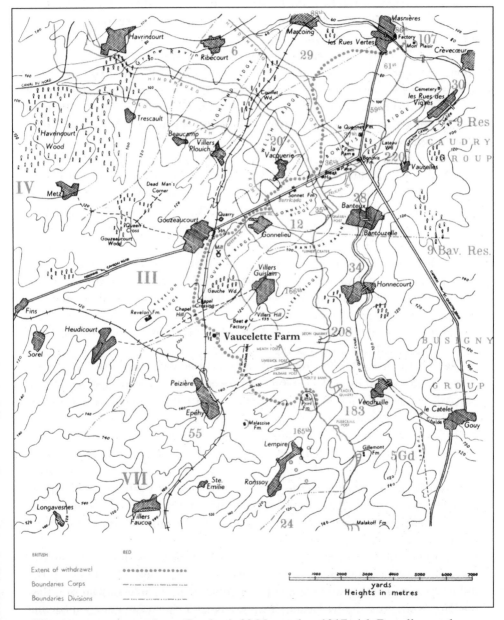

German counter-attacks at Cambrai, 30 November 1917. 4th Battalion took up positions at Vaucelette Farm.

by this time numbering only 1,400 men, about a third of its fighting strength, was brought forward by Major-General Jeudwine from reserves to build up a line of resistance extending from the left of the 9th Liverpools, who were occupying posts on the eastward side of Lempire. The first battalion of 164 Brigade to move forward that morning was the 4th King's Own. At 8.30 am they had moved to reinforce the right of 166 Brigade. Passing Epehy, the battalion pushed on north-eastwards and at about 11.00 am dug in some 500 yards in the rear of the positions held by the survivors of the 5th King's Own, who were still heavily engaged with the enemy. The 4th prepared to resist any German advance. Later in the afternoon, they were joined on their left by the 8th Liverpools. Gradually, a proper defensive line was beginning to be established. The 55th Division was also being reinforced by the reserve battalions of the 24th Division on their immediate right, who although under enemy artillery fire, were not being attacked so far by German infantry.

At Vaucelette Farm, just to their north, the 4th Loyal North Lancs had launched a remarkable counter-attack on the German troops advancing from Villers Guislan. Three weak companies had gone over the top, firing their Lee Enfields from the hip as they moved forward. The German advance began to falter.

The expected attack on the positions occupied by the 4th Battalion never materialized. At 3.30 in the afternoon, they were relieved and withdrew to dugouts along the railway line to the south-west of Vaucelette Farm, where they constituted a small reserve. The German forward thrust in this sector had succeeded in taking the forward British line, but thereafter began to meet determined resistance and lose much of its forward momentum. The enemy appeared to be content with the progress they had made and decided not to press their attack any further. Further to the north, the German counter-attacks were proving to be much more successful, and virtually all of the ground won on 20 November was lost again to the Germans over the next couple of days. Cambrai had proved to be another false dawn.

On 1 December, the battalion witnessed a remarkable counter-attack by cavalry along the Epehy–Villers Guislan road. It was a predictable failure. Horses were no more immune to machine gun fire than men. Later infantry attacks failed because of inadequate artillery support. At 4.30 pm, enemy artillery fire began to intensify. The battalion was relieved that night and moved back to St Emilie, under orders to move at thirty minutes' notice. The overall situation clearly remained highly unstable.

On 4 December, they were moved back into support positions at Sandbag Alley, expecting another imminent German infantry assault. At 05.30 the following morning they were 'stood to' in anticipation of an attack on their immediate front. Nothing happened. Two hours later they were marched back to St Emilie. The 4th Battalion's contribution to the fighting at Cambrai was now over. On 6 December they were marched to Longasvesnes where they proceeded by bus to Peronne, which was reached in the early evening. The following morning they travelled by train to Beaumetz. Over the next few days they marched in stages to Reclinghem, where they were to stay until the beginning of February 1918.

1918: backs to the wall and advance to victory

There they were to re-equip, rest, bathe and receive reinforcements. A total of nine new officers and seventy-five other men joined the battalion there. The battalion enjoyed their first Christmas out of the front line since their arrival in France. They had earned it.

New drafts continued to arrive in the battalion during January – forty-three in total. On 19 January, the First Army commander, General Sir Henry Horne, presented medals to those who had fought at Cambrai. In total, four MCs, four DCMs and five Military Medals were awarded to men of the 4th Battalion.

On the morning of 7 February, the battalion marched for four hours to Ligny in heavy rain. The next day they continued their march to Busnettes. Here they were joined at 10.00 am en route by six officers and 194 men form the recently disbanded 7th Battalion of the King's Own. The army was undergoing a major reorganization at this time. The supply of manpower was beginning to dry up and Haig had decided to rearrange the brigades into groups of three battalions rather than four. Under-strength battalions would be brought up to strength by merging them with others in the same regiment. The remaining men of the 7th Battalion were sent to join the 5th King's Own. It is not unreasonable to assume that the men from the 7th who were joining the 4th Battalion would have had some kind of connection to the Furness area. On 9 February, the strongly reinforced 4th Battalion reached Houchin, where it stayed for five days. They were under orders to go back into the front line on the La Bassee canal, the site of their very first trench duties on the Western Front. And it would be here they would take part in perhaps their most significant military engagement of the whole war. Unknown to the men of the 4th, they were heading straight to a section of the front line the German high command would seek to break in the Spring Offensive that was soon to be launched against the British Army in France.

All through the early months of 1918, the German army in France was being steadily reinforced by divisions that had previously been fighting in the east. Ludendorff, the German Army commander, planned to use these additional forces in a massive and overwhelming attack designed to separate the French and British armies from each other, and then roll up the British line in a push to the Channel ports. Cut off from supplies and on their own, the British Army would have to give up the fight in France and Belgium. The war would effectively be over. This assault would also have to be mounted before the fledgling US Army could take the field. The battle would start on 21 March, in just a few weeks' time.

The 4th Battalion moved into the support trenches on 14 February. The next three days were spent repairing the trenches. Two of the battalion runners, Privates Round and Jackson, captured two escaped German POWs at Westminster Bridge. One was shot dead trying to escape again. The battalion began wiring the so-called Village Line, an important trench in the reserve line, linking west to south. On 20 February they relieved the 4th Loyal North Lancs in the front line. The next few days were to see some shelling of their front-line positions by the enemy and some very active patrolling of no man's land, as efforts were made to secure intelligence about enemy intentions.

This tour of the front line was to continue until 2 March. But the casualties were fortunately very light. Only six men were wounded during the whole of February. No one had been killed. A further fifty men joined the battalion, bringing the total replacements during the month to 245. They were relieved by the 5th Lancs Fusiliers and moved back to support positions in the Village Line. The men were heavily employed on working parties, strengthening the front line against possible enemy attack. On 5 March they were driven by lorries into divisional reserve at Hingette.

Between 5 and 17 March, the battalion was engaged in training. Officers were sent to discreetly reconnoitre the Portuguese sector of the line, just north of the brigade's position at La Bassee, in case the battalion might be needed to provide any necessary support. When the German onslaught was finally mounted, the Portuguese defenders simply turned and ran away, leaving a gaping hole in the line which British troops had to fill urgently.

By 17 March, the battalion was back in the front line at Givenchy. Nine enemy observation balloons were up, meaning the whole deployment was witnessed by the German artillery. The men were heavily shelled all the way into their new trenches. Private James Bowfield of Anson Street, Barrow, died during this shelling. B Company in the support lines was shelled intermittently on 18 March, a pattern repeated again on the next two days. The weather was atrocious, with heavy rain and mist. On 21 March the back areas were shelled with gas for four hours in the morning.

The British positions at Givenchy were very strongly organized. The line had been in British hands for a considerable period of time. It consisted of a number of strongly wired outposts and redoubts as well as a large number of concrete machine gun posts, which had been sited so as to provide all-round rifle and Lewis gun defence. The intention was to make sure these posts could all be held independently if the enemy were to succeed in breaking through – a feature of the defence system which was to pay dividends in the fighting to come.

A unique feature of the defences was a 300 yard long tunnel which connected two positions which the 4th Battalion would soon be involved in defending: Givenchy Keep and Marie Redoubt. Running off the tunnel were a series of deep dugouts, 40 feet deep, big enough to hold up to two battalions, and with several exits to the support line behind. The men of the 4th were to practise endlessly at leaving the tunnels and dugouts to man their fighting positions as quickly as possible.

Major-General Jeudwine had also selected a 'Line of Resistance' to be denied the enemy at all costs. On the right of the division's position, this line ran along the actual front-line trench itself as the ground permitted the digging of proper trenches. However, on the left of the ground held by the 55th, the Line of Resistance was established further behind the front line. Here the ground was marshy. The front line, mainly sand-bagged breastworks, was constantly being levelled by German gun fire. The Line of Resistance was therefore sited along a subsidiary line connecting the villages of Le Plantin and Festubert. It would be known as the Village Line.

On 21 March, the Germans launched their major offensive. The main thrust was to be in the south, at the point where the French and British Armies joined at St Quentin. The Fifth Army, overwhelmed by the weight of artillery and infantry fire, were forced to retreat along a twenty-mile front of the line, to a depth of ten miles. It was the worst day for the British Army since the retreat from Mons. It would mark the end of General Gough's command on the Western Front. The 8th Battalion King's Own, part of 3rd Division, would be in the thick of the fighting. But for now at least there was no sign of any major activity on the section of the front line held by the 4th Battalion.

The following day, the British artillery opened up a heavy barrage on German positions south of the La Bassee canal. The day that followed was much quieter. On 24 March, the battalion serving on the right of the 4th launched a trench raid which was supported by all arms, left and right of it, including the 4th. Enemy prisoners captured during the raid stated that a big German attack on this sector of the front was imminent.

The 25th was another very quiet day. The Village Line was strengthened by extra machine guns, more barbed wire and by one company of the Lancashire Fusiliers. The next two days were quiet too. There was no sign yet of the expected attack.

The battalion was relieved during the night of 27 March. HQ and two companies went into reserve at Gorre. C Company were sent to occupy the Tuning Fork Line immediately north of the canal. D Company took over the Village Line with two platoons at Windy Corner and two at Pont Fixe. On 30 March the battalion enjoyed a day's baths at Beuvry.

At the beginning of April the battalion moved to occupy the front line in the right sector at the canal. The next two days were extremely quiet. A trench raiding party on 4 April entered the German line without opposition and found no Germans in occupation at all. The next day four patrols entered the German lines again, and the same pattern repeated itself. At midnight, the British shelled the enemy lines with gas and thermite rounds. On 6 April, three patrols – six officers and forty-five men – raided the opposing lines again and found them completely unoccupied. Far from an attack being just around the corner, it looked as though the Germans had withdrawn altogether from their front lines. There was no sign or sound of the enemy on 7 or 8 April either. The day that followed was destined to be one of the most significant days in the life of the 4th Battalion and the men from Furness.

There was a heavy fog as 9 April began. At 4.15 am the enemy opened a bombardment of gas and high explosive shells behind the front line. Soon the bombardment settled on the front line. At 07.30 the front-line positions were effectively destroyed by heavy trench mortar fire, inflicting very heavy casualties amongst the men. Here there were no deep bunkers into which they could retreat. The shelling was particularly heavy on Oxford Terrace and Bayswater. At 08.05, HQ was heavily shelled, causing serious casualties to HQ staff, including runners and pioneers. The barrage succeeded in inflicting major damage on the communications system between brigade, battalion, division and corps. Communications between battalion HQ and the front line had become tenuous, putting effective command and control of the fighting at real risk. At 09.15, Captain Ellwood sent an emergency request by runner for artillery fire support from his positions down near the cnal. It reached HQ at 09.30. At 10.30 it was becoming clear that the Germans were beginning to break through. A company of the 5th Lancashire Fusiliers were sent up to support the battalion in the Village Line.

During the fighting on that day at Orchard Keep, a young Second Lieutenant, Joseph Collin, who had joined the battalion in February when the 7th King's Own had been disbanded, was to win the Victoria Cross. He was not from Lancashire at all. He was born in Jarrow, and is buried at the Vielle-Chapelle Cemetery at Lacoutre.

Colonel Gardner, now in command of the battalion, provided this picture some years later, of the run-up to and the conduct of the chaotic fighting that was now to rage over the area for the next few hours.

The 164th Brigade moved up into the Givenchy sector on April 1st. For six nights in succession, patrols penetrated deep into the opposing lines without gaining contact with the enemy. On April 8th not a single shell fell on the Divisional front. At midnight on April 8/9th, the dispositions of the right battalion, the 4th King's Own were the following. Two companies, A and D held the outpost line from the most advanced post, Death or Glory Sap on the northern bank of the La Bassee Canal to the vicinity of Warlingham Crater, together with the main line of defence, Spoil Bank Keep–Bayswater–Oxford Terrace–Cambridge Terrace; two companies, B and C held the support line, Gunner Siding and the defended posts Orchard Keep and Mairie Keep. Battalion HQ was located in a couple of ruined houses on the west side of Windy Corner–Pont Fixe road about 200 yards south of Windy Corner. There was practically no shell-proof cover in the battalion sector. At HQ however, a small concrete dug out which had just been completed by the

Royal Engineers proved invaluable – it sheltered the HQ staff of two battalions during the remainder of the tour and served continually as an HQ until the forward movement in the autumn.

At 04.15 on April the 9th, the enemy opened a heavy bombardment on the gun lines, roads, HQ and back areas in general, phosgene instead of mustard being used. Conditions in the trench system were reported as normal except that there was a fog which reduced visibility to about 30 yards. Two hours later at 06.15 am the shelling of rear lines slackened and an intense bombardment of the trench system began. The enemy attacked actually at 8.45 am aided by a mist so thick that the SOS signal was rendered invisible. The first definite information which reached battalion HQ was the arrival shortly after 9.00 am of a runner from the platoon in Death or Glory Sap with an SOS message – the commander mistrusted the power of the SOS rocket to pierce the fog. The runner had made his way down the bank of the Canal unobserved by the enemy.

Captured German Divisional orders stated that the reduction of the Givenchy salient was to be carried out by two forces, each consisting of a regiment of three battalions, strengthened by storm troop and heavy machine guns. The salient was not to be attacked directly but to be outflanked and isolated. There was to be no frontal attack across the craters but machine guns mounted at commanding points were to engage the defenders while the enveloping attacks were in progress. On the northern flank, one regiment was to advance to the line Le Plantin South–Windy Corner. On the southern, another regiment was to penetrate by way of Spoil Bank Keep and Orchard Keep to Pont Fixe. One battalion of the northern force was ordered on reaching the line of Plantin South–Windy Corner to turn northwards along the Festubert Village Line and to clean it up in co-operation with an attack by one battalion of the reserve regiment. When these objectives have been gained, the two forces were to join hands along the Windy Corner–Pont Fixe road and then participate in a general advance against Gorre. This cut off, the main Givenchy position was expected to fall.

Owing to the absence of shell proof cover the 4th Battalion suffered heavily during the preliminary bombardment. The enemy advanced in great strength over the flat land between the Craters and the Canal, overrunning the lightly held outpost line and the main line of defence, Bayswater–Cambridge Terrace. But he was gripped and stopped on the line Spoil Bank Keep–Gunner Siding–Mairie Keep. Owing to the thickness of the fog and the strength of the wire defences the fighting resolved itself into severe local encounters in which individuals and small units behaved with great distinction. The weight of the attack was broken by isolated platoons and sections holding out in strong points and in defended localities. Three examples of conspicuous gallantry bear witness to the bitterness of the fighting.

The platoon which garrisoned Death of Glory sap, the outpost on the extreme right, resisted so successfully that all attacks were beaten off and very heavy loss was inflicted by enfilade fire on the troops advancing across the flank. The enemy never gained a footing in the post. Later on however, after having been completely cut off for several hours, the garrison made a sally and captured a machine gun and its crew. The wire in front of the sap bore grim evidence of prolonged and violent struggle. This sap was among the very few points or perhaps it was the only point in the whole of the British Line where the enemy failed to gain an entry during their offensive in 1918.

For conspicuous gallantry in the defence of Orchard Keep Second Lieutenant Joseph Collin was awarded the Victoria Cross. After long resistance in the Keep he was forced to withdraw with 5 men, the survivors of his platoon. Single handed he put a machine gun team out of action and sold his life very dearly when keeping a second hostile machine gun at bay.

Orchard Keep therefore was lost, but Spoil Bank Keep and Mairie Keep survived. The enemy entered Gunner Siding at its junction with Orchard Road, but further progress was checked by the garrison and by the crew of an anti tank 18 pounder gun posted in the trench. This gun, though damaged by shell fire so severely that the breach had to be opened by a pick, fired about 150 rounds at close range. The repeated attempts of the enemy to rush the gun by frontal and lateral attacks were beaten off by the infantry.

By about 10.45 am, the attack on the section of the front line held by the 4th King's Own had spent itself and the survivors were at large in the area between Mairie Keep–Gunner Siding–Spoil Bank Keep–Death or Glory Sap. As the enemy had not advanced further west than Gunner Siding there was no hand to hand fighting immediately around battalion HQ, but at Windy Corner, 200 yards further north there was a contest presently to be mentioned.

Against the 4th Battalion the enemy failed to take any of the strong points which covered the northern flank of Givenchy, but captured Le Plantin south and penetrated to Windy Corner. It was against a concrete pillbox in Cavan Lane that the enemy advanced, shouting 'Portuguese, beaucoup bombardo!' but the rouse was unsuccessful. The garrison, holding on in the rear compartment, fought the enemy through the gas curtain and kept up effective machine gun fire till relieved by a counter-attack from a neighbouring tunnel exit. At 9.45 am the enemy were attacking Southmoor Villas, the battalion HQ of the 4th Loyal North Lancs but by 10.00 am had been repulsed. They penetrated however to

Windy Corner, captured the aid post and canteen (which they looted) and established a battalion HQ there. About 50 officers and men were captured by the enemy at Windy Corner including the chaplains attached to the 4th Loyal North Lancs and to the 5th Lancs Fusiliers.

During the next five hours – from 11am till about 4pm, the 4th KORL and the 4th Loyals, reinforced by the support battalion, 5th Lancs Fusiliers, counter attacked and recovered the whole of their defensive system with the exception of the saps leading to the southern craters which had been destroyed by shell fire. At the outset, the work of recovery was begun by small parties acting on their own initiative, but when the Brigade realised that the surviving enemy were lodged in two deep pockets, orders were given for the mouth of the pockets to be closed. The support battalion co-operated very effectively in this movement. On the front of the 4KORL, a force moved up Cheyne walk, freed Death or Glory Sap and regained the main line of defence. The crater posts could not be recovered.

Invaluable support was given not only by the Divisional artillery, but also by two 18 pounder batteries of the 11th Division which were able to fire on the Brigade front. In addition there is indisputable evidence that fresh German troops assembled in a reserve trench were annihilated by a barrage which opened at 11.30 am and was designed to support the Brigade counter attacks.

Unfortunately, it appeared that the very same barrage killed twenty-three British prisoners captured by the Germans earlier in the day's fighting.

This account gives a very clear sense of the desperate fighting that took place on this fateful day. It was a period of incredible brutality, confusion, noise and violence for the men involved. Although the German offensive had pushed back the British lines in many places, at least on the front held by the 55th Division, little advantage had been gained by the evening. The German onslaughts began to be less and less successful. Their energy was being slowly spent. And at Givenchy it had floundered in the trenches held by the 4th Battalion and its sister units of 164 Brigade. This was a day when the individual actions of platoon and section leaders and their men would be decisive.

During the afternoon, two officers and fifty-eight men arrived as reinforcements and a company of the 5th South Lancs lent their support as well. Counter-attacks were launched against the invaders in the afternoon. By midnight, no German were left in any of the front-line positions. Patrols sent out in the early hours of the morning found nothing of the enemy. The 4th had resisted an attack of very superior numbers and had completely blunted the enemy's attack in this sector of the front. It was a magnificent performance. But it was won at a terrible price. On 9 April, the battalion sustained its heaviest losses in a single day's fighting on the Western Front. In total, 15 officers and 282 men were either dead, wounded or missing. Twenty-eight Military Medals were handed out to the men of the battalion. Lieutenant John Schofield of the 5th Lancs Fusiliers would also win a posthumous Victoria Cross for his actions during the counter-attacks of the late afternoon.

The 55th Division had been attacked by no less than three fresh German divisions. When the fog began to lift, the rows of barbed wire that had been so carefully put up by the 4th Battalion and other units of the Division were completely festooned by the dead bodies of German soldiers. Large numbers of German soldiers were trapped in the wire and were later captured as prisoners, including a band and their instruments.

The German records of the attack made clear the extent of the obstacle presented by the 55th Division that day: 'The enemy resistance could not be broken. The 55th Division offered obstinate resistance.'

There were many men from the Furness area in the long list of casualties. Lance-Corporal Jack Bennet was one of them. He had won the Military Medal at Cambrai. He lived in Hartington Street, Barrow, and had enlisted in 1915. Lance-Corporal John Brown lived in Kennedy Street, Ulverston. He was amongst the earliest recruits of the 4th Battalion in September 1914. Private Thomas Angrove was another man to die that day. He lived in Lindal Street. He was a labourer in the Vickers shipyard and been out since 1915. Corporal Robert Proudfoot was a Lewis gunner and had been with the battalion in France since June 1916. He too had worked at the shipyard, as a hammer lad. Also amongst the dead was Private Richard Moreton from Dryden Street, Barrow. He was 20 years old. Robert Adamson who had won the DCM earlier in the war and who came from Barrow was also killed on this eventful day.

Further to the north, the German attacks had made better progress and it would take many more days of hard fighting before the enemy attack could be fully checked. It was during these dark days that Haig had issued his famous 'backs to the wall' order to the British Armies in France. But the 55th Division had distinguished themselves on 9 April as a formidable fighting force, and no battalion was more involved in the fighting that day than the 4th King's Own. Here at least the enemy assault had been repulsed.

Patrols sent out later that evening into no man's land found no sign of the enemy at all, but the German artillery was still very active and there was a heavy bombardment of Le Plantin in the evening. Yet there was to be no repeat of the infantry attack of 9 April against the 55th. By 12 April, the battalion had been relieved by 5th Lancs Fusiliers and was moved back to the reserve positions at the Village Line. During the relief, Private Stanley Geldart, aged 24 from Barrow, was killed by shellfire. The next day again under shellfire, they were still able to send up working parties to strengthen the northern section of the front line. Sergeant Barnett Barrow from Coniston was killed on 13 April when a shell exploded in the doorway of the sergeant's mess. He died instantly. On 16 April they were relieved by the 1st Camerons and moved back to the support lines where they were picked up by buses on the Beuvry–Bethune road. They were heading for new positions at Marles Les Mines, arriving at 4.00 am on 17 April.

From 16 to 22 April, the battalion rested and re-equipped, but was nonetheless called upon to provide fatigue and working parties for the front and reserve lines. On the morning of 23 April, they once again went by bus on the road north-east of Marles Les Mines. The battalion – now around 500 strong thanks to heavy reinforcements during the days at Marles – was heading for the front line once again. The B team under Captain Batchelor went to Burbure. The rest of the men spent the day in and around the woods at Vaudricourt. At 7.30 in the evening, the fighting men of the 4th were moved by light railway to relieve the 1st Loyal North Lancs in the Givenchy sector. HQ company received ten casualties on the way up to the line as they de-bussed at Annequin. A, B and C Companies were put into the front line. D Company was in support.

Among the casualties that night were two men from Barrow. Lance-Corporal James Tomlinson had worked for Barrow Corporation and had enlisted in the first week of August 1914. He was 28 and lived in Rawlinson Street. Lance-Corporal William Johnson was 21. He had given up his apprenticeship as a joiner at Vickers to join the King's Own in 1915, as soon as he was old enough to enlist.

The 24th was fairly quiet. There was some enemy artillery fire in the evening. On 25 April, two fighting patrols in the evening got heavily engaged with the enemy and had to withdraw. The men were trying to reoccupy abandoned front-line outposts in some crater saps. The two officers leading the patrols were both wounded. Later that night a third attempt was made to occupy these positions. This time with the support of covering artillery fire the patrol rushed the posts. Unfortunately, the gun fire was not very accurate. The barrage came down behind the objective instead of on it, and the patrol could not advance against the hostile rifle and machine gun fire aimed at it. There were many casualties. The enemy, it seemed, was occupying the old British front line in some strength.

At 4.00 am on 26 April, again covered by gun fire, two platoons of A and D Companies rushed the enemy positions. This time they got into the German lines and heavy hand-to-hand fighting ensued. The men from the 4th were forced to retire under extremely difficult conditions, having a confronted a much bigger force. In the afternoon, further attempts were made to capture the crater saps – this time with more success. Once again, the men were engaged in some heavy use of their bayonets. Lieutenant Hunter was killed in the attack, but the men were able to retake their old positions. By six in the evening, however, the patrols were forced to retire. They were surrounded on three sides by the enemy. After bitter fighting they managed to withdraw successfully, inflicting further heavy casualties on the Germans. By 8 pm the withdrawal was complete. Lance-Corporal John Dickie, aged 26 and from Barrow, was reported missing, believed dead after the attack. His body was never found. The next day the Germans exacted their revenge by heavy artillery fire on the positions held by the 4th. By the evening of 28 April, the men had been relieved and moved back into support where they were joined by the B team. The total damage done by these days of trench raids was heavy. Four officers and 112 men were either dead, wounded or missing.

Lance-Corporal James Hewitson, a 26 year old from Waterhead Farm in Coniston, was to win the Victoria Cross for his actions on 26 April. Single-handed, he had attacked and overcome several enemy positions. He was to survive the war and died peacefully at Ulverston Cottage Hospital in 1963. Private John Watterson was not so lucky. The young soldier from Queen Street, Dalton, received a gunshot wound to the neck and died three days later at a field hospital. He was one of the first new recruits to the battalion in August 1914.

The battalion continued in support at Givenchy until 2 May when it was moved into brigade reserve at Verquigneul. It was joined by seventy-one new recruits and by General Jeudwine who had come to express his appreciation for the work of the battalion over the last few weeks. The men enjoyed a restful few days here, before preparing for further front-line trench duties. On 8 May, 2 officers and 135 men formed the B team and left for Allouagne. At 7.30 in the evening, the rest of the battalion moved up to Givenchy again, arriving in the early hours of 9 May. A, D and B Companies were in the front line, C in support. That day, enemy artillery fire increased substantially on Windy Corner, New Cut and Grenadier Road. The village of Givenchy itself, or what was left of it by now, was also shelled. The barrage also came down on the support lines as well. This pattern of heavy shelling continued without break for the next five days until the men were relieved again. In the support lines at Givenchy, they were required to supply men for working parties up the line. On 21 May, they moved into reserve at Verquignuel. On the 23rd they moved again into brigade reserve at Drouvin

They were to spend one more spell in the front line that month, during the period 26–31 May, where despite periods of heavy gun fire, there was no reported occasion where the opposing troops came into any contact with each other. On 31 May, Major Gardner took over command of the battalion from Colonel Balfour. Casualties for May had been quite heavy. Seven officers and fifty-five other men were either dead or wounded. These had, however, been more than made up by reinforcements of five officers and eighty-seven other ranks

The battalion spent the next two months in the front line at Givenchy with alternating periods in support and reserve. The front in this sector had become becalmed. The battalion was, however, fully engaged when it was in the firing line in aggressive patrolling. In June and July, the battalion sustained losses of eight officers and forty-nine men killed and wounded. During those two months, the battalion received ten officers and 163 men as replacements. Its fighting strength was being increased all the time. By the summer, it was clear that the German offensive launched in March had completely petered out. The BEF had held. Soon it would be time to strike back.

At the beginning of August, the enemy began to pull back slowly from his positions in the Givenchy sector. The 4th was once again in the front line. The battalion moved up to take over the ground without a shot being fired – the very same ground that had been so heavily fought over since April. On 4 August they moved back to camp at Drouvin, but were back in the line again by the 9th. By this time, the BEF had begun their offensive operations against the German lines at Amiens, further to the south, and were making significant headway against demoralized and lethargic opposition.

But in the Givenchy sector, although there had been a tactical withdrawal by the Germans, they were still full of fight. On 11 and 13 August the men were subjected to very heavy artillery fire. This would have partly been the result of actions further south, but it was also in retaliation for British artillery fire aimed at cutting the wire in front of their new positions on the Givenchy front. On 14 and 15 August, the gun fire became heavier still, as enemy nervousness about British intentions reached new heights. Some of his shellfire was falling short however, helping the British with their wire-cutting operations. There were forty casualties on 15 August from mustard gas shells. The position became much quieter over the days up to 20 August when the battalion was relieved by the 6th Liverpools.

They moved by bus to Vaudricourt, arriving in the early hours of 21 August. The next day, Brigadier Stockwell, commanding 164 Brigade, came to visit the battalion and outlined a new operation that was being planned to capture some craters along the Givenchy front – Red Dragon and Warlingham and the in-famous K sap. This was being planned as a joint mission by the 4th King's Own and the 5th Lancs Fusiliers. On 22 August, the battalions practised their planned attacks.

Zero hour was planned for 07.20 on 24 August. The operation was a complete success. Two companies advanced into no man's land without a protective barrage and launched a surprise attack on the craters. Ten minutes later, the British guns put down an intense barrage on the enemy reserve and support positions. At 10.30 the enemy counter-attacked, but his infantry was completely destroyed by the British artillery.

The following day was spent consolidating the newly won ground. Patrols were sent out to try and ascertain the enemy's positions. Contact could not be made. A desultory German barrage on the craters was launched early on the morning of the 26 August, but there were few casualties. They were relieved the next day. August had been a much more difficult month for the 4th Battalion. Four officers and 139 men had been either killed or wounded.

The battalion came back into the front line on 2 September. The preceding day, Major Gardner, the battalion CO, had broken his ankle in a soccer match involving officers against sergeants. The Germans were conducting by now a slow withdrawal from some of their positions in the La Bassee sector and on 4 September the battalion moved up into the old British front line to replace the battalion that had taken over the newly vacated German lines. But there was still a lot of hard fighting going on. On the 7 September, a minor operation by D and B Companies against some enemy strong points had been initially successful, but enemy counter-attacks in the afternoon had meant that some of this ground had to be surrendered. Enemy dugouts had been booby trapped by the retreating Germans, but had been cleared by the Royal Engineers. On 8 September, there was a good deal of fighting along the outpost line in very wet weather that was flooding the trenches of both sides. The next day there were heavy bomb fights around one of the German strong points which had, by now, changed hands several times over. That evening they were relieved by the 4th Loyal North Lancs and moved back to Drouvin for the next few days.

But by now it was clear that the British were gaining a decisive battlefield advantage over the Germans. The enemy had been forced back along a wide front from Ypres to the Somme. Further retreats in the La Bassee sector – perhaps as far as the Canal de la Haute Deule – were anticipated. The focus on training was beginning to switch back to open warfare. On 19 September the battalion was transported to Aix Noulette to witness a tank demonstration.

The next day the battalion was moved into the front line at Chappelle St Roche near Givenchy. The line was extremely quiet for the next four days the men were to spend there. There were no reports of hostile enemy action at all. After a few days in the reserve lines at Pont Fixe, they were back once again in the front line on 28 September, relieving the 4th Loyals in the outpost line alongside the canal.

The battalion sent out six daylight patrols and four evening patrols on 29 September, but made no contact with the enemy. September was much quieter for the battalion than August. Three officers and forty-five men had become casualties. Nine men were reported missing.

The enemy withdrawals began to gather pace in early October. On 1 October, the 55th Division advanced about 500 yards immediately to the north of the La Bassee canal. The next three days would be marked by significant progress, although the ground over which the Division was advancing over was heavily waterlogged. On the 2 October, information was passed to the battalion from captured prisoners that the Germans had begun to retire at 4 am that morning. The 4th Battalion began its hot pursuit. By then, the battalion was based at Pont Fixe with two companies to the north and two companies to the south of the canal. At noon on the morning of 2 October, B Company pushed through the village of La Bassee without encountering any opposition. Advanced guards were formed to push even further ahead. The men mounted a piquet line on the canal basin, having pushed through the southern outskirts of the village. There was no sign of the enemy at all. All of the bridges across the canal had however been blown. The men prepared for a further advance in the morning. The 4th Battalion was now acting as the advanced guard for the brigade. On 3 October, they pushed forward through Berclau where they made contact with the retreating Germans. Fighting took place. The men had advanced a further 2,000 yards during the day. Berclau itself was not taken. The battalion encamped at Sazume for the night.

Patrols pushed forward at dawn on 4 October from Hantay and drove the enemy back to the Canal de la Haute Deule. These patrols were strongly engaged by the enemy and the fighting was again severe. D Company attacked and captured Prevotre Farm. The enemy still held the western banks of the canal and the bridgeheads with machine gun fire. On 5 October further progress was made. But the battalion could not get across the canal, which was being held strongly held by the enemy. To make matters even more difficult, the Germans had flooded the area in front of the canal as well, making the conditions extremely hard-going. The 4th were relieved during the night of 5 October and marched back to divisional reserve at Pont Fixe and Givenchy.

For the next few days the battalion trained for open warfare and in rapid pontoon bridge building. But the end of the war was coming clearly into sight. On 10 October, the men received a lecture on the arrangements that would apply on the cessation of hostilities.

By 13 October, the battalion was positioned in the support lines at Marquilles. The front had advanced several more miles since they had been out of the line. The men deepened their dugouts and strengthened the wire in front of them. Battalion HQ was in the sugar factory, with two companies in the main line of resistance and two in support. They remained there until 16 October when they marched into billets at Sainghin. This time, their rest billets would be in front of them, not behind. The following day the battalion advanced again to Ancoisne, where they met recently liberated French residents for the first time. They had a 'most cordial' reception. They marched the next day to Houplines and then again in the evening to Templemars for the night. The reception was even warmer here. HQ was set up in the mayor's house.

On 18 October, patrols pushed out and finally managed to enter Peronne after strenuous fighting. The Germans were holding the line on the River Marque – 8 feet deep and 20–30 feet wide – in great strength. There was by now a great deal of shelling on both sides. Heavy mist had helped the British in their advance that day, but the mist had hindered the artillery in their endeavours. It was impossible to target the enemy batteries effectively and, although the fire was intensive, it was more in the nature of harassing fire. Putting on one side their lessons on pontoon bridge building techniques, under cover of darkness (although there was a full moon that night), the men used ladders to cross the river and then entered the village of Bouvines. In the first attempt the ladders broke and some men nearly drowned. The crossing succeeded at the second attempt. Machine gun and artillery fire forced the Germans to retire from the village just before midday. Twenty-three prisoners and three machine guns were captured in the village. The whole forward line now pushed through the village and established itself along the railway line to the east of Bouvines, with patrols out as far as Cysoing. The next day, the line was pushed forward further still by the 4th Loyals and the men were given a rest for the night in the village. The villagers were overjoyed by their liberation and helped the battalion and a field company of Royal

Engineers to begin the construction of a new bridge across the river that night. It was completed by noon the following day.

The battalion continued their march forward and by 20 October had reached the village of Esplechin, where they dug in about 800 yards to the north of the village. They were deployed in support of the 5th Lancs Fusiliers who were ahead of them. For the next few days the division made every effort to reach the River Schelde and to establish bridgeheads north and south of Tournai.

Enemy resistance began to stiffen considerably on 21 October. Severe patrol fighting took place. The high ground on the road from Froidmont to Tournai was initially captured by B Company in the afternoon but retaken again by the enemy at night. On the battalion's right, it met considerable resistance in the village of Ere, where a machine gun was firing on it from the church steeple. The church itself was mined. This was effectively a suicide mission by the German defenders. The machine gun position was eventually destroyed by artillery fire and the battalion finally pushed through the village which was heavily shelled all day. The Germans were making a stand on the north side of the River Scheldt. The shelling was particularly severe on both sides of the front line that night.

The 4th were relieved by the 4th Loyals on 22 October and transferred to the support lines at Ere where they were shelled with gas and high explosives. It was an extremely uncomfortable night. They sustained some casualties that evening. On the 23 October, the men were resting in farmhouses within easy reach of their dugouts in the support lines. A patrol of D Company attacked a German-held sunken road towards the east of the village without success. In the evening the German machine gun fire became very intense, wounding an officer and five men. The men of D Company were gathered together by their platoon sergeants and formed an outpost line on the eastern edge of a wood about 150 yards from the sunken road. The battalion was not to know that it had just fought its last engagement of the war.

On 24 October, the men were busy digging V-shaped trenches about 40 yards long on positions sited by the CO in the morning. They carried out this work all day, completing fifteen such trenches by nightfall. They were gassed during the day but sustained no casualties. Work continued the following day when they were relieved by the 4th Loyals in the evening. They then moved forward and relieved the 5th Lancs Fusiliers in the front line, with B and C Companies in the outpost line and A and D in support. The next few days were quiet with no fighting along the front held by the 4th, apart from sporadic and largely ineffective artillery fire. The last soldier from Barrow to die in the Great War in the service of the 4th King's Own was Private John Hart who was killed by shellfire on 26 October. Two days later the battalion was relieved by the 6th Liverpools and went to billets at Bourghelles.

They were to remain until 9 November, when they moved up to Esplechin, arriving at 11.30 am. The following day they marched forward to Leuze where they arrived in the early evening after a full day's march. Progress during the day was difficult as the main road had been blown up by German mines.

On 11 November, the Armistice was signed and the war came to an end. At 10.45 am the battalion paraded in the town square at Leuze. A few minutes before 11.00 am, Major Gardner, who was in command of the battalion since Colonel Balfour had gone to hospital a few days before, read out a telegram stating that the Armistice had been signed and that hostilities would cease at 11.00 am. A squadron of 1st Royal Dragoon Guards also in Leuze that morning then sounded the cavalry 'Cease Fire', the battalion gave the royal salute and its band played the National Anthems of France, Belgium and Great Britain to ecstatic cheers from the Belgian onlookers.

The battalion was to remain in the area for much of the next few months, billeting at Uccle from the middle of December. In February a party of four officers and 133 men went off to join the Army of Occupation at Bonne and the battalion was reorganized into two companies. The first demobilization party of fifty men was sent to England on 27 February, twenty-nine of these were bound for the Furness area. The survivors were on their way home at last. The final party of twenty-four, including Lieutenant-Colonel Gardner, left Belgium for England on 24 June. They arrived at Ulverston on 11 July and were met at the station by the battalion band and a large crowd of well-wishers. The next day there was a civic reception led by the mayor of Barrow and the chairman of Ulverston District Council. Afterwards, a procession marched to the parish church and the battalion colours, carried by Lieutenants Pritchard and Higginson, were deposited for safe keeping in the hands of the rector, the Revd Stuart Rimmer. The party then marched back to the Drill Hall, where many of them had enlisted four years earlier. How different everything must have felt and how poignant must have been the contrast with that distant day in August 1914 when the battalion had left Ulverston for Slough. Their world had changed for ever during those intervening years, and so had they.

Chapter 3

The 7th Battalion

The beginning of the battalion

Compared to the territorial battalions, the first few weeks of the war were very different for the new volunteers of Kitchener's Army. The territorials were already reasonably well trained, equipped and properly uniformed. Many of them had had regular army experience. The territorial battalions, like the 4th, were immediately mobilized and given military duties to perform guarding sites of strategic importance. They were operating within existing brigade and divisional structures. They were part of a clear regimental system. In short, although they had only been in existence for a few years, they were disciplined and effective soldiers with a clear mission and role to discharge. None of this applied to the New Armies. For these new recruits into the Army, they would have to start at the beginning and undergo a crash course in discipline, tactics and fitness.

Altogether five service battalions of the King's Own were raised during the war. The first of these battalions, the 6th, was raised during the first few days of August. It was to serve at Gallipoli and in Mesopotamia, and was one of the few Kitchener battalions never to serve on the Western Front.

The second of the new service battalions of the King's Own to be established later in August and early September was the 7th Battalion. This unit was to serve on the Western Front throughout its existence, until it was disbanded in February 1918 as part of a general reorganization of the British Expeditionary Force. It was to take part in some of the most significant military campaigns of the war, including the fighting at La Boiselle and the famous dawn raid at Bazentin Ridge during the Battle of the Somme, as well as the capture of the Messines Ridge in June 1917.

The men of the 7th Battalion began their initial army training at the regimental depot in Lancaster. Few had probably ever thought of being soldiers. They came from all walks of Furness life, from the shipyards and steel mills, from shops and offices, from the farms and small workshops that scattered the rural areas. What bound them together was the shared sense of purpose and mission. Their country was in danger. Some believed they were defending a noble cause in defending the rights of smaller nations from military oppression. Many were caught up in the huge drama and adventure of those extraordinary times. In those early, sunny days of August, they camped out under rudimentary canvas tents in nearby fields. They took part in route marches in country lanes around the city. They ate out in the open. It is likely that many of these men had never been out of the Furness district in their lives. It was an entirely different world they now found themselves in. Slowly, however, they began to come together as a body of soldiers.

Towards the end of September, the men travelled by troop train down to Tidworth on Salisbury Plain with other units who were eventually to form the 19th (Western) Division. The 7th Battalion was to become part of 56 Infantry Brigade of the 19th Division. The brigade was made up of volunteers from right across Lancashire, and many of the Lancashire regiments were to have service battalions serving with it.

At this stage of the war, none of the men who joined the New Armies in such a wave of heady patriotism had any uniforms and they had virtually no military equipment of any kind, including rifles. They may not have looked like an army but this did not dampen their enthusiasm. Nor did the fact that when they arrived in Tidworth they were ordered to pitch camp on swampy ground. The camp soon became an ocean of mud and filth. The men coped with all of these difficulties with amazing cheerfulness.

For the next three months the men underwent intensive military training. They learnt how to dig trenches and wire them. They were eventually issued with some of the older Lee Enfield rifles and began to master the art of musketry. They were drilled day and night. Food was rudimentary and in short supply. The men were grateful for the supplies of food sent by their families at home.

When the men arrived at Tidworth they were given the unpopular blue serge uniforms to wear. These came from surplus stock of Post Office uniforms. The men were far from pleased. There were no khaki uniforms to spare for the new army recruits. The newly mobilized territorials had first call on these. Specially minted regimental badges were however distributed to the men and they pinned them to their blue uniforms to give the semblance of regimental identity.

In early December the 7th Battalion was moved to better billets at Clevedon in Wiltshire. Here their war training continued. They received their first issues of the new Lee Enfields and their khaki uniforms. While the battalion was stationed in Clevedon, they were filmed by Pathe News marching through the town and undergoing training routines for a news reel film to be shown in cinemas up and down the country. They looked like a disciplined and fine body of men. However, they were not given any home leave for Christmas. They were to spend the first of several festive seasons away from their friends and families.

They stayed at Clevedon until the end of March when they returned to Tidworth. In the early summer months of 1915, the men completed their basic training and anxiously awaited news of their posting overseas. The new army divisions were beginning to move to France to replace the heavy casualties inflicted on the regular army units that went out to France in August 1914, and the eager soldiers of the 7th Battalion King's Own were keen to know their fate.

The war begins in earnest.

In June, the whole division paraded before the King George V on Salisbury Plain. The King was reported as commenting that the division was amongst the finest he had seen. These parades usually preceded an overseas deployment. And so it was to prove. On 7 July, the battalion was put on notice to be ready for active service overseas. On the 10 July, the men were given forty-eight hours leave. It is unlikely that many of the men would have had time to travel back and see their families in the Furness area. Many of them would have instead spent these final hours in London, enjoying the sights and sounds of a city few of them would ever have visited before.

At 10 pm on 14 July an advanced guard of 3 officers and 106 men left Southampton for Havre. The advanced party included the transport, quartermaster staff and the machine gun section. On the afternoon of 17 August the rest of the battalion left Tidworth on two trains for Folkestone. Later that evening they left for Boulogne on board the steamer *The Queen*, arriving in the early hours of the 18th. The total strength of the battalion on this fateful day was 30 officers and 914 other ranks. Their war service was set to begin in earnest.

They spent the first night in France in a tented camp 3 miles outside the city. The next day they were marched to the railway station at Pont de Bricque and headed east. On 21 July they marched to Ganspette. Over the next few days they marched via Wallon Cappelle, La Miquellerie, Regnier Le Clerc to Vielle Chapelle, arriving in their new billets near Armentieres on 3 August – a distance of over fifty miles.

The first few days in France were dominated by the condition of their feet. A few days before their departure from England the men had been issued with brand-new boots. The leather had not had time to soften or to become comfortable for long marches and they had a lot of marching in front of them. Motor transport was not yet sufficiently widely available to allow the troops to move in comfort from the rail heads to their billets or camps. On the first evening over 150 men complained about sore feet after their first route march. On their first day at Ganspette, nine men reported sick because of the condition of their feet. On the second day, another fifteen men reported the same problem. On 23 July, the men had to march a total of eighteen miles. There were dozens more cases of men who simply could not cope. Fourteen men were left behind at Moulle. The following day forty-three men were left behind at Wallon Capelle after a march of over 14 miles. On 25 July, the medical officer of the battalion had to dress 125 men affected by wounds to their feet.

General Sir Douglas Haig, then the commander of First Army, visited the battalion at La Miquellerie. He was the first of a long list of senior officers to inspect the newly arrived men from Furness. A few days later, General Willcocks, the commanding officer of the Indian Corps to which the 7th Battalion was now attached also paid the battalion a visit. The war diary records how impressed he was with the men's steadiness on parade. Given the condition of their feet, they must have endured a lot of physical discomfort in order to have created such a positive impression.

On 4 August, the men had their first experience of trench duties in the Neuve Chapelle area under the supervision of experienced troops of the Indian Corps. Six officers were conducted around the front-line positions held by the 1st Battalion, Connaught Rangers, in the morning, with the rest of their company following them in the evening. Each platoon was to have forty-eight hours of trench duty. Captains Chambers, Openshaw and Kendall and Major Wilkinson were the first company commanders in the 7th Battalion to undergo this ordeal. The battalion CO, Lieutenant-Colonel Bolton, and the adjutant spent their first night in the trenches on 5 August.

An eager party of Royal Engineers out in no man's land strengthening the wiring in front of their trenches drew a lot of German sniper fire onto the line held by the 7th Battalion. Fortunately, there were no casualties.

By 11 August three companies of the battalion were withdrawn to billets at Haverskerque. The first battle casualty was to occur the next day. One man was fatally wounded by shellfire in the afternoon. He was Private J Frith from Manchester. He died later that night in the field ambulance.

New drafts numbering two NCOs and fifty-seven other ranks arrived from the regimental training depot on 14 August, bringing the battalion up to its full war strength. For the rest of August and until 12 September, the battalion went through intensive training at Le Corbil and Festubert. It rained a lot that August and the men were frequently wet through. On 20 August ten officers of the battalion, under attachment to the Dehra Dun Brigade, underwent another forty-eight-hour tour of duty in the front-line trenches.

While the men were in billets near Festubert, they were heavily engaged in improving the local roads and water supply system. At night they were frequently sent out to dig new communication trenches up to the front line. Heavy manual labour like this was to become part and parcel of their daily routine in France for the next two and a half years.

On 13 September the 7th King's Own went into the front line again, relieving a battalion of the North Staffordshire Regiment. This time, they were on their own. They were to spend the next fortnight in the firing line. The men were holding the line at The Orchard, one a half miles east north east of Festubert, destined to be the scene of frenetic fighting involving their sister battalion, the 4th King's Own, in April 1918. This section of the front had seen bitter fighting in May and June. It was where the 4th Battalion had also had their first serious encounter with the enemy.

Three companies were in the firing line, with one in reserve. Early in the morning of 14 September enemy machine gun fire was directed at the front-line positions followed at 4 am by a grenade attack. One man was killed and six others wounded. The next day was quiet. The men could hear German working parties in front of them during the evening improving their wire defences. They could also hear the Germans underneath them too, digging mines towards the British lines. On 16 September the men again came under grenade attack from the Germans. One man was killed and seven others wounded. They were not able to retaliate as they had no grenades or trench mortars of their own to use. They had to rely on the Royal Artillery and its howitzers for fire support. At this stage of the war, the German infantry enjoyed clear weapons superiority over the British in all arms – bombs, mortars, machine guns and artillery. The men from the 7th were simply target practice for the enemy.

One young NCO serving with the 7th at this time was Lance-Corporal William Thornhill from Barrow. In a letter home to his family in October he wrote:

> I suppose you would like to know how we have spent the time since being over here. The first few weeks after landing it was all march, march, march and we all felt rather glad when we marched so near to the trenches that the next march took us in. We felt that at last we were going to do something. Our first two days in the trenches was with another battalion who were holding a certain part of the line. It was a bit quiet, but it got us used to hearing the bullets whizzing overhead and cutting through the sandbags. There was plenty of head ducking, but that soon wears off. After those two days we went back into billets. There was plenty more marching and heaps of trench digging. Often at night we had to go to the trenches and dig. It is all very exciting, especially when the Germans spot you and open up with their machine guns. You have to get down in quick style.

The openly optimistic tone of this first letter home reflected the gradual introduction of the battalion into the duties of trench warfare. It was not to last for long. During these first few weeks in France the battalion was undergoing the same experience as all those who were to serve in this theatre of operations: learning how to fight and survive.

In the history of the 19th Division, written in the early 1920s, the divisional historian Edward Wyrell confirmed the grim reality of these first few weeks on the Western Front: 'The business of learning how to make war within rifle shot of the enemy was vastly different from the training, (excellent though it was), on Salisbury Plain.'

The gruelling training referred to by Lance-Corporal Thornhill consisted of constructing trench defences, wiring, bomb throwing, sanitation and trench discipline. Out of the line the men learnt about trench mortaring, the use of gas helmets and bayonet fighting. Gas was a particularly deadly new threat facing the British Army for which it had not been prepared. In violation of international conventions, the Germans had first used poison gas during the Second Battle of Ypres in May 1915 with dramatic effect. Only a last-minute historic defensive stand by a Canadian battalion, Princess Patricia's Canadian Light Infantry, kept the British lines from being completely overrun. Both sides were to make much of this new weapon in the years ahead, but for now at least the Army had to learn how to stay alive in a gas attack. For Lance-Corporal Thornhill and all of his comrades in the 7th Battalion, nothing had quite prepared them for this.

Of his experiences in The Orchard, or The Glory Hole as it was known to the men, Lance-Corporal Thornhill was much blunter:

> Very soon we were again in the trenches for a long spell. The part where our company went to was called The Glory Hole. Hell on earth would have been a more suitable name. The German explosives are very high. In the daytime you can see the bombs and dodge them. They are like a big stick of charcoal about a foot long and several inches in diameter. We had three days in the Glory Hole and we were glad to get out. The Germans send all kinds of things over and always seem to be finding something new, like bombs, rifle grenades, whiz bangs and heaps of other things. At night times it is most lively, almost like a fireworks display, with the lights going up.

The battalion was in fact holding a line of trenches nearly 800 yards in length. For most of the time they had been under intermittent artillery fire which would periodically blow in sections of parapet and collapse the dugouts built into the side of the trenches.

Lance-Corporal Thornhill recorded what happened one night during an enemy bombardment:

> Two Sergeants of our platoon, Sergeant Hamilton and McKeever, both of Barrow, were in their dug out one night when a rifle grenade dropped in the trench right opposite the opening. A piece of it hit Hamilton in the stomach, but McKeever was unhurt.

Sergeant Hamilton was to recover from his wounds. During the day and at night, patrols were sent out into no man's land to gather intelligence and to complete reconnaissance and observation missions.

> One day a patrol of us went out in broad daylight and managed to get right up to the German trenches without a shot being fired at us. I cut a piece of their barbed wire which I'm keeping as a souvenir. It is very thick and has more spikes on than ours.

During the course of this tour of trench duty, significant developments were to take place on the British section of the Western Front. Throughout the summer, the French and British military commanders had been planning a major new offensive operation on the Western Front in order to help relieve the pressure on the failing Russian campaign. Disaster threatened the Russian army after it had been pushed out of Poland and a new front established sixty miles to the east of Brest Litovsk. But there were sharp differences between the British and French commanders over the nature and shape of any such action.

Lord Kitchener, the British Secretary of State for War, had hoped to avoid any further major offensive on the Western Front during the remainder of 1915, after the heavy losses at Neuve Chapelle, Festubert, and Aubers Ridge. He had instead been hoping to build up the BEF with the new armies and launch an attack on the Germans in 1916. But with defeat after defeat on the Eastern Front and the desire of the French commander General Joffre to renew operations against the Germans in France and Belgium, Kitchener reluctantly agreed to the new strategy.

On a visit to Sir John French in August, Lord Kitchener told him that the Allies must resume the offensive on the Western Front. He had decided that: 'We must act with all energy and do our utmost to help France in their offensive even though by doing so we may suffer very heavy losses.' The French wanted the BEF to attack the German positions between the mining village of Grenay, just south of Lens, and the La Bassee Canal to the north. They suggested that the main thrust of the attack should focus on the area between Loos and the canal, avoiding the built-up mining villages around Lens. Subsidiary attacks would be mounted by British forces to the north of the canal. These would be designed as diversions, confusing the enemy and keeping him from reinforcing the main positions being attacked. The French Tenth Army would launch a massive attack involving over seventeen infantry divisions south of Lens. The French Second Army in the Champagne region would mount a simultaneous attack involving over thirty infantry divisions and eight cavalry divisions. The French believed that the power and force of an attack that went in side by side with the British south of the La Bassee Canal would allow the German main defences to be ruptured. The cavalry could then exploit the gap thus created and advance possibly as far as Mons. The German forces in the huge salient around Noyons would be effectively cut off. It could be the decisive victory of the war.

The Allies were divided over both the strategy and the tactics. French and Haig in particular had not been enthusiastic about these plans. They felt the ground over which they were being encouraged to put in their offensive was totally unsuited to such an attack. Nor had they been able to assemble enough men and materiel to launch a successful attack against positions which had been rapidly strengthened during the summer – largely in response to the British attacks at Neuve Chapelle and Festubert. The Germans were anticipating another British operation in the general area.

The British high command would have preferred an attack launched north of the La Bassee Canal, designed to capture the high ground of the Aubers and Messines Ridges. This was rejected by Joffre and the French government.

Separating the two attacks would in their view undermine the success of both. Sir John French then proposed to support the main French attack south of Lens by artillery fire at first and then await developments. If the prospects of an infantry attack looked promising after such a bombardment he would then, and only then, commit his troops to the action. This plan was also rejected by Joffre, as it was seen to fail to provide the necessary military as well as political support for the French forces.

Under pressure from Kitchener and the French government, Sir John French was effectively compelled to join the offensive and to commit his forces south of the canal. By the middle of September, at a conference at Chantilly, the plan of attack was confirmed. The BEF would commit up to nine infantry divisions to the offensive, with five cavalry divisions ready to go in and exploit any breach of the German lines. The plan was similar to the one hatched earlier in the summer. The only real difference was that now the main thrust would come from French attacks in the Champagne region. The French and British attacks in the Artois were to be scaled down, although it was here that the German defences were the strongest.

The British were to attack on a six-mile front with six divisions in the front line and with over 100 heavy guns. The attack was to be directed on the village of Loos. The French would attack with twice this number of guns behind them. To make up for this deficiency, the British would use poison gas on a large scale for the first time. The troops would advance after a heavy preliminary barrage and the gas had been deployed against the German front-line positions. Maximum violence would be the principal tactic. The infantry would advance in successive waves, forming an irresistible mass that would simply overwhelm the German defenders.

The British forces would be under the command of Haig. However, the British reserves, including the newly arrived 21st and 24th Divisions of the new army, would be under French's control. Unfortunately, these troops were not close enough to the battlefield to be deployed quickly enough if the opportunity arose. This separation in the command and control arrangements would have appalling consequences as the battle developed. The Indian Corps in which the 7th King's Own was serving was to have a subsidiary role supporting the attack at Loos with an attack just north of the canal.

On 25 September, the Battle of Loos began. The battle was to be another costly failure and was to give rise to the 'lions lead by donkeys' charge that was to become part of the folklore of the Great War. The ground was far from ideal for infantry attacks. It was mining country, with small villages built for the miners providing a complicated and cluttered battlefield as well as an important and intrinsic advantage to the defenders. The Germans enjoyed the vantage points of the huge spoil heaps from which they could direct fire onto any advancing infantry. There was little obvious cover for the attacking troops. The gas used at the beginning of the attack blew back into the British trenches and was more of hindrance than a help. The artillery bombardment was to prove largely ineffective. Troops of the 47th, 15th and 7th Divisions did manage to penetrate the German lines but could not be properly reinforced in time by the reserves of XI Corps which French had held back too far from the battle.

Two of the divisions of XI Corps, the 21st and 24th, were new army units that had only just arrived in France. The 21st arrived on 9 September and the 24th on 30 August. They were even greener than the units of the 19th Division. They had long route marches to make to get even near to the battle zone and could not be fed before they were ordered into action. They were effectively destroyed in the battle. Tired and confused, they failed to deliver an effective intervention and many of their battalions were annihilated by German artillery and machine gun fire. The British were eventually forced back to their original lines. The cavalry were stood down. Despite the extraordinary bravery of the soldiers themselves and over 20,000 casualties, the battle plan had failed. Minor territorial gains had been made, but they were not of any great significance. There was to be no decisive breakthrough. Disappointment and frustration set in. The war would not be over quickly after all.

Watching and listening to the sounds of battle were the men of the 7th King's Own. Fortunately for them, they were to be bystanders to the action on their own front. The 19th Division had been ordered to support the 2nd Division on their right who had launched their own diversionary attack at 05.50 am, 40 minutes before the main attack at Loos: 5 Brigade of 2nd Division attacked north of the canal in two places half a mile apart; near the canal and near Givenchy. Both attacks failed. Gas had blown up from the south and into their trenches. The troops were met by heavy machine gun fire when they went over the top. In the wet conditions their grenades were almost useless as they needed to be lit by fuses. They couldn't be ignited.

The 7th King's Own was positioned in the very same trenches opposite the Rue d'Ouvert in which the 4th King's Own had begun its own baptism of fire three months earlier. 56 Brigade took over the trenches occupied by 58 Brigade as these units mounted their attack of the Rue d'Ouvert at 6.30 am. The men of the 7th watched this attack fail also. After advancing about 200 yards the young soldiers met very heavy machine gun fire and took cover as best they could. There was confusion about the whereabouts of the attacking troops of 58 Brigade on their right. They had been told they had occupied the German trenches being attacked. The opposite was true. At midday two further battalions of 58 Brigade were ordered to advance to reinforce their comrades sheltering in no man's land. They too were forced back and at noon the whole attack was cancelled. The brigade suffered over 800 casualties.

The trenches held by the 7th King's Own came under heavy German artillery fire throughout this attack. However few casualties were sustained. One man was killed and twenty wounded. The following day they were relieved at 11.30 pm by 1st Battalion, Loyal North Lancashires, and went into reserve lines at Rue d'Epinette, a few miles to the rear. The next two days were pretty miserable for them. It rained heavily and constantly. But the main fighting for 1915 had effectively come to a halt with the end of the Battle of Loos. Winter was setting in early. The conditions on the battlefield became quickly unsuited for any serious infantry action. In any case, the BEF, reluctantly drawn into the fighting at Loos against its own preferences, had sustained heavy casualties throughout the late spring, summer and now the autumn, and needed time to re-equip and reinforce before it could contemplate launching any new offensive against the Germans.

On 1 October the battalion moved back into new billets at Rue de Chavatte, in a row of cottages either side of a small country lane two miles to the north of Festubert. By the early evening they had begun to settle in. The billets were cramped and full of rats, which the men began energetically to hunt down and kill. They were issued with fresh underclothes on 3 October as a prelude to moving back into the front line near Festubert that evening, relieving the 7th East Lancs. The weather continued to treat them harshly. It poured with rain for the next few days without a break. The enemy suffered from the same fate and as a result there was little hostile action between the two opposing armies while these conditions prevailed. Their time was instead spent improving the drainage at the bottom of the trenches and repairing parapets which were constantly falling in because of the wet conditions. The battalion sent out some patrols into no man's land but failed to encounter any enemy soldiers. The next day saw the weather begin to improve and hostilities recommenced. The battalion snipers claimed two hits on German trench periscopes which drew retaliatory rifle grenade fire from their opposite numbers. There were no reported casualties. For the next few days there was regular trench mortar and artillery fire from both sides. On 14 October, ten men were badly burnt by smoke bombs which prematurely detonated as the battalion mounted a feint attack on the German lines to confuse the enemy. Sergeant Lancaster from Barrow rescued a box of grenades from a fire caused by sparks from the smoke bombs, badly burning his hands in the process. His actions undoubtedly saved the lives of many of his friends and comrades.

The following day the battalion was relieved and moved back into the support lines at Rue d'Epinette, a little to the north of Festubert. There was to be no rest for the men. A working party of 300 was sent back to the front lines in the evening to help repair and improve the firing line. The same happened the following two nights. On 19 October the battalion was sent to the divisional baths at Vielle Chapelle and around 400 of the men were issued with clean uniforms. In the evening, more working parties were called for. This pattern of resting during the day and working all night continued until 24 October when they moved into reserve positions at Locon, a small village three miles north of Bethune. But the heavy duties imposed on the battalion continued. Every evening, working parties were sent out to improve the front and support trenches. On 27 October, a working party spent twelve hours in the front line. The buses arranged to take them back to Locon failed to turn up. The men had to march six miles to their billets before they could rest. They arrived cold and wet through.

Notwithstanding the pressure these heavy night-time fatigues must have imposed on the men, the battalion continued to devote its daytime and energy to the business of combat training. Throughout the first week of November the battalion continued to drill and practice as they sought to protect themselves from the terrible effects of the cold and rain. On 9 November, the battalion received orders to return to the front line at the crossroads in Festubert. Before they left their billets that evening, they covered their feet and legs with whale oil to prevent trench foot. That evening they relieved the 8th North Staffs in pouring rain and the worst possible conditions. They marched up over open country as the communication trenches were unusable because of the wet conditions. They managed to avoid any casualties, even though their arrival must have been heard by the Germans.

The trenches were once again in an appalling condition. The trenches and dugouts were flooded as it rained heavily all day. Ration parties coming up that evening with food and water were also compelled to cross over open country. This time the Germans spotted them. Two men were killed and two wounded by machine gun fire.

The rain continued for the next two days. The conditions in which the men had to live became even worse. Dugouts frequently collapsed, often trapping their occupants for several hours. Those who came to their rescue were then subjected to sniper fire from the German lines. On 11 November, two men were killed by these snipers. The repairs would collapse again almost as soon as they had been completed. One of the battalion's young subalterns, Second Lieutenant Humphreys, was wounded in the abdomen whilst supervising a working party repairing the parapet. He died the next day at the dressing station at Chocques. This was the 'attrition' that was now the daily price to be paid for holding the front line. It was as far away from the glory and glamour of the early days of the war as it is possible to imagine.

On 13 November the rain finally stopped. But it was soon replaced by a severe frost. The men had to rely on their greatcoats for warmth as they had not yet been issued with the new goatskin jerkins which were becoming widely used in the army. If the weather was bad, at least the serious fighting had more or less come to a halt. There was the occasional shelling and sniper fire to contend with, but casualties for this period were generally very light.

Under a bright moon, the battalion was relieved by the 7th East Lancs during the evening of 16 November and by 10 pm was in fresh billets at Le Hamel, a tiny village two miles to the north-west of Festubert. At last, they had a roof over their head, fires to keep them warm and hot food again. For the next three days the battalion spent the time reprovisioning, cleaning up and furnishing the inevitable night-time working parties. On 20 November they were ordered into the reserve trenches at Festubert and Le Plantin. During this time, the men were employed on digging a new battalion HQ. After two days, the battalion was relieved by the 6th Gordon Highlanders and the 4th Cameronians and by midnight had moved to rest billets to the south of Calonne, nine miles to the north of Bethune, and safely out of range from most of the German artillery. It was a long march in difficult conditions. The roads were wet and slippery and one of the battalion cookers was damaged during the progress from Festubert.

The battalion was to spend the next eleven days at Calonne. Its war training continued. The men underwent medical inspection and inoculations and refitted. Early in the morning of 3 December, the battalion received orders to move. The 19th Division was to replace the 46th Division in the line near Neuve Chapelle. They moved out at 11.30 am to billets south of Paradis, a march of about three miles, in extremely wet conditions, marching over flooded roads. On 4 December they moved up to Richebourg St Vaast, starting off before dawn and arriving over six hours later – a distance of only seven miles. Later in the afternoon they marched off again to relieve the 7th Sherwood Foresters and a battalion of the South Staffordshires in the line from Copse Street to Oxford Street, south of the village. The relief was completed at about 8 pm.

The next three days were very quiet. Both sides were content to 'live and let live'; to hold their own positions and not provoke the other side into any heavy retaliatory action. The trenches around Neuve Chapelle would in fact remain almost entirely static now until the great German spring offensive of 1918, with little movement and no great fighting other than the regular shelling and patrolling of trench warfare.

As a result, the battalion fortunately sustained only slight casualties over this period. Four men were wounded by shellfire. On 8 December, the battalion was relieved by the 7th East Lancs and retired to billets around Croix Barbie. Over the next two days, the men could clean up and visit the baths again. On 11 December, journalists from some of the national newspapers visited the 7th King's Own and got a taste of trench duty. Shelling in the afternoon killed one man and wounded fifteen others including Captain Hoyle. The following day the battalion was back in the same section of front-line trenches they had held a few days earlier.

The battalion's snipers continued to be active on this front, claiming four German victims on 13 December. On the same day the battalion acted as instructors in trench warfare for another newly arrived new army battalion, the 10th Welch Regiment, with one of its platoons going to each company of the 7th King's Own in the line.

But this spell of front-line duty was not to be without incident or casualties. Battalion HQ came under artillery fire on 14 December, forcing its occupants including the CO to seek cover in disused trenches nearby. A few days later Lieutenant-Colonel Bolton, the battalion CO who had been with the battalion since its arrival in France, would hand over command to Lieutenant-Colonel Tudor Fitzjohn from the 1st Battalion, Worcestershire Regiment. Three men were also killed in an early morning bombardment when shells landed in the firing line. One of these men was Private Michael Bayliff from Cark who had joined the battalion in Ulverston in August 1914. A patrol in no man's land engaged a German listening post with grenades and rifle fire.

In the evening of 16 December, which was a very quiet day, the battalion was relieved again by the 7th East Lancs and returned to its billets at Croix Barbie, four miles to the north. The battalion spent the next ten days here, where it was joined by eighty-one new drafts. Twenty men were allowed home for Christmas leave. For those who remained, Christmas Day was spent quietly. It was a wet and windy day, but the battalion was not disturbed by any enemy shelling. There was no church service. On Boxing Day a working party was sent into the front line to improve the trenches and dugouts.

On 27 December the battalion took over a section of the front line held by the 10th Royal Warwickshires on the left of the brigade front from Farm Corner up to Copse Street. Once again the conditions were terrible. The weather made it extremely difficult to maintain the trenches and shelters in anything like a reasonable and comfortable state. The enemy shelled the front line intermittently throughout the next four days. The high explosive shells did further damage to the outposts and trenches. On 28 December, one man was killed and one man wounded from artillery fire. These were the only casualties during this stretch of duty and on 31 December the battalion was relieved by the 7th East Lancs and retired to reserve positions around Richebourg.

1916 and the Battle of the Somme

1915 had therefore come to a fairly quiet end for the 7th Battalion, King's Own. They had spent their first five months in France in and around the Neuve Chapelle/Festubert section of the Western Front but without being heavily engaged in any major fighting. They had sustained the relatively light casualties associated with holding the front line in a largely defensive mode. They had certainly been worked hard in relation to improving the state of this part of the British front. But they had also found time to improve their military effectiveness as a fighting unit through extensive training in tactics and weapons. All of this would prove to be of enormous value to the battalion as it prepared for 1916 and the major campaigns that would mark a year of sacrifice and struggle on a colossal scale for both it and the BEF. This was planned to be the year of decision on the Western Front, with strongly reinforced British forces and their French allies delivering the blows that would bring the fighting to a victorious conclusion.

For the next few days the battalion was again heavily engaged in providing working parties for the front line. On 4 January it was back in the same section of the front line it had held in December. It was immediately involved in helping to remove seventy-nine gas cylinders from the firing line. The weapon was no longer needed for imminent hostilities and, because of the dangers posed by enemy shelling, presented more of a danger to the men themselves than to the Germans. The next two days turned out to be very quiet, with little enemy action of any kind. On 6 January the battalion was relieved by the 19th Welsh Fusiliers and returned to billets at Richebourg. Forty-nine new drafts arrived as replacements for the dead, sick and wounded.

The next day the battalion marched eleven miles to new billets at Les Lauriers near Merville, the HQ of First Army, eight miles to the north of Bethune. The billets were very dirty according to the war diary and the next day was spent cleaning them up. On 10 January, the battalion went on a seven mile route march to improve its fitness levels.

On 11 January, the battalion provided two officers and twenty men for a raid on German trenches. The raid was designed to gather intelligence and hopefully some prisoners for identification purposes. Unfortunately, the artillery barrage was not very effective and only served to put the enemy on alert. The attack began at 4.30 pm. The enemy positions were found to be very strongly held and no entry into them could be effected. The men threw 130 grenades into the German trenches and then withdrew without any prisoners or information. Three men were slightly wounded. The raiding party returned to their billets at Les Lauriers at 3 am on 12 January.

That day the battalion exchanged billets with the 2nd Coldstream at Rue des Vaches. Here they were to stay until 31 January. The men continued their training throughout this quiet period for them. They were reinforced by two new officers and sixty-seven other ranks on 15 January. But for most of this time the men could enjoy the peace and relative quiet of being out of harm's way. The working parties never stopped however the continuous work of strengthening and repairing the front line and the routes up to it. On 31 January they marched to Witternesse and then on 1 February to Quernes. The battalion was on its way back to the front line at Neuve Chapelle.

On 2 February, the battalion marched a further fifteen miles to Rue des Vaches. They would spend another fortnight here, undergoing more training, inspections and inoculations. Captain Kendall gave a demonstration on how to complete wiring work at the double and there were lectures for the men on sniping. On 17 February, the men moved once again, this time back to their old and familiar billets at Croix Barbee, arriving at noon. At 10.30 pm the next day they relieved the 7th East Lancs in the front line south-west of Neuve Chapelle on the La Bassee road at Port Arthur, where the Indian Memorial now stands. It was a wet and windy night. Three companies were in the firing line with one in reserve. Two men were wounded that evening by shellfire.

Nothing very much had changed since they had last been in the front line in December. The Germans were generally content to remain on the defensive and so were the British. There was little hostile action of any kind between the two sides. The 7th King's Own spent most of the time strengthening the section of the line they held with new strong points and dugouts. The drainage and sanitation systems were improved. On the evening of 20 February they were relieved by the 7th East Lancs and returned to billets at Croix Barbee. Two men were wounded by machine gun fire during the relief. The next day 350 men attended the divisional baths.

For the next two days it snowed during the day and froze at night. On 22 February they were back in the front line at Port Arthur. A platoon of a new army battalion of the Royal Scots was attached to each company for induction into trench warfare. The novices had now become the masters. The following day was spent improving the wiring in front of the lines: 275 yards was put up during the night.

The weather continued to be bitterly cold. Enemy shelling during the day killed one man and wounded three others. The battalion was relieved late in the evening of 24 February and retired to Croix Barbee where they had access to the baths again and could clean up and re-equip.

The 26th saw them back once more in the front line at Port Arthur for another quiet and uneventful tour of duty. A thaw had set in and the trenches soon became a quagmire of mud and filth. Conditions were very poor for the men and with great relief, they were relieved by the East Lancs on the night of 28 February, without casualties and retired to their familiar billets at Croix Barbee.

By the evening of 1 March the battalion was once more back in the front lines, having themselves replaced the East Lancs at Port Arthur in Plum Street and Liverpool Street trenches. They served another very quiet tour of duty which ended on 3 March. There were no casualties reported. For the next few days the men were rested. They received instruction in the latest German weapon, the fearful *flammenwerfer* which had just come into use. On the evening of 7 March they were back in the front line, replacing the 7th East Lancs again.

The trenches needed major work in order to preserve them from the wet and damp weather and to this task the men forcefully applied themselves. On the afternoon of the 9 March, British artillery fire on the German lines in the Bois du Biez attracted a heavy retaliation on the trenches held by the 7th King's Own, killing Captain Berrington who had only recently joined the battalion and another man. Second Lieutenant Simpson took out a patrol with a view to cutting the German barbed wire as a prelude to a trench raid. The wire was found to be too thick and strong and the party returned after two hours without making any real progress. The trench raid was cancelled as a result. There was more enemy artillery fire on 10 March but the day passed without any further casualties. On the evening of the next day the battalion was relieved but came under heavy enemy machine gun fire in the process. Battalion snipers claimed four German victims over the course of the tour. They marched four miles that evening to new billets at Les Lobes, a string of cottages on the Bethune–Lestrem road, a mile to the south-west of Vielle Chapelle. The billets were cramped and dirty.

The men were allowed a late morning on 13 March. A new draft of twenty men arrived from the regimental depot. It was a beautiful warm early spring day and the men were out of range of enemy gun fire. On 16 March they moved to nearby La Gorgue. For the next week the men would enjoy some well-earned rest and recuperation, punctuated by the occasional route march and company training duties. They were issued with new boots and clothing on 17 March and on the 20th, the corps commander, Lieutenant-General Haking, inspected the battalion. At 5 pm on 23 March, they moved off to rejoin the front line at Neuve Chapelle, which was eventually completed at 9.30 pm without casualties.

It snowed heavily during the night of 24 March which continued all day, leaving three inches of snow by the early evening. The snow covered no man's land with a soothing blanket that concealed the horrors beneath it. The day itself was extremely quiet, with hardly a shot fired by either side. It was as if neither Germans nor British could bear to spoil the peace and calm that had descended onto the battlefield of Neuve Chapelle.

The snow did not last long. The next day it had virtually all disappeared. All day the German guns fired on the British trenches, the gun fire reaching a crescendo between 2 and 4 in the afternoon. It was the heaviest shelling the men had experienced for several months. The parapets were badly smashed in all along the line. Miraculously, there were only four casualties. The British artillery remained silent. The shortage of munitions from the factories at home meant that the gunners were under strict orders to economize and were supplied with only a limited number of shells each day. The men of the 7th Battalion had no choice but to grin and bear it. The shelling continued all day on 26 March but had died down by the 27th. That night they were relieved by the 7th East Lancs and retired to billets at Croix Barbee. There were no casualties during the relief.

For the next three days, the men were heavily employed in providing working parties under the supervision of the Royal Engineers. They helped drain the water-logged support trenches leading up the front line, build new concrete machine gun emplacements and erect fresh barbed wire defences. In the evening of 31 March they were back in the front lines at Neuve Chapelle. This time their tour of duty would be extremely quiet and uneventful, with no reports of enemy action of any kind. During their relief on 4 April, one man was wounded by enemy shellfire on the La Bassee en route to their billets at Croix Barbee.

From 4 to 9 April the men were again used as labourers in the constant effort to maintain the strength and adequacy of the front, reserve and support lines. On 6 April, Sergeant George Poole of Ulverston saved the lives of many of his comrades when, during a bombing training exercise, he managed to pick up a live grenade that had been accidentally dropped into a trench and threw it clear. For his action he was to be awarded the Military Medal.

By the early morning of 9 April, they were back in the front line at Neuve Chapelle. That day was very quiet, but one soldier, Private James Rodda from Haverigg, was killed by shellfire. At 2 am on 10 April, a patrol was sent out to try and capture a prisoner for interrogation. The patrol was spotted by the Germans and forced to retire empty handed. This raid did not attract any retaliatory action. The next day saw similar patrolling and a lot of sniping.

At 2.15 am the following day there was another trench raid, led by Lieutenants Simpson and Hunt, and twenty-four men with blackened faces entered the enemy's front-line trench through a gap in the wire. Most of the German soldiers had already evacuated the position but sharp fighting ensued, with the men engaging enemy soldiers hiding in shell holes. Ten Germans were claimed as kills. Private Robert Starkie, originally from Nelson but who had joined the battalion in Barrow in August 1914, was killed in the fighting, one soldier was reported as missing and five others were wounded. The raiding party returned at 4.15 am in daylight with no prisoners. That night they were relieved by the 7th East Lancs. The total casualties for this tour were given as one killed, ten wounded and one missing. Two of the wounded subsequently died of their injuries.

On 13 April, the men were back in billets at Croix Barbee. They came under shellfire that evening. Second Lieutenant Moore was badly injured in the wrist and was evacuated to the dressing station. On 14 and 15 April the battalion visited the divisional baths and on 16 April marched fifteen miles back to Merville. On 17 April they moved to billets at nearby Rue des Vaches. They spent the next two days here, cleaning up and refitting. On 19 April they marched to the First Army Training area at Ligny sur Les Aire, where they would spend the next fortnight heavily engaged in assault training, night operations and battalion manoeuvres. Unknown to most of the men, the battalion was being prepared for the Big Push on the Somme. Their nine-month tour of duty on the Festubert/Neuve Chapelle front had come to an end.

At 1.45 pm on 7 May, the 7th King's Own marched to Lillers and went by train to Amiens, which was reached at 1 am on 8 May. They immediately marched to their new billets eight miles north-west of the city at St Vaast en Chausee. Here they would spend the rest of May, getting ready for active operations on the Somme. Every day was devoted to training, fitness and tactical operations. By now, it is unlikely that anyone in the battalion had any doubt that they were to play a role in a major new offensive operation against the enemy.

On 2 June, the battalion began the final stages of their deployment for the Battle of the Somme. At 8 am they began a long hot march to Flechincourt, arriving at 1.30 pm. The battalion strength was over 800. On 3 June, they moved again to a campsite west of Albert. The men spent the afternoon erecting their bivouacs. The weather was sunny and hot. On 5 June the whole battalion bathed in the glorious warm waters of the River Ancre, the first time they had done such a thing since they arrived in France the previous July. That night and the following day they were employed digging assembly trenches in Becourt Wood, in anticipation of the assault on the German positions along the southern flank of the Somme battlefield. The weather was, however, far from settled. Further digging planned for 7 June had to be cancelled because of the heavy rain that had begun to fall. Digging resumed on 8 June and by the 12th, the battalion had dug over 1,300 yards of assembly trenches, three and a half feet wide and over six feet deep. This represented a huge achievement for the men.

The battalion returned to Flechincourt on 13 June and then marched to Fleschelles the following day. The billets were in a poor condition. A fresh draft of sixty-seven new men arrived to strengthen the battalion ahead of the forthcoming battle. On 16 June the men were marched to Molliens Au Bois north-east of Amiens and began several days of last-minute preparations. They rehearsed mounting an attack through woodland – a common topographical feature of the Somme area – as well as bayonet fighting and trench mortar training.

While the 7th King's Own finalized their combat training at Molliens Au Bois, the preliminary bombardment for the Battle of the Somme began. On 24 June the war diary records the beginning phase of this fateful encounter. The noise was earsplitting, even though the men were several miles from the front itself. All through this time, the men would have had a clear sense that they were waiting for their turn to join the battle. It could come at any time, and with very little notice.

Over the next few days in the run-up to 1 July, the battalion moved up closer and closer to the British front line, in readiness to join the offensive. On 26 June they moved to Bazieux Wood. The next day they moved into bivouacs near Henencourt Wood, three and a half miles west of Albert, where they spent the next two days in final preparations. That night, their sister battalion in 56 Brigade, the 7th East Lancs, was given permission to light fires in the wood in order to help the men get dry after torrential rain had fallen during the march into their new positions. Twenty fires were lit and were reported to have reached the top of the trees. This must have attracted the attention of the German observers. Luckily, the wood did not come under artillery fire. On the eve of the battle, the battalion moved into trenches near Albert, the British Intermediate Line. Half of the officers were left behind in Henencourt. These officers would help to reform the battalion in the event of it sustaining heavy casualties in the battle ahead.

The 19th Division would act in support of the 8th Division of III Corps, which had been ordered to launch the first wave of the British attack on the village of Ovillers, which lay just to the north of the Albert–Bapaume road, two miles north-east of Albert. The road dissected the Somme battlefield. The British effort on this central part of the front line was aimed to push the Germans off the Pozieres Ridge and so open up the opportunity for the cavalry to advance into Bapaume itself. It was here that the main breakthrough was to take place. But if this was to occur, it was essential that the infantry should overwhelm the entire enemy trench system both at Ovillers and the nearby village of La Boisselle from which the Germans occupied commanding positions overlooking the British forces. The plans for the first day of the battle in this sector required the two attacking divisions to capture two fortified villages, six lines of German trenches, and to advance two miles into the German positions on a front of 4,000 yards. It would in fact be more than six months before British troops were to reach Bapaume. And hundreds of thousands of British soldiers were to become casualties in the process.

Both of these villages had been turned into defensive fortifications of very considerable strength. The ancient village houses had deep cellars, ideal for the protection of troops from shellfire and for the creation of reinforced machine gun nests. The wire around both these villages was also very strong. However the artillery plans for the pre-attack bombardment were focused on some of the more distant obstacles in the path of the planned cavalry advance into Bapaume. By splitting the targets allocated to the British gunners in this way, the bombardment of the barbed wire defences around La Boisselle and Ovillers was seriously weakened. Between Ovillers and La Boisselle ran a long, narrow declivity which the British called Mash Valley. Any attack at this point would come under immediate enfilade fire from both villages. The section of trenches held by III Corps was also covered by two German strong points: the infamous Nordwerk and Leipzig Redoubt. If these were not neutralized by suppressing artillery fire, then the attacks on La Boisselle and Ovillers would face even further difficulties.

The British plans suffered from one further handicap. Behind the front line, the British troops enjoyed virtually no natural cover at all from the land. The area to the immediate rear of the front line was barren and fully exposed to German observation. The bare, gentle slopes of open countryside, culminating in the Tara/Usna hills through which the Albert–Bapaume road crossed would inevitably attract heavy German artillery and machine gun fire as soon as any attack was launched.

The plans for the attack on La Boisselle were to be underpinned by the explosion of two huge mines, involving 100,000 pounds of ammonal. These mines, at a position north of the village known as Y Sap and at the Schwaben Hohe (Lochnagar Crater today) to the south were designed to remove two particularly strong positions and demoralize and confuse the enemy.

The attack on both these villages on 1 July was a total failure and resulted in huge losses to the British with no territorial gains of any significant kind whatsoever. The British barrage immediately lifted at zero hour on to the German second and third line trenches, providing the attacking infantry with no effective cover at all. It soon disappeared into the distance and could not be recalled owing to problems with maintaining communication lines in the chaos of the battle. In any event, the barrage was not designed to match the pace of the infantry advance. Instead, it was designed to deal with every obstacle that might lie in the way of the advancing troops – a perfectly sensible idea but one that relied absolutely on the assumption that the attacking infantry were at least making some forward progress. When this did not happen, the British troops were left horribly and fatally exposed. The British commanders were clearly aware before the assault began that the German defences had not been destroyed by the barrage. As a result, a battery of eight Stokes mortars was specifically detailed to open fire on

La Boisselle at zero hour. It effected some damage, but not enough before it was knocked out by German counter-battery fire.

There was also a serious problem with the quality of the gun ammunition, especially the heavy howitzer shells. These would have been ideal for dealing with some of the deep dugouts sheltering the German machine gun teams. Unfortunately, many of these shells failed to explode, weakening still further the intended impact of the protective barrage. The official history reported that an officer of an adjoining battalion claimed that there was a 'dud shell every two or three yards over several acres of ground'.

At zero hour the mines were exploded on time successfully, but the Germans were given a precious five minutes to recover their senses before the infantry began their attack. La Boisselle itself was attacked with smoke bombs rather than real bombs. The smokescreen failed to materialize as the wind was blowing in the wrong direction. Whole battalions, like the 11th Suffolks and the 9th Lincolns were effectively wiped out, with wave after wave of attacking troops being simply mown down by machine guns that were firing without any let or hindrance. 103 Brigade, the Tyneside Irish, suffered 70 per cent casualties simply moving over the Tara/Usna Hill on its way up to the British front-line trenches. Where the British did succeed in gaining a foothold in the German lines they were soon ejected. It was virtually impossible for reinforcements to cross no man's land to provide either combat support or supplies of ammunition and materials. Communication with battalion, brigade and division was non-existent. The artillery fire could not be redirected to provide vitally needed covering fire. Effective command and control ceased to exist. It was a brutal firefight fought at close range in impossible conditions. In these circumstances, there could, in truth, only be one outcome.

The attacks on La Boisselle and Ovillers, more than anywhere else perhaps, showed the total failure of tactics, preparation and staff work on the first day of the Somme battle. The attack of the 34th Division cost over 6,000 casualties alone. In front of La Boisselle and Ovillers, where the 8th Division had suffered a similar catastrophe, lay nearly 12,000 dead or wounded British soldiers. At Ovillers, the British had to cross nearly 800 yards of no man's land. They were simply slaughtered. The 8th Division was destroyed as a fighting unit on 1 July and would take three months of recuperation and refitting before it could retake the field. One battalion of the 8th Division, the 2nd Middlesex, suffered over 90 per cent casualties. Many battalions of the new army were annihilated on their very first day of serious fighting. It was into this maelstrom that the men of the 7th King's Own would now be deployed.

At 7.30 am on 1 July, at the moment these attacks were launched, the battalion had in fact moved up to the Tara/Usna Line in support of the 8th Division advance on Ovillers. The noise and fury of that time can only be imagined. The sense of fear must have been palpable too. This was, after all, the first major operation the 7th Battalion had been involved in since its arrival in France almost exactly a year before. They would remain in these support lines all day, waiting for the command to go forward. The sights and sounds of the battle must have created the unavoidable conclusion amongst the officers and men of the King's Own that things were going seriously wrong. The Germans had not been overwhelmed by the force of the artillery barrage aimed at them. There was to be no stroll across no man's land. The wounded and dying would have been passing through their lines all morning and afternoon.

At 5 pm, 56 Brigade was ordered to attack the village in one final last attempt to clear the way for the advance on Bapaume. The order was very quickly cancelled. The high command had finally realized the hopelessness and futility of another infantry attack in these conditions. The following day the 12th Division was put into the front line to relieve the shattered 8th Division and 56 Brigade moved back to positions south-west of Albert, arriving at 1 am on the morning of 2 July. They rested during the day. In the morning, the 7th King's Own was transferred to 58 Brigade in support behind the Usna Line.

South of the Albert–Bapaume road, around Mametz Wood and Montauban, the British forces, fighting alongside the French XX Corps, had enjoyed much greater success, securing their first objectives and driving the Germans back in disorder and confusion. It was in this sector that the British would focus their main efforts over the next few days and weeks of the battle. Generals Haig and Rawlinson were anxious however to strengthen their positions in the centre of the front around La Boisselle and Ovillers. A further move to capture these villages was therefore sanctioned.

In the morning of 2 July, the 19th Division, having replaced the 34th Division, began preparing for another attack on La Boisselle: 57 Brigade would attack on the left with 58 Brigade on the right; 56 Brigade, with the 7th King's Own back in its fold, was to remain in support. During the day, patrols of the 7th King's Own established contact with elements of the 21st Division on their right around Contalmaison. Second Lieutenants Mercer and Rutherford did particularly good work.

The attack was hurriedly organized. There was little time for effective reconnaissance. It was decided that the attack would take place at night in order to minimize casualties crossing no man's land. However, the division had never taken part in or trained for night operations before. And the artillery bombardment was desultory and lasted for only an hour at most. Although early gains were made, the attacking troops of 57 and 58 Brigades were quickly driven back. They dug in about 100 yards from their original start line, occupying a position running through the shattered remains of the church in the centre of the village. The division suffered over a thousand casualties. Two of the battalion COs in 57 Brigade were killed in the fighting for the village. Altogether, three VCs were awarded to men of the 19th Division during this period – an exceptionally high number. Undoubtedly, this second action was undertaken with extraordinary bravery. The division did make further progress than proved possible on 1 July.

But it is hard to see what lessons, if any, had been drawn from the failure of the original assault. Heavy and predictable casualties were sustained by the attacking battalions.

The 7th King's Own moved up into the front line during the early morning of 4 July, replacing 58 Brigade in the line. At 8.30 am they were ordered to attack and consolidate a line south of La Boisselle – an advance of about 500 yards. They attacked without any artillery cover and with their left flank in the air as the adjoining 57 Brigade was late in leaving its start lines. The men attacked three old German communication trenches with supporting fire provided by the battalion's Stokes mortar guns and rifle grenades. The advance was held up by strong machine gun fire from the north-east of the village. By 2.30 pm, the men had managed to advance about 300 yards, beyond the village, which now lay entirely in British hands except for a few ruins in the northern end. The scene no longer resembled anything that could truly be called a 'village'. It was instead a scene of total devastation. Little remained of any of the houses except red brick dust forming a bloody layer over the ground. Body parts, abandoned equipment, shell holes and craters created a hellish environment that few who fought there would ever forget. On the green in front of the church in present-day La Boisselle now stands the memorial to the bravery and heroism of the men of the 19th Division.

During the attack made by the 7th King's Own, sixteen men were killed and sixty-six were wounded. Two men were reported missing. One soldier from Maryport, Private William Kirkbride, who had enlisted with the battalion in Barrow, was killed. Lieutenants Simpson and Overton were wounded. Given the horrendous casualties suffered by other battalions, the 7th King's Own had come through these dark days remarkably lightly. They had achieved a considerable success on 4 July. But more was to come.

At 2 am on 5 July the battalion was relieved by the 7th East Lancs and moved back to the Tara/Usna Line in very bad weather. The heavens had opened and deluged the whole area with heavy rain, turning the trenches into knee-high torrents of filthy muck and slime.

The following day was spent cleaning up and reorganizing. But the respite was to be brief. During the day, the battalion provided a bombing party under Lieutenant Wigley to support the 7th East Lancs in capturing two enemy strong points and pushing the line forward a short distance. By the early morning of 7 July, they had themselves relieved the 7th East Lancs in the same positions they had won on 4 July. That morning the battalion mounted another attack on the German lines designed to advance the British lines by another 350 yards. The British commanders were convinced that the Germans' resolve was weakening. They were keen to maintain pressure in the southern sector of the front where the greatest gains had been made. To protect the advances planned here, it was felt necessary to continue the pressure on the front held by the 19th Division, stretching from La Boisselle to the village of Contalmaison, a mile and a half to the west. Here, the two divisions of III Corps, the 23rd and the 19th were both to attack simultaneously on a line running from Bailiff Wood to the north-eastern corner of La Boisselle.

The day had started with brilliant sunshine. However heavy rain had set in and the battlefield around La Boisselle soon became clogged with mud and water, making movement extremely trying. The infantry assault began on time at 8 am and involved not only the 7th King's Own but the 9th Welch from 58 Brigade. The attacking forces were ordered to 'approach the objective as near as possible before the bombardment lifts'. This instruction was carried out to the letter. But disaster ensued. The war diary of the battalion states clearly that the British artillery barrage failed to move forward as planned and as a consequence 30 men from the 7th King's Own were hit by their own gun fire. The official history described the barrage as accurate and effective, but that 'owing to some mistake in the timing, the infantry ran into the barrage almost at once and considerable loss and disorganisation ensued'. This rather suggests that the infantry commanders were themselves to blame for the tragedy by mistiming their advance. Whatever the origins of these events, at least on this occasion, communications with the gunners remained intact and the necessary corrections were soon effected. The barrage which eventually landed on the German lines proved to be highly effective, with numerous enemy casualties reported to be thick on the ground around the dugouts being assaulted. The advance was restarted at 9.15. C Company on the right began the advance which was immediately followed by the whole battalion charging across the open ground with fixed bayonets. The enemy trench was carried after some hand-to-hand fighting. The companies on the centre and left made slower progress against stiff opposition but reached their objectives too. The battalion eventually took up a position on the road running north-east out of the village where they dug in. Here they were joined very quickly by the brigade machine gun company which gave them the heavy fire power they would need to repel any counter-attacks. They were shelled heavily throughout the day.

The battalion took over 400 German prisoners as well as several machine guns and a considerable amount of war materiel. Second Lieutenant Conway was killed and six officers were wounded, including Captain Openshaw and Second Lieutenant Wigley. Fourteen other men were killed, 122 were wounded and 13 were reported missing presumed dead. One of the dead soldiers was Private William Hullock from Barrow. His body was never recovered from the battlefield and his name is recorded on the Thiepval Memorial

Overall, the attacks in this area failed to secure all their objectives. Bailiff Wood was not captured and although some progress was made in the direction of Contalmaison, which was entered by soldiers from the 1st Worcestershires of 23rd Division, it could not be held due to the ferocity of German artillery and the difficulties in getting supplies of ammunition up to the men in the newly won front line. After the disaster of the first day, the Somme battle had now become a series of localized assaults, such as the attacks of 7 July on the German second-line positions delivered principally to advance the line south of the Albert–Bapaume road. The line of advance would take the British forces first towards Mametz Wood and then on up the slopes towards Delville Wood and High Wood, the scenes of horrific fighting. The next two months would prove to be amongst the most difficult and costly of the whole war. This would certainly be the case as far as the 7th King's Own was concerned.

But for now at least there was some relief at hand for the men from Furness. They were relieved at 4 am on the morning of 8 July and went back to billets in Albert. They would spend the next ten days refitting, resting and resupplying. On the evening 9 July they marched to Henencourt Wood for baths and fresh clean uniforms. During this period sixty-six new drafts arrived to replace those who had become casualties in the recent fighting. On 18 July Major-General Bridges, the general officer commanding the 19th Division, inspected the battalion and passed on his thanks for the contribution they had made to the battle so far. He also brought them news of their renewed role in the battle.

During their time out of the front line, the British had been moving slowly forward. They had captured Mametz Wood and the German positions around Bazentin le Petit and le Grand and were now beginning to engage the enemy in Delville Wood and High Wood. Ovillers had finally been captured. But there was no sign of the imminent collapse of the German forces. Far from it. The Germans had heavily reinforced their defences with fresh troops and artillery. Every inch of ground was being bitterly contested and when they were forced to withdraw immediate counter-attacks were always mounted. The battle had become a slogging match in conditions that were indescribable. Any notion of a dramatic breakthrough had long since evaporated. Instead, the battle had effectively become one of attrition; of wearing down the enemy with a series of powerful blows designed to maximize battle casualties. It meant that progress was now being measured in small steps rather than in giant leaps.

On 19 July, the 7th King's Own was moved on at an hour's notice to rejoin the fighting. On 14 July the British had succeeded in driving a 6,000 yard salient into the German lines at Bazentin after an attack which involved the night assembly and deployment of troops from four divisions. On the right of this new salient lay Delville Wood and Longueval. Until these positions were captured they could threaten the left of any British thrust towards Guillemont and the east. Until High Wood and the trenches around it were subdued there could not be any further success in the centre either. Both of these woods and the village of Longueval presented enormous obstacles to the advancing forces of the Fourth Army.

The King's Own were on their way to the front line at Bazentin le Petit. They were ordered to move into the support lines in the old German trenches on the south-western corner of Bazentin le Petit Wood. Unfortunately the guides that had been sent to direct them to their new positions made a fateful mistake. They found themselves in the front-line trenches instead. Here they came under heavy artillery fire and suffered forty-seven casualties. They eventually arrived in their proper positions at 6 am on the morning of 20 July, a few hours after a major assault was launched on High Wood by XV Corps, involving the 7th, 5th and 33rd Divisions. They spent that morning burying the dead from previous attacks – 70 British and 48 German soldiers.

All day on 20 July the fighting raged. By the early evening, after chaotic scenes, the British had been forced out of the wood by heavy German counter-attacks as well as fire from machine gun emplacements in both corners of the wood and from a strongly held German trench known as the Switch Line which cut through the north-east side of the wood.

That evening further plans were devised for a renewed assault on the wood, which was finally agreed would take place at 12.30 am on 23 July The artillery began to focus its attention on the Switch Line. The job of the III Corps and the 19th Division in particular was to prepare for a flank attack on the Switch Line on the western side of the wood towards Martinpuich. In the mean time, much work was needed to prepare for this new assault.

On the night of 20 July the 7th King's Own began to dig an advanced trench and new jumping off positions, north of Bazentin le Petit. The work started at 9 pm. The working party came under immediate artillery fire. Captain Hammond Wright, commanding the working party, was killed as he marked out the positions for the new trench. The shellfire was heavy and accurate. Two other men were killed and fourteen wounded. One of these was Private Isaac Coward from Dalton. Slowly however, the trench began to take shape. The work continued the following night. A hundred men were engaged in the digging. About 200 yards were completed before the men realized that they had been given the wrong line and that most of the work had been wasted. It was a costly mistake. Two more men were killed that evening and nine wounded. One man was missing presumed dead. On 21 July, whilst supervising this work, Second Lieutenant Rutherford, who had shown exceptional bravery and leadership qualities at La Boiselle, was killed by shellfire. He was only 22 years old. Prior to the war, he had been a teacher at Barrow Island School and had played soccer for Barrow Island FC. His father worked in the Collections Department of Barrow Corporation.

The hard labour continued on 22 July when the trench was finally completed. At 12.30 am the attack of the 19th Division was launched on the German Intermediate Line, which lay about 600 yards north of Bazentin le Petit, between the village and the main Switch Line behind it. It proved absolutely impossible to make any progress. Heavy artillery and machine gun fire from High Wood took a heavy toll. Men sheltered in shell holes wherever possible but never managed to get into the Intermediate Line itself. The attack was made by battalions from 57 Brigade and by the 7th South Lancashires and 7th Loyal North Lancashires of 56 Brigade. The 7th King's Own were acting as brigade reserve. They suffered some casualties from shellfire; two men were killed, ten were wounded and one man was missing. Two companies were placed at the disposal of the 5th South Wales Borderers and a bombing party under the 7th Loyals. They were not used. It was realized that no attack under these conditions was likely to succeed unless the opposition in High Wood could be dealt with. Between 3 and 4 am a general withdrawal was effected and the men retired to the trenches dug by the 7th King's Own.

During the night of the 23/24 July the battalion moved back into tents in Mametz Wood. The next day was a quiet one. The men were employed improving the trenches in and around the wood. Mametz Wood was a staging area for men heading up to the front line, and was full of stores, dumps and artillery. As a consequence it was under regular German gun fire designed to disrupt the British build-up. On the afternoon of 25 July the battalion came under heavy shellfire between 1.30 and 6 pm. The Germans were firing both high explosive shell and shrapnel. Seven men were killed and nineteen others wounded, including Major Philips, the battalion CO. A working party of 150 men who were trying to lay cable lines were unable to work because of the shelling. There was no respite at night either. In the evening and throughout the night the Germans fired gas shells into the wood. The men were very shaken. All the while the battalion was under 10 minutes notice to return to the front line. It was one of the most uncomfortable nights they had spent in France.

One of the dead soldiers was Private John Nelson Willacy of Sedgewick. He had enlisted in the summer of 1914. In a letter home from one of his mates, Private John Tyson, his parents were told:

> He was laid to rest by his comrades. We all grieve the loss of Nelson. He was well liked in the company by officers and men.

His CO, Lieutenant Cook, wrote:

> He was killed by a shell together with 3 others. His end was painless. He was always a good and steady soldier. He has served a long time in the bombers and has done good work.

Another casualty of the shelling was Private James Wilkinson from Barrow. The following day the battalion was moved to safer position west of the wood and for the next two days provided working parties in preparation for the next attacks on High Wood and Delville Wood.

On 29 July they were back in the front line again at Bazentin le Petit, this time under the command of 57 Brigade. D and B Companies were in the firing line with A and C in support. Haig had agreed with Generals Foch and Fayolle, the commander of the French Sixth Army, that the British would support a major French offensive south of the Somme from Lihons to Barleux with an attack on Guillemont. The French were naturally reluctant to push forward until

Guillemont was in British hands as the left flank would otherwise remain at risk from serious enfilade fire. General Rawlinson had also promised Foch that he would provide further assistance by undertaking as many offensive operations as possible along the front of the Fourth Army at the same time. The job of the III Corps and the 19th Division would be to press on with its attacks against the Intermediate and Switch Lines.

This time the 7th King's Own would be in the leading wave of the attack. The Switch Line itself and the north-western corner of High Wood received particular attention by the corps heavy artillery ahead of the attack which was scheduled to start at 6.10 pm. A smoke cloud was laid down to screen the right-hand side of the planned advance. This would prove to be of real help to the men of the 7th King's Own. They were attacking on the right and the smoke would successfully shield them from German observation in High Wood.

A minute before zero, an intensive artillery bombardment opened up on the Intermediate Line. The battalion advanced in one wave and lay down as close as possible to the hostile positions as they could get. The second line troops advanced simultaneously. When the barrage lifted the troops rushed the German lines which were taken almost without opposition. They took up a line 50 yards in advance of the occupied Intermediate Line and began to consolidate. The battalion, along with the 10th Royal Warwicks, had in fact captured half of the Intermediate Line and the strong point at its eastern end nearest to High Wood, together with over 30 prisoners from the German 75th Reserve Regiment. Private John Richardson from Barrow died during this attack. He was 24. His body disappeared and was never found. His name is recorded on the Thiepval Memorial. On the left, however, little progress was made by the 8th Gloucesters and 10th Worcesters. For some reason, they had launched their attack slightly after the King's Own and came under murderous machine gun fire. Their losses were heavy and their assault failed entirely. The attack further to the south on Guillemont also failed with heavy losses.

The success of the King's Own attack was largely the result of their getting as close as possible to the barrage and the German lines. And on this occasion the phone link to battalion HQ and the corps and divisional artillery was kept open the whole time the assault was under way. The captured position was consolidated with the help of the brigade pioneers, the 5th South Wales Borderers and the 81st Field Company, Royal Engineers. A counter-attack was successfully repulsed, aided by the accurate fire of the gunners. German gun fire during the evening and morning of 30/31 July was making movement difficult. Communication with the front line was hampered as cable lines were destroyed by shelling. It was during this period that an act of extraordinary bravery took place.

On 31 July Private James Miller was to win the battalion's only VC of the war. Miller had been ordered to take a message back to battalion HQ during a break in communications. The *London Gazette* contained this entry of the events that day:

For most conspicuous bravery. His battalion was consolidating a position after its capture by assault. Private Miller was ordered to take an important message under heavy shell and rifle fire and to bring back a reply at all costs. He was compelled to cross the open and on leaving the trench was shot almost immediately in the back, the bullet coming through his abdomen. In spite of this, with heroic courage and self sacrifice, he compressed the gaping wound in his abdomen, delivered his message, staggered back with his answer and fell dead at the feet of the officer to whom he delivered it. He gave his life with supreme devotion to duty.

James Miller was born on 13 March 1890 at Taylor's Farm, Houghton, near Preston, Lancashire. The family had moved to Withnell near Chorley when he was a boy and he had taken up employment in the local papermill at Withnell Ford. He had enlisted at the outbreak of the war along with several of his mates. James is buried in Dartmoor Cemetery near Becordel. In honour of his memory a Celtic cross was erected on the edge of Withnell village churchyard. It was paid for by public subscription. His posthumous VC was presented to his father at Buckingham Palace by King George V later that year.

During the attack and on the following day the medical officer, Captain Knowles, and Second Lieutenant Clue were killed and six other officers were wounded, including Captain Kendall, one of the most experienced officers in the battalion, who had been out since July the previous year. Sixteen other men were killed, eighty-seven were wounded and ten were missing. One of the dead soldiers was Private John Woodhouse from Dent. In a letter to his parents, his platoon commander, Lieutenant Nichols wrote:

I was with him at the time, he was killed instantly and died without pain. Being his section officer I should like to tell you that I considered him my most valued NCO. He had a fine soldierly spirit and was a very hard worker and there is no one I regret more the loss of. You have the deepest sympathy not only of myself but of the whole company.

At 5 pm on 31 July they were relieved by the 16th Royal Scots of the 34th Division – the famous McRea's Battalion raised in Edinburgh which included many of the professional footballers of Heart of Midlothian FC amongst its ranks. They moved to bivouacs south of Becourt Wood.

For the time being, the battalion's service on the Somme was to come to an end. They were heading north, away from the horrors of that battlefield. It would be November before they were to return again for the final stages of the campaign.

They spent 1 August resting and cleaning up and in the afternoon marched to billets at Franvillers. That day, the army commander General Rawlinson sent this message to the 19th Division:

I desire to convey to every officer, NCO and man, my congratulations on their successes and gratitude for their gallant conduct during the Battle of the Somme.

In capturing La Boisselle and the trenches in the neighbourhood, as well as during the hard fighting in which they were engaged near Bazentin le Petit, the Division showed a determination and fine soldierly spirit which was wholly admirable. The co-operation of the artillery as well the dash of the infantry indicates that a high standard of training has been reached and their success is largely due to the careful and thorough system of training which has been carried into effect.

It is a matter of regret to me that the Division is leaving Fourth Army and I trust that at no distant date I may again have the honour of finding them under my command.

The following day they were inspected by the commander of III Corps, Lieutenant General Sir William Pulteney. They were able to bathe and clean up. In the afternoon they began a long hard march to Ailloy les Haut Clocher arriving at 4.30 the following morning. News came through that Corporal Richardson had been awarded the DCM for his actions at La Boisselle.. On 6 August they marched again to Longpre railway station and went by train to Bailleul, in the Second Army front south of Ypres, where they arrived in the early hours of 7 August. They marched to Locre and into divisional reserve.

For the next two days they were at last able to rest and recover from their hard labours. Ninety-five new recruits arrived on 9 August. The war diary records that these men were 'below the standards of the battalion'. It is probable that these men came from the depot at Etaples. For the next few days the battalion was under OC companies. On the 14 August the King visited the area. Captain Hoyle and Sergeant Fane were presented to him at corps HQ. The King would later drive along the Locre–Bailleul road where he was greeted and cheered by the whole battalion. Later that night the battalion relieved the 7th East Lancs in the front line east of the Lindenhoek sector. Compared to the Somme, this sector of the front was an oasis of calm. There was little or no hostile action for the next six days and no casualties at all were recorded. They moved back to huts at Kemmel Shelters.

The next six days were spent providing working parties under the supervision of the Royal Engineers. Ten new officers arrived. On 26 August they once again relieved the 7th East Lancs at Lindenhoek. A Canadian battalion was attached to them for training in trench warfare. There was intermittent shelling by both sides over the next few days but it was generally quiet. On 1 September they marched back to Locre and into divisional reserve.

The next two days were spent resting and cleaning up. On 3 September they moved to fresh billets at Nieppe. The following day they relieved the 8th Yorks and Lancs in the right reserve trenches at Ploegseert Wood, south of Messines.

This section of the line had been generally quiet for some considerable time. There had been bitter fighting here in the winter of 1914, but in 1916 at least it was not considered to be a particularly hot spot. It rained heavily all day on 5 September. German machine guns fired on the wood all day long. A working party of 200 men was sent up to the front line under the supervision of the Royal Engineers. The medical officer went away for instruction in the use of the new box respirator which had just become available for use against gas attack.

The German guns fired on the wood and on Ploegsteert village for most of 7 September, but inflicted no real damage and no casualties were reported. On 8 September the battalion relieved the 7th East Lancs in the front line east of Ploegstreet Wood. They would spend the next six days holding these positions. The opposing lines at Ploegsteert were close together – a distance of no more than 50m. It was too close for the front-line trenches to be subjected to artillery fire as the risk of the guns firing short and hitting their own men was too great. But trench mortars were heavily used by both sides. The normal pattern of hostilities was for the trench mortars to fire during the day, with the machine guns used more often at night to disrupt any working parties.

These six days were generally fairly quiet, particularly 10, 11 and 12 September. On 13 September, Second Lieutenant Crone died of wounds inflicted by machine gun fire.

They were relieved the next day by the 7th East Lancs and moved back into support lines in the wood. But there was to be no rest. For the next two days the battalion furnished large working parties for both the Royal Engineers and for the tunnelling companies that were busy in the area. The new box respirators were issued to the men together with a blanket for each soldier as the evenings were getting colder. On 17 and 18 September, the men were allowed to visit the baths at Papot and were excused from any more working parties. In fact they were to enjoy a three more days of rest before they moved on 21 September to billets at Nieppe. On 22 September they were on the move again to Outtersteene, where they would serve out the rest of the month. Over 130 new drafts were to arrive over the next few days, which were spent on route marches, and training exercises. These new recruits were considered to be of much greater quality than the more recent arrivals.

This welcome routine of rest and training continued until 4 October. At 10.30 am the next day, the battalion went by train from Bailleul to Doullens, arriving at 6 pm. They then marched to billets at Rossignol Farm near Coigneux. The battalion was being prepared for another big attack on the Somme, where the battle had been raging unabated since their departure in August. The British and French were making painfully slow progress, and the casualties were continuing to rise. The battle had become a series of localized offensives designed to secure more limited objectives such as the straightening of the line or the neutralizing of strong points and villages. Coordinating the timing of these attacks and securing the flanks for any advance had proven to be an extremely difficult task for the staff. The attacking troops would frequently find themselves being subjected to enfilade fire from both flanks as attacks did not always begin at the same time. And localized attacks allowed the German artillery to concentrate their fire onto the small sectors of the front being attacked with devastating effect. Counter-battery fire from the British was not providing the cover that the infantry desperately required if they were to be confident of completing the tasks they had been set. As the battle moved into October, the gunners found it increasingly difficult. They could not rely any longer on effective support from the air. Pilots could see little through the mist and rain, impeding even further the accuracy of counter-battery work. Any prospect of a rupture of the German lines in these conditions had long since disappeared and Bapaume, the first day's objective, was still firmly in German hands. But there had been some notable successes. Guillemont had been finally captured, as had High Wood, Delville Wood, and Thiepval. The British were making progress around Morval and Les Boeufs, but any further prospects here were being hampered by the slow progress of the French forces on their right.

In the time the 7th Kings Own had been away from the Somme, tanks had been used for the first time with dramatic effect, but they had not proven to be the decisive new weapon many, including General Haig himself, had hoped for. There were still few of them and they were prone to mechanical failure. The heavily cratered and mud-soaked battlefield meant that it was often difficult to deploy them successfully. At High Wood, the tanks had found it virtually impossible to penetrate the dense carpet of broken tree stumps. They were also very slow and cumbersome machines. Their maximum speed was only a couple of miles per hour. As a result, the tanks attracted heavy German gun fire which would jeopardize not only the tank crews themselves but the supporting infantry as well. The stalemate could not be broken. And with winter beginning to arrive, the final moves in the battle would have to be made quickly. The struggle now was to secure maximum tactical advantage and positioning ahead of a renewed assault in the spring of the next year. This was the context for the arrival once more into the battle of the 19th Division and the 7th King's Own.

On 7 October, the battalion marched bivouacs near Sailly aux Bois. For the next three days the whole battalion, over 600 strong, was engaged in heavy working parties. They were engaged in laying new signal cables – a sure sign of fresh action. On 11 October the battalion moved once again, this time to huts near Couin. Here they were to train intensively for their new role in combat operations on the Somme. Between 12 and 15 October the battalion took part in joint assault training with the 7th South Lancashires. On 16 October, the battalion practised similar operations, this time on their own. The next day, the battalion moved a step closer to the front line. They marched to billets at Harponville. The following day, the senior officers went to observe other units of 56 Brigade practice for the forthcoming assault.

On 19 October the brigade began to move to its new area around the Brickfields west of Albert. They had got as far as Warloy, when their move was postponed for twenty-four hours. On 20 October there was another twenty-four-hour delay. It was the 21 October before the battalion arrived at their new camp at the Brickfields. On 23 October the battalion replaced troops from the 11th and 13th Royal Sussex Regiment from the 39th Division in Stuff Trench north-east of Thiepval, which had been captured along with adjoining Regina Trench in heavy fighting earlier that day. The fighting around Thiepval was designed to prepare the way for a more general advance astride along the north and south banks of the Ancre River. The capture of the Thiepval Ridge would give the British perfect observation up the Ancre for the main assault. The objectives were the spur running north from Miraumont and then on to Serre. A subsequent advance would secure Pys and Irles – a distance of just over two miles. It was a limited battle plan, designed to push the Germans from the high ground and create a front line that could be more easily held for the winter.

Plans for the main assault were severely impeded by the heavy rain that had been falling on the battlefield since 19 October. It had been planned for the main assault to go in on 25 October. It was eventually postponed indefinitely until the weather improved.

While the senior army commanders wrestled with these momentous decisions, the job facing the 7th King's Own was altogether more simple and straightforward. After the heavy fighting around Thiepval their immediate task was to improve the trenches they now held, to secure them from counter-attack and to prepare for the next phase of the British advance. This involved heavy digging duties and carrying parties, bringing up supplies of material and ammunition. All the while, their positions were under continuous gun fire. The night of 23 October and the early morning of the 24th was however generally quiet. The men dug a new communication trench during the night without being impeded by any enemy fire. They were relieved at 10 am in the morning by the 7th East Lancs. The relief was slow and difficult and took nearly three hours to complete. The conditions were extremely difficult. The ground was a quagmire. The mud in the trenches came up to their thighs. The men moved back into reserve positions at Wood Post and Leipzig Redoubt. It was a timely relief, however. In the early hours of 26 October, the 7th East Lancs were heavily attacked by a strong German force. It was repulsed, with heavy losses being inflicted on the attackers and with some casualties for the East Lancs.

The 25th was spent trying to get the men dry and clean. Two officers, Second Lieutenants Doulton and Ross, were wounded by gun fire the next day. On 27 October they were relieved by the South Lancs and moved back to billets at Aveluy. For the next two days the men were allowed to rest. They were issued with new underpants, which in the circumstances must have been a particular delight.

On 30 October the men were back into the front line again north-east of Thiepval, relieving a battalion of the Cheshires. It had rained heavily every day since they had left the trenches on the 24th. They were in a terrible condition. There was two feet of mud in the bottom of the trenches. But at least the enemy were quiet. There was some intermittent shelling, but nothing that caused the men any particular anxiety. The 31st was a dry and clear day. The village of Grandcourt, over 2,000 yards away, was clearly visible as was the valley of the Ancre itself. The men did the best they could to improve the trenches, but the conditions made any really serious work almost impossible.

The battalion was relieved on 1 November by the 7th East Lancs. It was, once again, an extremely difficult relief because of the trench conditions and because of heavy enemy artillery fire. The relief had started at 10.30 am but was not complete until 7 pm. One man was stuck in the mud for seven hours before he could be dug out. The battalion eventually retired to Wood Post and Leipzig Redoubt.

On the following day, a small working party of fifty men helped carry bombs up to the front line, but the rest of the battalion was allowed to rest and clean up. On 3 and 4 November officers attended a series of lectures on the planned offensive. The starting date was still not clear and would not be for several more days.

On 5 November the battalion was sent to relieve the 9th Royal Welch Fusiliers in Regina Trench on the right of the divisional front. A and C Companies were in the front line with B and D Companies in Hessian Trench in support. The next day was quiet day, with only light enemy shelling. German soldiers could be seen moving behind the village of Grandcourt. Conditions were similar on 7 November. Regina Trench was shelled intermittently, but Hessian Trench was fired on throughout the night. Patrols in no man's land found no presence of the enemy.

The Germans were active all day on 8 November. German artillery fire was heavy and accurate, scoring several direct hits on the front and support lines. The trenches were full of water and mud because of the continuing heavy rain and the parapet would fall in at the slightest provocation.

That evening the battalion was relieved by the 10th Worcesters and moved back to huts near Ovillers. Here they were greeted by mugs of hot soup, clean socks and, at last, with new leather jerkins. It had been a particularly unpleasant tour of duty in the front line, although there is no record of the extent of any casualties. On 8 November, however, it had finally stopped raining and colder weather had set in. Now at last, the British commanders could come to a view about when they might be able to mount their planned attack along the Ancre.

Since its return to the Somme, the 19th Division had been part of the Fifth Army, commanded by Hubert Gough, probably one of the most controversial commanders of the war. He had always enjoyed the confidence of Haig, if not other senior officers, because of his commitment to ambitious offensive operations. On Friday 10 November there was still some dispute as to when the attack could be launched. On the 11th Gough, who wanted to commit his troops to the offensive in one final act of the Battle of the Somme, decided that he would attack on 13 November, with zero being fixed for 05.45, an hour and a half before sunrise. On the 12th, the preliminary bombardment began. Haig, notwithstanding his general support for Gough, was still not convinced that conditions on the battlefield would support a successful operation. Haig visited Gough at Fifth Army HQ that afternoon to express his reservations. Although he was anxious for a success in order to boost morale at home and to provide support to the Allies (especially the Russians and Romanians), he did not want to risk too much. He was also worried about further heavy casualties and the political repercussions that night flow from them. Despite these concerns, Gough was able to persuade Haig to lend his endorsement to his planned operation.

Gough was in fact planning to mount only a limited assault designed to reduce the head of the German salient between the Albert–Bapaume road and village of Serre to the north of Beaumont Hamel. North of the river, four divisions of V Corps, including the 3rd Division in which the 7th's sister battalion, the 8th King's Own, formed part, would attack the German lines around Beaumont Hamel and Serre. The German positions here had been attacked with disastrous losses on 1 July. Although operations since then had shortened the distance between the two sides to no more than 250 yards in places, the Germans remained very strongly in possession of these formidable positions.

II Corps, including the 19th and 39th Divisions, would attack simultaneously south of the river. Its task was to clear the enemy from the positions between the Schwaben Redoubt and the fortified village of St Pierre Divion (securing the so-called Hansa Line) and then to establish a line facing north-east abreast of Beaucourt.

On 11 November the 7th King's Own relieved the 9th Welch Fusiliers in Leipzig Redoubt and Wood Post. The men were fitted out in full battle order. It was a dull day with a lot of low cloud and mist. Visibility was very poor. In the early hours of the 12th, the battalion moved up to its assembly positions. And C Companies were in the Schwaben Redoubt, B and D in Bainbridge Trench and battalion HQ was in dugouts in Zollern Trench West.

At 05.45 on 13 November, after a very heavy artillery bombardment, the 39th and 19th Divisions began their attack. Forming the right of the II Corps attack, the 7th East Lancs and the 7th Loyal North Lancs of 56th Brigade advanced from Stuff Trench, safeguarding the right flank of the 39th Division on its left. The 7th King's Own was to act in close support.

There was a heavy fog that morning providing very useful extra cover in the darkness. Before zero, the leading waves had assembled outside their front trenches in order to take maximum advantage of the artillery fire on the German front lines. Eight machine guns from the brigade's machine gun company had also been placed in no man's land during the night in order to provide covering fire.

The barrage proved to be highly effective and the troops secured their objectives quickly and with few casualties. In fact the enemy put up very little organized or protracted opposition at all.

At 07.50 am D Company was placed at the disposal of the 7th Loyals to reinforce their right flank and occupied a former German communication trench. Here they would spend the night consolidating their new position. At 08.30, B Company was made available to the 7th East Lancs, with C Company being pushed up into Bainbridge Trench to replace them. In support of the East Lancs, two platoons of B Company pushed into Lucky Way, a sunken road that ran north-eastwards through the Grandcourt Line and eventually down into the village itself and established forward positions there.

The total casualties for the brigade during the attack were less than 200. Over 150 prisoners were captured and enemy losses in killed and wounded were considerable. There were no infantry counter-attacks on either 13 or 14 November.

The rest of the battalion was used to provide carrying parties from the beginning of the attack on 13 November until 8 pm on the 14th when the battalion sidestepped to the left and took over the main Hansa Line which had been captured by 118 Brigade of 39th Division. The battalion war diary describes this manoeuvre as the most difficult relief operation it had conducted since the 7th had arrived in France. It involved a march without guides, across the enemy's front, over very heavily cratered ground in the pitch dark. It was eventually completed by 4 am on 15 November.

The 15th was marked by violent and accurate German gun fire on the Hansa Line which started at dawn and continued at intervals during the afternoon and evening. The 7th sustained casualties under this barrage, but the precise numbers are not recorded. There were direct hits on many of the dugouts. Work began that day on consolidating an advance line some 60 yards in front of the Hansa Line. An advance post of one platoon and a Lewis gun team was established in the Hansa Road. Another post of one section together with another Lewis gun was put into Beaucourt Mill. Second Lieutenant Weber was killed during this operation. On 16 and 17 November the work of consolidation continued. The battalion came under occasional shelling, and in the evening of the 17th they were finally relieved by the 7th East Lancs and moved back to Marlborough huts. But the Battle of the Ancre was not quite over yet.

V Corps north of the Ancre had found things much more difficult. Success here had been patchy. Beaumont Hamel had finally fallen to the 51st Division, but the attack on Serre had been a failure and Beaucourt village still held out. Gough therefore laid new plans for a renewed assault by V Corps the following day. II Corps continued to develop its plans for an advance on Grandcourt village itself.

Between 14 and 18 November, further attacks were launched against the German lines north of the Ancre. Beaucourt village was captured on the morning of 14 November, and these gains were then successfully consolidated, but little progress was made in the attacks on the Redan Ridge beyond Beaumont Hamel. Casualties were once again beginning to mount and Haig was expressing doubts about the likely success of continuing the attacks. Gough wanted to continue with two more days of offensive operations starting on 17 November, with the principal role being conferred on II Corps south of the river. Gough wanted II Corps to move against the German trenches around Grandcourt. The advance was a fairly limited operation, involving a forward movement of 500 yards and the capture of the western edge of the village. Haig finally consented, after his chief of staff, Lieutenant-General Kiggell spoke to him in Paris while he was on his way to the Allied Powers planning conference at Chantilly.

Unfortunately, Gough's orders for this attack kept changing at the last minute. Some of these changes were the result of fresh intelligence reports that came in to his HQ. In particular, reports from air reconnaissance indicated that the Germans had abandoned important defensive lines. This led Gough to believe that he might be able to move even further ahead than he had planned, moving through Grandcourt and crossing the Ancre which curved behind it, to take the position known as Baillescourt Farm, a renowned German strong point. He issued orders to this effect. The attack would begin on 18 November.

These last-minute changes to operational orders had been a source of friction between senior commanders for much of the Somme offensive. Lieutenant-General Jacob, commanding II Corps, had in fact received very different information about German dispositions. His view was that the enemy had not withdrawn form any of his front-line trenches. About midnight on 17 November patrols from 56 Brigade reported Germans working on the wire in front of Grandcourt, which indicated strongly that the trenches were still occupied. He protested to Gough about his new orders for his corps. These protests were in vain. These eleventh-hour alterations also made it very difficult for effective planning by local commanders, fatally affecting the prospects for a successful attack. Guns could not be accurately reregistered onto new targets. Officers had not been given the chance to scout the ground to be attacked. Effective coordination between different units often proved impossible. The attack of 18 November would prove no exception.

Major-General Tom Bridges, commanding the 19th Division, was totally opposed to the operation. In his view, the whole trench system held by the division was a quagmire and the men were in no fit state to attack. The artillery had to fire over a steep hill and form a barrage on the downward slopes – an extremely challenging task. At the corps conference he predicted the failure of the attack and urged that it should be more in the nature of a demonstration. He was overruled as well.

The II Corps assault would involve the 19th, 18th and 4th Canadian Divisions. At 06.10 on the morning of 18 November, the assault of the 19th Division began. The task of 57 Brigade was to capture the whole of Grandcourt trench system south of the village. The 7th South Lancs of 56 Brigade was to advance up the

Ancre valley itself to the western edge of Grandcourt village. After these objectives had been consolidated, the brigade would assault the village itself and secure the passage of the Ancre beyond it in order to reach Bailliescourt Farm. The 7th King's Own were once again to act in close support.

It is impossible to exaggerate the appalling conditions in which this attack took place. During the night of 17 November, the first snows of the winter had fallen. On the morning of 18 November, the men advanced into swirling sleet and rain. A thaw had in fact set in. They could barely see in front of them as they groped their way through half-frozen mud and slime. The protective barrage was soon lost and all of the discernible features of the battlefield itself, cloaked in snow, became almost impossible for the men to identify. Direction was hard to maintain and the attacking units became mixed and confused. However, some progress was made despite these terrible conditions.

The attack of 57 Brigade had mixed success. The 8th North Staffs became cut off and most were taken prisoner, including their commanding officer, Lieutenant-Colonel Andersen. Only 70 men from this battalion were to eventually make it back to their own lines later that day. The 10th Royal Warwicks suffered extremely heavy casualties in front of uncut wire. A few men entered the German trenches in front of Grandcourt where they were joined by the 8th Gloucesters. The 8th Gloucesters went on to enter the south-west corner of the village – a heroic achievement in the circumstances.

The 7th South Lancs reached the western part of Grandcourt and made contact with the 8th Gloucesters. Because of the failure of the 57 Brigade assault, no effort was made to take the whole village. Instead, strong points were constructed on the road to the entrance to the village and along the railway embankment running alongside the river. The 7th East Lancs got as far as the South Lancs positions in Grandcourt but could make no real progress towards Baillescourt Farm, owing to heavy machine gun fire still coming from the village. Here they dug in.

Later in the day, all of these forward positions were put under the command of 56 Brigade. Consolidation was undertaken under heavy and continuous gun fire.

On 19 November, the Germans began to counter-attack. An attack was repulsed by the 7th South Lancs at the western edge of the village. Major-General Bridges, commanding 19th Division, ordered a new position to be constructed from the Ancre parallel to and about 500 yards west of the Grandcourt Line, the main German trench system defending the village. All of the troops of 56 and 57 Brigade were withdrawn to this line in the evening. The ground they had captured during the hurriedly arranged assault of 18 November was still overlooked by the Germans from both sides of the Ancre valley and was clearly untenable. The sacrifice of 18 November had been largely in vain.

The 7th King's Own were ordered up to take over this newly dug position, which now represented the limit of the British advance in the Battle of the Ancre.

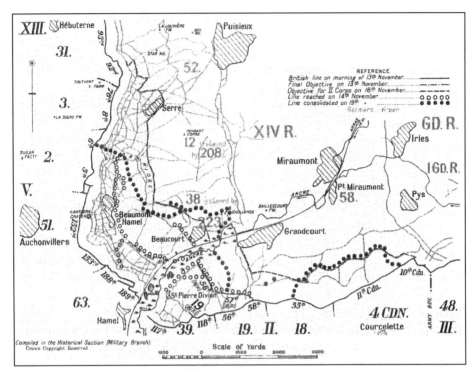

7th King's Own action during the final stages of the Somme Battle, November 1916, showing the trenches occupied by the battalion after the attack on Grandcourt.

They had moved at 30 minutes notice to the road junction east of Hamel village, arriving at 21.30, and then into the new position astride the valley. The men of the South Lancs, East Lancs, Gloucester and Royal Warwicks passed, exhausted and weakened, through the ranks of the 7th King's Own. The right of this position was in the air, but 58 Brigade were reported to be less than 200 yards away. There was no way of knowing what would happen next. The 7th King's Own were holding hastily constructed and exposed positions at the very tip of the British advance. The men must have expected the worst at any moment.

The next day the battalion worked flat out to improve and strengthen their new line. They lay as quiet as possible during the day and worked at full pressure during the hours of darkness. Patrols brought in a number of wounded men from no man's land. But there were to be no counter-attacks. Both sides had had enough. Winter had arrived with a vengeance and there was no possibility of any further offensive operations. The Battle of the Somme had finally come to an end.

On 21 November, the 7th King's Own, now only about 300 men in total, were relieved by the 9th Sherwood Foresters and moved back to Crucifix Corner. Four men were slightly wounded during this relief.

Brigadier Jeffreys, commanding 57 Brigade, described the battle in these terms:

> The conditions were, I think, the worst I ever remember in the war. The shell fire was continuous, the ground a mass of slimy mud, which, in such trenches as there were, was up to and sometimes beyond a man's knees. There were shell craters full of water in which a man could easily be drowned. Yet with it all, somehow or other, the men managed to keep up an extraordinary spirit and put up with hardships, dangers, and the filth in a spirit which was very different from what is sometimes described in some very bad war books that have appeared. What was unfortunate was that the Army Commander and the personnel of Army headquarters could not realize the state of affairs in the front line and the exhaustion which was produced in merely staying in the line under conditions of ground and weather well nigh intolerable. If they had been able to realize it, I feel that the attack of 18th November would never have been ordered.

Over the next few days, the battalion moved from Warloy to Contay, Gezaincourt, finally arriving at Candas on 25 November. They were joined en route by 180 new recruits. They would spend the whole of December at Candas resting and cleaning up. A further 162 new men joined the battalion during this time. Throughout December they were engaged in route marches, training exercises, drill and working parties. Absorbing so many new recruits in such a short time was a major challenge to the battalion. It now bore little resemblance to the body of men who had arrived in France the previous July, although its connection to the north-west of Lancashire remained strong and clear. The division had now passed under the control of V Corps and its commanding officer, Lieutenant-General Fanshawe, inspected the battalion on 20 December. Private Richard Willcock of Barrow was awarded the Military Medal for bravery during the Battle of the Ancre. Christmas was spent quietly. The men had a full Christmas dinner with plum pudding and beer.

1917: Messines Ridge and Third Ypres

The battalion was to remain at Candas until 9 January, when they moved to new billets at Terramesnil. The next day they marched to Famechon into billets taken over from the 12th Yorkshires. For the following ten days, the battalion was engaged in yet more training and exercises, including route marches. On 22 January 56 Brigade relieved 57 Brigade in the front line at Hebuterne, at the northern end of the original Somme battlefield. The 7th King's Own moved to Bayencourt where it formed the brigade reserve. The next two days were training days for the battalion and on 25 January they were moved up to the front line itself in the left subsector at Hebuterne. It was from these trenches that the 56th

Division had launched its heroic diversionary attack on Gommecourt village – only a few hundred yards from Hebuterne – on the first day of the Somme battle, an attack that was secondary to the main thrust to the south and which was designed purely to confuse the enemy about where the main British offensive would be directed. Despite horrific artillery and machine gun fire, the attack succeeded in gaining entry into the German front-line trenches, but was eventually driven out again before the end of the day. In the process, over 1,300 men from the division lost their lives. This sector of the front had, since these fateful encounters, remained fairly quiet. There had been no major engagements between the opposing forces apart from the 'normal' routine of trench warfare.

The next two days in the front line were very quiet. There was a little reciprocal shelling but nothing serious. The men worked on improving the trenches. On 28 January the battalion was relieved by the 7th East Lancs and moved back to the support lines at Hebuterne Keep and Sailly, about two miles west of Hebuterne village. For the next two days the men were required to provide working parties for the front line. But 200 men were able to enjoy hot baths and an issue of clean clothes at Sailly. On 31 January they were back in the front line at Hebuterne once again.

This was also to be a generally quiet tour of duty. On 3 February, however, a raiding party of 16 men, led by Lieutenant McClelland, attempted to enter the German front-line trenches in order to capture enemy prisoners for intelligence purposes and to do as much damage as possible to the enemy's positions. The mission was a failure. Betrayed by the bright moonlight, the raiding party, even with their blackened faces, was soon discovered by the Germans and they had to withdraw under a torrent of hostile gun fire. Two men were wounded. The battalion was relieved that night and was moved back to brigade reserve at Bayencourt. They spent the next three days resting and cleaning up. They were back in the front line again on 6 February for another three days, after which they were positioned in the support lines around Hebuterne and Sailly. There are no reports of any casualties during this period.

The battalion completed one more period of front-line duty in February with little incident. On 20 February they moved into hutted billets at Bus les Artois, four miles to the south-west. Here at least they were to enjoy a couple of days' rest. But on 22 February, the battalion was split up into two groups. A and D Companies were moved to Beussart, two miles away, where they were attached to 252 Tunnelling Company of the Royal Engineers. Their job was to work on the construction of command posts. C Company was sent to nearby Acheux to mount the guard at a prisoner of war camp. B Company remained at Bus but half of the company were detached for working parties. Only two platoons were left to enjoy their rest at the camp.

On 27 February, the whole battalion reassembled to work on improving and repairing the railway lines at Lealvillers near Varennes, an important supply route for the troops on the Somme. The work was to last for the next fortnight. On 10

March, the battalion marched to new billets at Gezaincourt to the south-west of Doullens. The following day they marched once more to the Bouquemaison area where they were divided between accommodation at Beuvoir and Bonnieres. The men were able to rest and train in peace and quiet, out of the range of enemy guns.

On 16 March, they moved to Febvin and then over the next four days to Tournhem – into the Second Army training area – via Guarbecque and Lynde. From 21 to 31 March they were engaged in intensive infantry assault training alongside the 7th East Lancs. The battalion was heading north. By 2 April they had arrived at Scherpenburg, a small village near Mont Kemmel, a few miles to the south-west of Ypres. From 4 to 16 April the battalion was employed on working parties and cable laying for the signallers.

On 16 April, the battalion was posted to the front-line trenches around Diependaal, about 1,000 yards to the south-west of St Eloi at the foot of the northern slopes of the Messines Ridge. The trenches here ran alongside the Diependaal Beek, a small stream running down the slopes of the ridge. The ground was wet and the trenches were largely breastworks requiring constant repair and attention.

Once again, the men were to enjoy the good fortune of being in a relatively quiet sector of the line. However, this would in the next few weeks be transformed into one of the most active sections of the whole British front. The relative peace and quiet lasted until 19 April, when they came under very heavy machine gun fire all day and rifle fire throughout the night. At 7.30 pm the following night the enemy began heavily shelling the 7th King's Own with trench mortars as a prelude to trench raid of their own. The Germans were planning a raid on an adjoining section of the line further north. The British guns came into action in retaliation. The heavy gun fire lasted for three hours, but the 7th King's Own saw no sight of any enemy infantry at all. In the evening they were relieved by the 7th East Lancs and went into brigade reserve at Murrumbidgee. The next three days were spent in the familiar pattern of resting, cleaning up and enjoying hot baths.

On 24 April, they were back in the front line again at Diependaal. On 25 April, two patrols were sent out to gather any intelligence possible on the enemy's whereabouts and dispositions. The men entered the enemy lines and found them unoccupied. The same thing happened again the following night. This time, however, they exchanged bombs with the Germans. No prisoners were taken. On 27 April they were relieved and moved back to Ridge Wood in the support lines. The next day virtually the whole battalion, 450 men, was engaged in working parties. The battalion's position in Ridge Wood was far from comfortable. On 29 April the enemy shelled the wood in the evening. Two men were wounded. The wood had to be evacuated and the men took cover in nearby trenches. The next day saw over 200 men employed on working parties.

The battalion was getting ready for a major offensive operation. The Allied high command had decided at the end of 1916 to make Flanders the decisive battleground for the coming year. The general plan was designed to drive the

4th Battalion, officers' group, Bedford, 3 May 1915, just before the battalion left for France. Rear row, left to right: 2nd Lieutenants J Fisher, H R Sykes, H A Brocklebank, R H Steinthal, E Spearing, Lieutenants G F Taylor, E H Hewitt, A A Wright, 2nd Lieutenant W C Neill, Lieutenant J Fisher, and 2nd Lieutenant T W Dugdale. Middle row, left to right: Lieutenants R Gardner and J Crossley (Quartermaster), Captains W G Pearson, J V Barrow, G B Balfour, J M Mawson, R D Morrel, Lieutenants H Y Huthwaite, W H Walker, and 2nd Lieutenant G B Bigland. Front row, left to right: Captain W D Barrett, Major A F Rutherford, Major R Thompson (Second in Command), Lieutenant Colonel W F A Wadham (Commanding), Captain V A Jackson (Adjutant), Major N E Barnes and Captain R P Little. (KO0428-01)

4th Battalion men taking a break during a route march, Tonbridge, March 1915. (KO01408-07)

4th Battalion arriving in Tonbridge, March 1915. (KO01691-03)

A group of 4th Battalion men, autumn 1914, probably taken during the period the battalion was guarding the Great Western railway.

...sels, January 1919. 4th Battalion led the march past in a victory parade before the King of the ...ians (mounted on the white horse). (Q3503)

...sh troops advancing during the Battle of Morval, September 1916. 4th King's Own men would ... moved over this terrain. The Somme battlefield had become a featureless landscape of blasted ...h after three months of heavy fighting. (Q1312)

...w Head Copse, September 1916. Trones Wood in background. 4th Battalion launched their 8 ...ust attack on Guillemont from this location. (Q53169)

B Company officers, 7th Battalion, King's Own, France, October 1916. (KO0883-256)

Battalion in Clevedon in February 1915, Captain Openshaw on horseback, leading his company.
01769-01)

oon of 7th Battalion men taken at Lucknow Barracks, Tidworth, June 1915. Private James Miller VC
th from right on the back row. (KO01851-01)

7th Battalion in France, summer 1917. (KO01586)

7th Battalion in training at Clevedon, spring 1915. The men are seen laying a bridge across a small stream. (KO01769-01-019)

La Boisselle, 3 July 1916. Taken from in front of Ovillers, village on extreme right. Bodies of British soldiers killed on 1 July clearly visible in middle foreground. (Q67)

7th Battalion, marching through Candas, band playing, late summer 1915. (Q17336)

7th King's Own men take captured German prisoners to the rear after the successful attack on La Boisselle. King's Own badges clearly visible on steel helmets. (Q761)

Oblige Trench, captured by 7th King's Own, Battle of Messines, 7 June 1917. Notice in German reads 'Telephone Exchange, entrance permitted only to men on duty'. (Q3088)

8th Battalion Sergeants' Mess, autumn 1914. Some of the men still do not have their proper uniform. (KO01011)

Major Berry, CO of the 8th Battalion, interviewing a sergeant about demobilization, Cologne April 1919. (Q3796)

Troops of 76 Brigade travelling on light railway, Pilckem Ridge, 25 September 1917. (Q5998)

Sergeant Tom Mayson VC

gueval village, September 1916. Scene of bitter fighting involving the 8th Battalion in July. (Q1260)

mplete devastation; Delville Wood, September 1916. (Q1259)

11th Battalion on parade, Blackdown Barracks, June 1916. (KO094-1)

Battalion officers, Blackdown, June 1916, taken as the battalion prepared to leave for France. (0094-02)

Battalion Sergeant's Mess, Blackdown, June 1916. (KO094-03)

Platoon, A Company, 11th Battalion, Blackdown, June 1916. (KO002590-45)

Looking north from the positions held by the 4th Battalion at Givenchy, April 1918.

Looking back towards Trones Wood from Arrow Head Copse, from which 4th Battalion launched the attack on Guillemont on 8 August 1916. There is life in these fields again now. In 1916 they were full of death.

Road leading north-east from La Boisselle along which the 7th Battalion advanced after taking the village on 4 July 1916.

7th Battalion marched together for the last time down this road into Lechelle on 4 March. Ytres in the background.

Scene of the 7th Battalion advance towards the Intermediate Line, August 1916. High Wood on the left, Delville Wood on the horizon.

8th Battalion retreated through the village of Neuville Vitasse, church steeple visible on the left, in March 1918 after heavy fighting. The men took up positions behind the village and dug in.

The area around Avelette Bridgehead defended by the 8th Battalion, April 1918. Trenches would hav run through the far end of the field.

...w from The Orchard at Delville Wood, showing the ground over which the 8th Battalion advanced ...ly 1916. Note the screw picket in the foreground. These were widely used by both sides on the ...tern Front to fasten barbed wire and are still widely used by farmers on the Somme today.

...ely Trench, sited in the middle distance, running left to right, to the south of Guillemont, was ...cked unsuccessfully by the 8th Battalion in August 1916.

...ntry Hill looking north-east from Monchy Le Preux. The 8th Battalion captured German positions ...e middle foreground in May 1917 and held them against counter-attacks until they were relieved.

Scene of the advance of 11th Battalion into Beaucamp on 25 April 1917. The village is in the backgrou

Eastern edge of Bourlon Wood, attacked by 11th Battalion, 25 November, 1917.

Germans from the Belgian Channel ports and so ease the pressure on Allied convoys. German submarines operating from these ports were inflicting major losses on the merchant navy and unless these were reduced, the British Armies in France might begin to run seriously short of vital war materials. The whole course of the war might be affected.

To succeed in this endeavour, the German lines around Ypres would have to be assaulted and breached. The Germans, however, held all of the high ground around the city and the British forces were confined to a dangerous salient over which the enemy had total observation. The Messines Ridge to the south also represented a major threat that would need to be overcome first if the main attack at Ypres stood any chance of success.

Here the Allies would enjoy a major tactical advantage. Mines had been dug underneath the ridge and were primed with vast amounts of explosive. Deep tunnels had begun to be dug at the beginning of January 1916. An attack at Ypres had been planned for the summer of 1916, but these plans had eventually been put on the shelf as the main focus switched to the joint Anglo–French advance on the Somme.

These tunnels were dug 80 to 120 feet below the German positions on the Messines Ridge. At this depth they would be virtually impossible for the Germans to detect. The mines, twenty-four in total, stretched in an arc from just north of Ploegsteert Wood in the south to Hill 60 in the north. The work was conducted in total secrecy. The Germans had literally no idea that they were sitting on top of such a deadly stockpile of high explosive.

In addition to the mines, over 2,000 guns and howitzers had been assembled for the operation, nearly 800 heavy guns and 1,500 filed pieces. Nearly 150,000 tons of ammunition had been supplied for them to fire.

The final plans for the operation at Messines were agreed at the beginning of April, when the 7th King's Own were in billets at Scherpenburg. The attack was to be on a broad ten mile front, from St Yves to Mount Sorrel. The final objective was strictly limited to an advance of one to two miles into the German lines. The enemy would be driven from the high ground on the ridge by the combined effect of the mines, an overwhelming artillery bombardment and a rapid infantry assault. Having captured the high ground there would be another advance down the eastern slope of the ridge to capture the German second line and thus secure the ridge itself. Three corps of General Plumer's Second Army were to be employed. The II Anzacs Corps would take the southern shoulder of the ridge and village itself. The IX Corps, including the 19th Division, would capture the central section of the ridge. The 19th Division would attack north of the Vierstraat–Wytschaete road, opposite two woods, the Grand Bois and Bois Quarante. The attack would involve two of the division's three brigades – 58 and 56. The 7th King's Own would be placed directly in the front line of the attack. On the left, X Corps would secure the northern sector of the ridge. XIV Corps was in reserve.

The German positions on the ridge formed a very exposed salient. As a consequence, the troops of IX Corps had to cover about 2,000 yards to reach their ultimate objective – the most that any of the attacking troops would have to cover. But all of this ground was under direct artillery and machine gun fire. If the attack was to have any chance of success, and if casualties were to be kept to a minimum, then surprise and speed of assault would be critically important. The positions to be assaulted were very strongly constructed and strongly held. The Germans had been in possession of the ridge for over two years and had turned it into a veritable fortress. Careful training would be necessary if this audacious plan was to succeed, as there could be no absolute guarantee that the mines planted so long ago would detonate as planned. If they didn't the attack would still have to go on.

On 1 May the 7th King's Own were relieved by the Irish Fusiliers and marched back to new billets at Curragh Camp and then the next day to Montreal Camp near Poperinghe. For the next six days the men were briefed for the attack and began to prepare themselves for their role in it. On 9 May, the men marched to the La Clytte area near Scherpenberg. Here special training areas had been marked out. At Scherpenberg itself, a large model of the ridge, the size of two croquet lawns, had been constructed showing the precise ground to be traversed and the enemy positions to be captured. Over the next few weeks the battalion planned its assault with meticulous detail. Wearing full kit, the men were to make several dummy runs of their attack. The ground was marked out with flags and tapes to mirror the position of the German lines and strong points. The assault itself was scheduled to begin on 7 June.

In between this intensive infantry training, the men were still needed to provide labour for the necessary preparations for the offensive. They helped dig assembly trenches, lay new pipe lines for water supplies and worked on establishing new dugouts and strong points. On 13 May they were back in the front line again at Diependaal. The British guns had become much more active, although the preliminary bombardment itself would not commence until 21 May. But on 14 May, the King's Own men could not help but get a feel for what the future would hold for them. British artillery began searching for enemy targets in earnest. The guns were trying to cut the enemy wire and were systematically shelling enemy positions. The tension amongst the men must have risen sharply as the unmistakable signs of the battle to come were all around them.

On 17 May, they were relieved by the 7th East Lancs and moved back to brigade reserve. On 20 May they marched again to La Clytte. Here they stayed until the 25th, going over and over again their part in the attack. On 26 May they marched to Westoutre and were inspected by General Shute, the new commanding officer of 19th Division. They practised their assault again on 27, 28 and 29 May. The men were being trained in how to attack the pillboxes that dominated the German defensive positions. Small parties of infantry would mount suppressing fire while others moved to isolate the pillboxes from both flanks.

On 30 May, the officers of the battalion went to see a demonstration of the tanks in action at Wailly, south-west of Arras. The battalion had not yet gone into an attack alongside these new and increasingly significant weapons. The next day was spent finalizing the last details of their attack plans.

On 2 June, the battalion went back into the front line at Diependaal. The early morning of 3 June passed off peacefully. No man's land between the two front lines was heavily patrolled but there was no sign of the enemy and it was not being contested by the Germans. They were clearly content to remain on the defensive. The British guns were pounding away at the enemy all night long. Over 2,000 burning oil drums were fired into the German positions at Grand Bois on the night of 3/4 June. The sound and noise was deafening. Six men were wounded by German shellfire. On 4 June, preparations for the infantry advance were being put into place. An outpost line of six Lewis gun teams at 100 yard intervals was pushed out near to the German wire. Second Lieutenant Lancaster, Sergeant Rooney and three men carried out an effective patrol which succeeded in identifying which trenches and shell holes were being manned by the Germans. The patrol was spotted by the enemy and had to withdraw under rifle and machine gun fire, wounding Lieutenant Lancaster. Another patrol was sent out to observe the enemy wire.

The artillery bombardment continued remorselessly all day. There was only light enemy retaliatory fire. Some gas shells – in this case tear gas – landed near the trenches being held by the 7th King's Own and the men were forced to keep their respirators on for long periods of time. Although these devices undoubtedly saved many lives, they were uncomfortable and claustrophobic and their prolonged use must have added to the general discomfort of the troops as they prepared for the attack ahead.

Under cover of an artillery barrage, a trench raid was carried out on the Bois Quarante by a hundred men of A Company at 3 pm on 5 June. The raid was mounted in order to help identify the units of the German Army defending their front line. It was a huge success. One officer and forty men were taken prisoner and four enemy soldiers were killed. Captain Openshaw, who had been in France with the battalion right from the beginning, was wounded, as were Second Lieutenants Grant and Backhouse. One man was killed and three others wounded.

On the eve of battle, 6 June, the battalion moved up to its final assembly positions in the front line at 9.30 in the evening. Zero hour had been set for 3.10 the following morning. The men would have to endure a wait of nearly six hours before they were to go 'over the top', not knowing whether or not their presence might have been spotted by the enemy. If it had, they would be highly vulnerable to artillery fire. The wait must have been agonizing. Few if any of the men would have had very much sleep. The sound of the barrage intensified.

At about midnight on the evening of 6/7 June, after a brief but violent thunderstorm earlier in the evening, the moon again shone brightly in a clear sky. At 2 am,

British aircraft began to fly up and down the German lines to drown out the sound of the approaching tanks that were moving up to their start positions.

The British artillery fire had been heavy throughout the night. Half an hour before dawn, a peculiar calm set in. Nightingales could be heard singing. The official history records what one eye-witness described as the moment the mines were detonated:

> Suddenly at 3.10 am great leaping streams of orange flames shot upwards, each a huge volcano in itself, along the front of the attack, followed by terrific explosions and dense masses of smoke and dust which stood like great pillars towering into the sky, all illuminated by the fires below.

The German official history describes the scene equally graphically:

> Nineteen gigantic roses with carmine petals, or as enormous mushrooms rose up slowly and majestically out of the ground and then split into pieces with a mighty roar, sending up multi-coloured columns of flame mixed with a mass of earth and splinters high into the sky.

Each of the mines had exploded without failure. The shock wave was felt many miles back on both sides of the front line. The mines had not however all exploded simultaneously. The last mine exploded 19 seconds after the first creating a cumulative effect that magnified the impact of the explosions and helped further destroy the morale of the defending soldiers. Most of the German front-line trenches and their defending garrison were instantly obliterated.

As soon as the mines detonated, the huge weight of the 2,000 British guns opened up on the German front and support lines and on the German artillery positions. The gun flashes were so close together and continuous that the whole of the western horizon seemed to be alight. It was at this decisive point that the men of the 7th King's Own were ordered to advance on the enemy. C and D Companies went over the top first, followed at 30 yard intervals by B and then A Companies.

The effect of the explosions and the artillery barrage was to drown the battlefield in smoke and dust. Visibility was down to 50 yards. But the men managed to keep their sense of direction, helped by the fact that the dim outline of the hillside below the ridge was lit up by the green and white flares sent up by the remaining defenders pleading for artillery support. The British barrage had however been massively successful on this occasion. The deluge of both gas and high explosive shell had effectively neutralized the German guns and their barrage was largely ineffectual and late. The German shells did not begin to fall on the British trenches until several minutes after zero, by which time the troops were well on their way.

In front of the 7th King's Own, three mines had exploded simultaneously at Hollandscheschurr. It had the effect of eliminating the German position known as the Nag's Nose which lay on an outlying spur of the ridge. The diary of the 19th Division records: 'There was little resistance from the Germans, who either ran forward to surrender, or, if they could do so, ran away; very few of them put up a fight.' Those who did manage to run away were caught by the British barrage.

The men attacked the German strong points with trench mortars, Lewis guns and rifle grenades. Parties of riflemen and bombers worked their way around the flanks from shell hole to shell hole and surrounded the defenders. The men had trained for these tactics intensively in the run-up to the assault, and it was now to yield a handsome dividend. The German front line was easily overrun. The first objective was secured within the first half an hour of the attack. In total, the battalion had attacked and seized three lines of German trenches. By 4 am the men had begun to dig in, in advance of their final objective on the top of the ridge. The 7th East Lancs passed through these positions at 4.15 am, helped secure further objectives along the ridge and then began to move cautiously down its eastern slopes towards Oostaverne. In this initial assault, the battalion had sustained precious few casualties – far less than the 50 per cent that had been originally

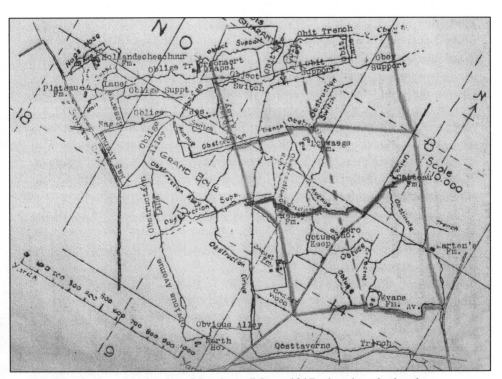

7th King's Own battle plan, Messines, 7 June 1917, showing the battle objectives and final position of the battalion at the end of the attack.

estimated for the first wave of the attack. Five officers had been wounded. Eight men had been killed, ninety-five wounded and sixteen were missing, believed killed. These figures bear testimony to the successful planning and execution of one of the most effective military operations conducted by the British since the war itself had begun three long years before.

For the infantry, the morning's work had been an unqualified success. Even more so when it is realized that most of the 48 tanks assigned to support them had failed to keep up with the speed of the advance and had therefore made only a minimal contribution to the territorial gains made.

II Anzac Corps and X Corps had enjoyed a similar experience to that of the troops attacking in the centre. By 9 am British troops were established along the whole length of the ridge. They had successfully beaten off the predicted counter-attacks. The defenders had been comprehensively routed. In the bright and warm sunshine, and in their shirt sleeves, the men began to dig in.

But because of the slight casualties sustained in the advance, the ridge was now crowded with troops which now presented excellent targets for the German guns. Casualties began to mount.

During the afternoon of 7 June, the battalion moved across the ridge to occupy some advance posts held by the 7th East Lancs. All through the afternoon, repeated German counter-attacks were broken up by concentrated machine gun and artillery fire.

On the evening of 8 June, the battalion relieved the 8th Gloucesters in the new front line from Polka Estaminet to the adjoining road and they began to strengthen their trenches and dugouts. The relief took place under heavy gun fire and was not completed until 3 the next morning. Enemy artillery fire continued throughout the day, which was bright and sunny. But it was neither heavy nor very accurate. There was more trouble caused by enemy aircraft flying low above them, spraying their positions with machine gun fire. The men retaliated with Lewis and Vickers guns. Small parties of the enemy were successfully sniped. The enemy shelling continued on 10 June, becoming heavier in the evening. But only three men were wounded on these two days.

On 11 June the battalion made another minor advance forward down the eastern slopes of the ridge. They made this advance under fire. Seven men were killed and seventeen wounded. Captain Stockdale and Second Lieutenant Backhouse were also wounded.

Enemy gun fire was intermittent again on 12 June. There were no infantry attacks mounted against the new lines held by the 7th King's Own. Enemy aircraft were once again very active. At 10 pm they were relieved by the 7th East Lancs and moved back to brigade reserve in trenches on top of the ridge. Battalion HQ was positioned in dugouts in what was left of Onraet Wood which ran along the main road from Messines to Ypres. Two men were killed and three wounded during this relief as the men came under high explosive shell fire. On 13 June, the battalion was lightly shelled as the men enjoyed a period of rest out of the front line. One man was killed and seven wounded from shellfire. Three more were killed and seven wounded on 14 June, the final day of military operations on the Messines Ridge. The battle had seen a great victory for the British forces and the scene was now set for the major offensive planned at Ypres to begin as soon as the necessary preparations could be made. The Germans had been driven from the high ground dominating the southern aspects of the Ypres salient. Over 140 officers and 7,000 men had been taken prisoner. German battle casualties were estimated to be over 23,000. Forty-eight guns, two hundred and eighteen machine guns and sixty trench mortars had been captured. Most of the British casualties were incurred not in the battle for the ridge itself, but during the crowding that took place on the ridge after its capture. This was also true for the 7th King's Own. This could and should have been avoided. Of the 24,000 Allied casualties, over half were in II Anzac Corps. In IX Corps, there were over 5,000 men killed, wounded or missing.

The total casualties in the battalion for the whole Messines operation were 9 officers wounded, 30 men killed and 157 wounded. Sixteen men were missing. One of these was Private Richard Lytham from Market Street, Dalton. He was one of three brothers serving with the King's Own in France. Private J Davies from Barrow was killed on the first days of fighting at Messines. Private Davies was a member of the Cemetery Cottages Working Men's Club at Ormsgill. He was 24 years old.

For the 7th Battalion, this action would prove to be one of their most significant of the war. They had taken part in the historic first few hours of the battle, leading the assault of the 19th Division. They had performed their allotted tasks with distinction and bravery. Their training proved decisive. Everything that had been asked of them they had delivered. Once again, their combat effectiveness as well as their hard labour had made a huge contribution to the overall success of the British forces at Messines. The men of Furness had much to be proud of. They had demonstrated their mettle again.

On 15 June, the battalion was employed in battlefield clearance, salvaging as much equipment as possible and identifying and burying those that had fallen in the attack. In the evening they were relieved by the 8th Gloucesters and moved back to the Curragh camp at Scherpenberg, a march of over six miles in the warm evening sunshine and into divisional reserve. Every man would have been reflecting on their good fortune to still be alive and to feel the sun on their faces. On 16–17 June they were allowed to rest and recover from their efforts at Messines. They visited the divisional baths and had good hot food. On 19 June they were briefly attached to 57 Brigade, the reserve brigade during the attack of 7 June, which had now taken over the whole divisional front along the ridge. The battalion was stationed in the old British front line and in the captured original German front-line positions.

On 19 June, the division was relieved by the 36th Division and moved back to Locre.

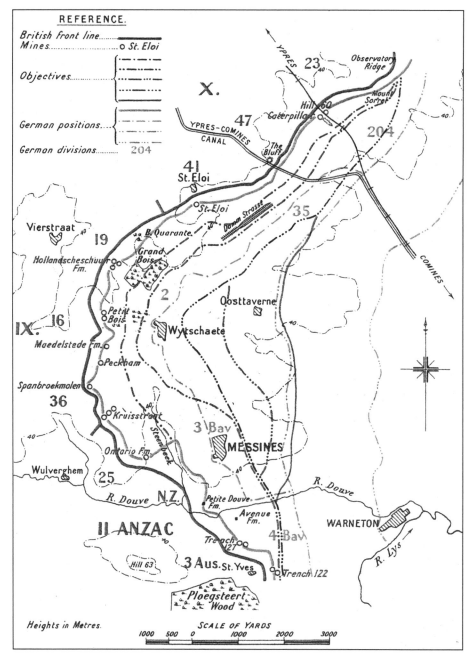

Attack of the 19th Division at Messines, 7 June 1917, 7th King's Own in the first wave.

On this day, Second Lieutenant Backhouse was awarded the Military Cross for his bravery throughout the period of the battle and in the run-up to it. He had been in the thick of the action and had been wounded twice. Sergeant Walter Chambers and Lance-Corporal Birch of Heywood, Lancashire, were both awarded the Military Medal. Private John Booth was awarded the Distinguished Conduct Medal. The battalion was to stay at Locre until 11 July, where it was allowed to rest and recuperate after its hard fighting at Messines.

But the Messines operation was always designed as the forerunner of a much more aggressive campaign, to be launched by General Gough's Fifth Army, against the Germans on a broad front around the Ypres salient. The planned offensive would be on a fifteen-mile front from Frelinghien (just to the north of Armentiers) to Steenstraat north of Ypres. The Second Army, to which 19th Division was still attached, was to capture the remaining outpost strong points in front of the Warneton Line. The attack was designed to create the impression of a major assault on the Warneton Line itself, thereby threatening Lille and so holding the German reserves there, while the main attack of the Fifth Army went in further to the north.

The 7th King's own were alerted to their possible new role in this scheme early in July. On 11 July they moved from Scherpenberg to billets at Kemmel Shelters, near Mont Kemmel. For the next few days the men formed large working parties in the forward areas around the Messines Ridge. They helped lay new signal cables and improve the roads. In between they took part in assault training. On 18 July they relieved the 9th Royal Welch in the support lines around Oostaverne Wood. During the relief the enemy attacked and captured a position known as Junction Buildings, a group of houses a couple of hundred yards in front of the British lines in no man's land which provided both a useful observation and fire control post. The buildings had been held by a company of the 9th Cheshires. The buildings were fought over during the course of the day but the enemy managed to hold onto them. One company of the 7th King's Own was ordered to act as support for the attacks but was not committed to the fighting.

On the 20 July, the 7th King's Own replaced the 9th Cheshires in the front line opposite Junction Buildings. For the next few days things were pretty quiet. There were no further attacks on Junction Buildings. During the day the men came under occasional artillery fire and at night enemy machine gun fire would rake their front parapet.

Divisional HQ however wanted to take back Junction Buildings before the main attack, which would eventually commence on 31 July. If the buildings were left in German hands, then losses during an assault over this ground could be high. On 22 July, therefore, the 7th King's Own and the 7th South Lancs launched two raids designed to recapture them. The right raiding party from A Company was formed under Second Lieutenant Wickham; the left party came from B Company under Second Lieutenant Britton. The A Company party advanced but found no sign of the enemy. Small parties were observed further away and were engaged by Lewis gun fire. The B Company party found the enemy holding a position in small shelters behind a hedge. They captured four prisoners and killed two soldiers of the 31st Reserve Infantry Regiment. The raiding party from the South Lancs found Junction Buildings strongly held and were driven off by heavy machine gun and rifle fire. They suffered heavy casualties in the attack. Amongst the 7th King's Own, six men were killed and eighteen wounded. It had been a disappointing setback.

At 10 pm they began to be relieved by the 8th Gloucesters. The relief was completed by 3.15 am the following morning, and they moved back to a campsite at Butterfly Farm, six miles to the west on the safe reverse slopes of Mont Kemmel. For the next few days the battalion trained intensively for the new assault it would be asked to perform on 31 July. On the 29th, they returned to the front line again, taking over from the 8th North Staffs in trenches just to the right of Junction Buildings. The battalion strength was 20 officers and 452 men. In general 29 and 30 July were quiet days before the storm. On 30 July, two men were killed and six wounded by shellfire.

In the early hours of 31 July, the men moved into their attack positions, completing this at 3.20 am. Zero was set for 3.50 am. All four companies were in the line. The battalion would attack on a frontage of about 700 yards. Their objectives were to take Junction Buildings and other strong points in their line of advance and to push the British line forward as far as possible. The main German line was not to be assaulted. The barrage was provided by the 18-pounders firing shrapnel. The advanced waves would be followed by 'moppers up' who would deal with any enemy left behind in the initial advance.

As soon as the barrage began at 3.50 am, the battalion moved forward. No man's land was about 200–300 yards wide. On the left, good progress was made. All of the objectives were quickly secured and the men met very little resistance. Junction Buildings – the scene of bitter fighting a few days before – fell quickly. Three German officers and eighteen men were taken prisoner. Tiny and Spider Farms – both of them strong points and machine gun positions – were captured along with several other prisoners. But the mopping up was not done well enough. An enemy machine gun opened up on men from C Company from behind and had to be dealt with by a bombing party. Having taken these positions the men began to consolidate and put up a considerable amount of wire in the next two hours – defences that would help them deal with the inevitable counter-attack.

On the right, the position was less clear. The men had made initial progress, but the battalion on their right had come across their front, causing confusion and delay. The fog of war had descended. They were under continuous and heavy fire from the German main position – the Warneton Line. At about 6.30 am, the enemy counter-attacked with a force of about 300 men. The battalion on the right was driven back to the original start line by the force of this counter-attack. The right flank of the 7th King's Own was completely in the air. Of the men attacking on the right, only one officer and twelve men managed to get back to Tiny Farm, where they occupied a strong point newly constructed by the Royal Engineers. The enemy drove through the gap that had now been created. Although their immediate flank had been effectively turned, the other companies held their ground stoutly. They inflicted heavy casualties on the German attackers with rifle and Lewis gun fire. At 8.10 am, a company of the 7th South Lancs, under the command of the King's Own, attempted to move up to provide further support. They could not get out of their trenches in the original British front line as they were met by murderous machine gun fire. But the British gunners knew exactly what was going on in front of them and their fire broke up repeated attacks on the front line held by the 7th King's Own men. Two officers were killed (Lieutenants Wigley and Beachcroft), four were wounded and two were missing presumed dead; 34 men were killed, 134 were wounded and 42 were missing – most of these were dead. The battalion had sustained nearly 50 per cent casualties, the heaviest of the war so far. In total, the line had been pushed forward about 500 yards. Amongst the dead that day was Private Richard Ainsworth of Hall Street, Barrow. He was 27 years old. Lance-Corporal Frank Rice was another Barrow man to die in this attack.

In the evening, it began to rain. It would rain incessantly for the next three days and nights, turning the battlefield into a complete swamp of mud. The conditions in which the 7th King's Own held onto their newly won positions were described in the war diary as 'indescribably bad'. It was extremely difficult even to evacuate the wounded as stretcher bearers could not carry their desperate loads through the mud safely. Instead, the men held on under severe enemy machine gun fire. There was virtually no communication possible between the front line and battalion HQ. At 10 pm the battalion began to be relieved by the 9th Welch. It took over five hours to be completed. The tired and exhausted survivors marched back to Haringbeek camp – a position just behind the old 31 July front line, about five miles away – where they arrived at six in the morning. Later on 3 August they were moved back again to Kemmel Shelters, three miles away to the west.

On 4 August, the scale of the battalion's losses were brought home to all of the survivors. Companies were reorganized into one complete platoon each of thirty-six men. Each company would normally consist of four platoons of over fifty men each. The remainder of the men, about fifty, were formed into sections to be turned into platoons when the reinforcements arrived.

The next day was spent quietly. There was a church service in the morning and a concert party in the evening. In the afternoon, the men visited the baths. On 6 August the battalion marched to new camps at Berthen where they took part in drill and rifle training. The same routine was repeated again for the next three days. On 10 August the men moved by rail to the Lumbres area. They marched to Bailleul station and then by a further train to Wizernes. From there the men marched to Coulemby for the night. The next morning the battalion marched to fresh billets at Le Wast, a few miles from Calais. The following day was given over to resting and refitting. On 13 August, the battalion was inspected by the army commander, General Plumer, at Longeville.

On 15 August, the first of the new reinforcements arrived: 180 men from the base camp. At a stroke, the size of the battalion nearly doubled. The next day, the battalion began to assimilate its new recruits. It spent the day drilling and training. The next day saw a further forty-seven men and two new officers join the battalion – Second Lieutenants Lyons and Willis. Four more subalterns were to arrive over the next few days and 18 August was spent in training the new recruits.

The following afternoon the battalion took part in a sports day in the grounds of Colembert Chateaux. On 21 August, the battalion was to enjoy a rare treat. It was taken by lorries to the sea at Ecault, a few miles south of Boulogne. The men would swim in the warm sunshine. The officer commanding Number 10 Convalescent Camp in the village had kindly arranged for swimming costumes to be provided for the men. These were waiting for them on the beach.

The next day the men marched to Coulemby again and went into billets in the village. Field Marshall Haig inspected 56 Brigade the following day at Harlettes and paid tribute to their service at Messines and on the first day of the fresh Ypres offensive. The battalion trained extensively for the next few days, before moving on the 29 August, first by train to Bailleul and then by route march to Carunna camp near Westoutre. The battalion was returning to positions around the foot of the Messines Ridge. It would soon find itself back in action again, fulfilling the familiar role of supporting the continuing operations in the Ypres salient.

The Ypres offensive, under the command of General Gough, was making very slow progress. Every yard of ground was being strongly contested by both sides. The conditions on the battlefield itself were beyond anything that had been experienced so far in the war. The incessant shelling had churned up the ground. The rain had converted the landscape into an ocean of mud and filth. The ground began to dry out however in September, after three weeks of warm sunshine.

But after several weeks of fighting, it was obvious that there would be no break-through to the Channel ports. The fighting had become another battle of attrition designed to inflict as much damage as possible on the Germans and to secure as much of the high ground around Ypres as possible – ground that might allow further operations in 1918 the chance to succeed where others had failed. If this strategy were to succeed, then the British would have to drive the Germans off the Gheluvelt plateau to the south-east of Ypres astride the Menin Road. Here the Germans had concentrated much of their artillery which had been causing the British troops in the salient so much misery since the battle had started on 31 July. Repeated attacks on the plateau had failed miserably. Now Haig had turned to General Plumer to succeed where Gough and the Fifth Army had failed.

The Second Army would assault the plateau in a succession of 'bite and hold' operations, over several days, beginning with the capture of its eastern slopes. The plan of attack would rely heavily on assembling an overwhelming superiority in heavy guns which would smash the machine gun nests and concrete shelters of the defenders before turning their attention to the German batteries themselves. The southern flank of this attack would be mounted by IX Corps with one division – the 19th – in the front line. Plumer was determined to apply the tactics that had prevailed at Messines in June. The infantry would attack and outflank the pillbox defences in small groups. Each group had its task and was trained as a fighting unit. The forward movements would each be strictly limited so that fresh troops could carry on the assault, passing through the recently won positions but not so far so as to lose the protection of the artillery barrage. This would protect the advancing troops from enemy counter-attacks.

The battalion remained at Westoutre for the next few days. Every moment was spent practising for their new operations. On 7 September they moved to Dranoutre, on the south-west slopes of Mont Kemmel, and 250 men were employed on working parties. Over the next week, most of the battalion was engaged in preparing the ground for the new offensive. Stores were moved up to the front line. Cables were laid. It was hard labour for the men without any rest. On 18 September the battalion moved closer to the front line. They camped at Bois Confluent, very close to their old positions at Diependaal.

On the eve of the battle, the men moved up to their assembly positions on the northern bank of the Ypres–Comines Canal, four miles to the south of Ypres. Two companies were placed in Buffs Bank and two companies in Gaspers Cliff. There was a little light shelling during the night, but the forward movements were completed without a hitch. It rained throughout the night. The 19th Division occupied a frontage of about 1,600 yards on the line from Klein Zillebeke to Hessian Wood near the Comines Canal. Zero hour was fixed for 5.40 am, when it would just about be light enough to see for about 200 yards.

The main attack on the plateau succeeded in securing all of its principal objectives after a day of hard fighting. By midday the Second Army had completed its first step across the plateau and the Fifth Army on its left had also come up alongside it. Repeated German counter-attacks had been rebuffed.

On the southern flank held by the 19th Division, good progress was also made. The line was pushed forward by about 600 yards. The division attacked with 57 and 58 Brigades in the front line and 56 Brigade and the 7th King's Own were in reserve. The right flank of 58 Brigade came under immediate heavy machine gun fire from the nearby railway embankment which ran alongside the canal. The centre of the attack was checked by machine gun fire from Hessian Wood. Both these centres of opposition were soon overcome and the objective, which ran along the eastern edge of the wood, was secured. 57 Brigade encountered some very difficult conditions as it advanced across no man's land. Deep mud in front of Belgian Wood slowed down its progress and they soon lost the protective cover of the British guns. But by about 8 am, the entire objectives of the division had been achieved. Losses had been heavy. On 20 September the division sustained nearly 2,000 casualties.

Patrols were pushed out to clear the immediate foreground of the enemy. Major-General Bridges, commanding the division, was severely wounded at around midday as he went forward to congratulate his men.

The 7th King's Own were not called for until about 11 am. Two companies were ordered to move up to positions near the railway embankment to replace one company of the 9th Royal Welch Fusiliers who had moved up to the front line. At 2 pm, D Company also moved up to the embankment. The whole battalion was now in close support to 58 Brigade. One officer and fifty men went forward as a carrying party for the 9th Cheshires in the front line at Hessian Wood.

The battalion remained in these positions overnight. At 5.10 am they relieved the 6th Wiltshires and the 9th Royal Welch in the front line from the canal to about 150 yards north-east of Hessian Wood. Throughout that day and the next the battalion was under constant heavy shellfire. Gas shells were also being fired at them. And there was continual sniping and machine gun fire. But there were no enemy infantry counter-attacks. On 23 September the battalion put out a number of patrols seeking to make contact with the enemy. They couldn't be found. The shelling, however, continued non-stop on both sides. During the night, they were relieved by the 7th East Lancs and moved back to safer positions 3,000 yards in the rear at Spoil Bank, on the canal near Voormezeele. For the next two days the battalion stayed at Spoil Bank, resting and repairing. On 26 September they were back once more in the front line at Hessian Wood, the relief being completed in the early hours of the 27th, which was to be a very quiet day, although Private John Fallows from Barrow was killed by shellfire. Some of the heat of the last few days had been dissipated. On 28 September a patrol under the command of Lieutenant Vincent, moving south along the railway embankment, came across a party of Germans and killed three of them. On 29 September it was their turn to be relieved and they moved back into divisional reserve at Vierstraat at the Brasserie on the Kemmel–Ypres road. Over the period 19–30 September, one officer had been killed – he was Second Lieutenant Lyons, who had only joined the battalion in August – 22 men were dead, 68 were wounded and 3 were missing presumed dead. One of the dead was another young man from the Furness area – Private John Langsteth from Flookburgh, the son of a local fisherman.

This action would prove to be the last serious engagement of the war for the 7th King's Own. For the next two days, the men took it in turns to visit the baths at Siege Farm, a mile and a half away towards Kemmel. On 3 and 4 October the men took part in weapons training and assault practice and on the 5th the battalion moved into the left sector of the divisional front, taking over from the 10th Royal Warwicks in brigade reserve. The men were spread out between Kemmel Shelters, Larchwood Tunnels, Bois Confluent and Lock 8 on the canal. For the next two days the men were tasked to dig a new reserve trench and were given the inevitable carrying party duties to fulfil. On 8 October, they relieved the 7th East Lancs in the right subsector of the brigade front in

Shrewsbury Forest on the Gheluvelt Plateau south of the Menin Road. The relief was complete by 4 am.

The next day, the battalion sent patrols out as far as the Basseville Beek without spotting any the enemy. The Beek itself was flooded and was only passable with the aid of special pontoons. The men were deployed in a series of fortified shell holes forming an outpost line in front of the main trenches. The Germans shelled this outpost line for two hours in the morning, killing one man and wounding two others. A British infantry attack north of the Menin Road brought enemy artillery fire down on to the 7th King's Own on Shrewsbury all day.

At dawn on 10 October, the British guns opened up on the German lines in front of the battalion, which attracted some retaliatory fire in return. Lewis guns fired on small parties of German soldiers seen moving about in the open. Three men were wounded and one soldier was reported missing.

The following day an officers' patrol crossed the Basseville Beek and moved 500 yards up the Zandvoorde Ridge. Only one small enemy patrol was spotted, which disappeared from view as soon as they were fired upon. There was very little hostile artillery fire during the day, but this became heavier on the back areas at night. In the evening of 11 October, the men were relieved by the 7th East Lancs and moved back into brigade reserve at Bois Confluent. Four men were killed and six others wounded by gun fire during the day.

For the next two days the battalion provided the men needed for the endless working parties that were required to keep the front line supplied and secure. On 14 October battalion HQ and C Company assembled at Lock 8. The remainder of the men stayed at Bois Confluent. The battalion was acting in close support to 58 Brigade in the front line. Between 14 and 18 October, the men were employed full time on carrying and working parties in the forward areas. There were no reported casualties for this period. The front had become relatively quiet in this sector, as the main British effort focused further to the north and the capture of the Passchendale Ridge. Having driven the Germans off the Gheluvelt plateau, the Second Army had removed some of the immediate threat posed to British operations in the salient by the German guns. Their job now was to consolidate and secure the area, but not to make any further advances against the Germans, as it was not thought that this would bring any obvious advantages. The high command had instead been focusing on smaller attacks on particular points in the German line, rather than trying to make any advances on a broad front.

On 20 October the battalion reassembled at Kemmel Shelters and was formed into companies on a two platoon basis. The men trained in platoons and companies until the 27 October. On the 26th, Lieutenant-Colonel Bowan took over command of the battalion from Major Bromlow. The next day the battalion relieved the 9th Welch in the front lines east of Shrewsbury Forest. They were driven by lorries to St Eloi – a rare luxury for the men – and then marched to the trenches, arriving at 9 pm. By now, most of the heat had disappeared from this section of the line. For the next few days there was light intermittent shelling.

Some patrols went out into no man's land, but there was little contact between the two opposing front-line forces and there was no dispute over the territory being occupied by each side. On the evening of 31 October they were relieved by the 7th East Lancs and marched back to Hill 60 to act as brigade support. Only two men were wounded during these four days in the front line, one of the lowest casualty rates for any tour of duty the battalion had completed since they arrived in France over two years before.

On 1 November, salvage parties were sent out to recover any possible materiel from the forward areas. Two companies were working on establishing a new front line east of Shrewsbury Forest. Another company was employed in cleaning up the Larchwood Tunnels. A small trench raid was planned and executed that night by two groups of men – 28 in total – led by Lieutenants Holmes and Second Lieutenant Conheeny. The battalion war diary contains a detailed account of what happened that evening (see box).

This was a well executed, carefully planned raid. Effective artillery support had isolated the German dugouts and prevented them from being reinforced during the attack. The raid had overcome the difficult conditions on the ground – particularly the mud and flooding. The attackers had succeeded in retaining the element of speed and surprise and overcame defenders who enjoyed all of the natural advantage of cover and superior fire power. The whole action lasted little more than a quarter of an hour. In short, this raid confirmed the effectiveness of the battalion as a fighting unit. Although there were by now very few men left who had started out with the battalion in France, the battalion was nonetheless a battle-hardened and experienced outfit.

Lieutenants Holmes and Conheeny were both awarded the Military Cross. Corporal Walter Storey was awarded the DCM. Corporal A Woods, Private Robert Eastwood and Private Tom Broxholme were all awarded the Military Medal.

On 2 and 3 November the battalion was again employed in battlefield salvage east of Shrewsbury Forest. On both days the enemy artillery fired sporadic high explosive and shrapnel at the battalion's positions, but there were no casualties. On 4 November, however, battalion HQ on Hill 60 was subjected to severe mustard gas shelling. Forty-six men of HQ Company became casualties, along with eight men from B Company. None were fatal. Later that evening they were relieved by the 10th Royal Warwicks and went into divisional support at Bois Confluent and the Moated Grange, a large farm complex half a mile south of Voormezeele.

For the next few days the men provided the labour required for numerous carrying or working parties, helping to bring up stores and materials as well as work on the trenches themselves. They visited the baths again at Siege Farm.

On 8 November they moved back again to Dranoutre, behind Mont Kemmel. They were moving away from the front line altogether in order to re-equip and retrain as a battalion. On 9 November, the men marched to Bailleul and then the

Account of a raid from the battalion war diary:

Following on the information obtained on patrol by Lieutenants Holmes and Conheeny regarding the occupation by the enemy of a group of dug outs across the Basseville Beek, it was decided to carry out a raid with the object of obtaining identification and inflicting casualties on the enemy. The raiding party consisted of Lieutenant Holmes and Second Lieutenant Conheeny and 28 other ranks. It was split into two groups each with one dug out as an objective. They left Company HQ at Hill 60 fully equipped at 4.45 pm and proceeded to Company HQ in the line in Bulgar Wood. At 6.45 pm they passed through the outpost line and made for the southern edge of Bitter Wood. Duckboards were placed across the Beek and a Lewis gun was placed in position covering the crossing. Two men were also left at the crossing with a whistle to attract the attention of the party when returning.

The raiders crossed the Beek in small parties at ten minute intervals and by 7.50 pm had successfully worked their way into a position of assembly about ten yards west of and parallel with Rifle Road – about 80 yards from their objectives. At 8.20 our barrage opened on the whole chain of dug outs which were not being attacked. At 8.24 the barrage lifted 150 yards east of the northern group and each party rushed forward to its objective. Dug outs 1, 2, 3 and 5 were found to be unoccupied. Dug out 4 was defended by a machine gun section which in the endeavour to escape was driven by Corporal Woods and his party into the barrage and probably suffered casualties.

Lieutenant Holmes went for dug out 6 and found an entrance on the far side guarded by 2 sentries. These he promptly shot and they fell back blocking the doorway. The occupants of the dugout were firing through the entrance and prevented our men from getting in. A bomb was therefore thrown in. A machine gunner who opened out through the loophole was shot through the loophole by one of men.

Corporal Storey in the meantime was dealing with dug out 7. Lieutenant Holmes went to his assistance and eventually 6 prisoners were extracted. A further attempt was made to enter dug out 6 by Lieutenant Conheeny but he was held up by fire from within.

The object of the raid having now been accomplished, Lieutenant Holmes sounded the signal to withdraw and the whole party were safely back across the Beek with their prisoners by 8.40. Our casualties were nil.

following day, they were moved by train to Ebblinghem. From there they marched to Sercus, a small village to the south-west of Hazebrouck, arriving at 2 pm. Here they were to stay for the rest of the month and for the first week of December, drilling, training and preparing for whatever they might be called upon to do in the future.

Towards the end of the first week in December, the battalion was told to prepare for a move to the Cambrai front. The fighting there had subsided, and between 4 and 6 December, the British forces had withdrawn to the Flesquieres line in order to take possession of a more favourable defensive position for the winter. In so doing, the British had withdrawn from the dangerous and exposed salient created by their original thrust into the German lines. But the salient, although greatly reduced, was not entirely eliminated by this withdrawal. The new line, on the forward slopes of the Flesquieres Ridge gave the British good observation over the German lines, but it would take considerable work for it to be converted into the main line of defence. These trenches had been constructed by the Germans in order to oppose an attack from the south-west. Now they would have to be strong enough to face the enemy from the north-east.

The battalion paraded at 5.30 am on 6 December. They marched to Steenbecque where they set off by train at 8 in the evening. They travelled south to Saulty, arriving at 3 am. The men then marched six miles in the freezing early morning mist to Bellacourt, arriving three and a half hours later. They arrived to a hot breakfast. They rested on 7 December and then moved again the following day to a camp at Courcelles le Comte, arriving in the late afternoon.

In the morning they marched on to Etricourt. They marched all day in the rain and sleet. Their new camp at Etricourt turned out to be located in a sea of mud. The conditions were appalling and the men were tired after three days of solid marching. Their blankets did not arrive until 4 am the following day.

On 10 and 11 December the men were allowed some rest. But in the conditions they now found themselves, this could not have been easy. On 12 December, they went into divisional reserve, relieving the 9th Cheshires in a central section of the old Hindenburg Line south-west of Cambrai, near Ribecourt. This section was probably the weakest and most vulnerable of the British positions in the now reduced salient, and the fear of counter-attack was thought to be very real. The battalion was on a high state of vigilance and under orders to be ready to reinforce the front line at short notice. But no attack was forthcoming. Both sides had had enough fighting for the moment.

On 13 and 14 December the battalion helped strengthen the line around Ribecourt. The village itself was riddled with ancient cellars and catacombs and these were used to establish strong points and machine gun positions. On 15 December they were relieved by the 8th Gloucesters. The 7th King's Own became the support battalion to the brigade. They were heavily shelled during the relief, but there were no casualties. A and B Companies were detailed to be the immediate counter-attack force in the event of the enemy attacking the brigade's positions in front and to the south-east of Ribecourt. C and D Companies had to produce the men needed for the endless nightly working parties.

The battalion was back in the front line in front of Ribecourt on 21 December. Three companies were placed in the front line, with one in support. They held the line until 26 December, with no reported casualties. Patrols into no man's land found neither sight nor sound of the enemy. Christmas Day itself passed uneventfully, with no signs of fraternization of any kind between the two opposing armies. On 26 December they were relieved by the 7th East Lancs and went back into the cellars of Ribecourt village itself. Two men were wounded during this tour of duty.

Ribecourt was heavily shelled from 10 am to 3 pm on 28 December, especially HQ Company at the Brasserie. A direct hit on HQ injured six men, killing several. One of these was Sergeant Crabtree, who had been the battalion pioneer sergeant since March 1916. The following day, the battalion moved into reserve positions at Havrincourt Wood, a mile and a half to the rear of Ribecourt. The men were now under canvas. The weather was still bitter during the day and freezing at night. On 29 December the men enjoyed hot baths at Neuville and 30 December was their Christmas Day. The men had roast chicken and plum pudding. Beer and rum completed a fine feast. However it was also the day that the Germans launched a successful attack on the 63rd Division who held the line to the south of Ribecourt at La Vacquerie. The attack had been preceded by very heavy gas shelling of the British artillery positions, followed by a destructive bombardment of the front lines. The enemy infantry, clothed in white and armed with the fearsome *flammenwerfer*, had succeeded in entering the British lines in several areas. The fighting became extremely intense.

The 7th King's Own were placed under the orders of 63rd Division in the late afternoon. At 6 pm, having received an hour's notice, the battalion moved up into support positions at the village of Metz, three miles to the west behind the front being attacked. Here they were ready to move again at an hour's notice. They stayed the night at Metz but were not called on to engage the enemy. The 63rd Division – the Royal Naval Division – although losing some ground, managed to hold on and the Germans did not seek to exploit their successes.

As the position remained uncertain, the battalion remained under the command of 63rd Division at Metz until 3 January.

The final few weeks
On 3 January 1918 they were moved back into the front line at Couillet Wood, along the railway line in front of Marcoing. The cold and freezing weather continued unabated. The next three days were a struggle against the elements rather than the enemy. There was little hostile action of any kind. On 7 January, a thaw set in and the trenches soon became deep in mud. The men were issued

with gum boots. However these boots could not be handed out as no one had dry socks. The next day, a 'drying room' for wet socks was created in an old German shelter. The gum boots could now be issued, much to the men's relief and satisfaction.

The men were busy improving the defences in front of their positions. German intentions were still unknown and the prospect of further enemy counter-attacks was considered very likely. On 9 and 10 January, a great deal of new wire was put up in no man's land, with the battalion's trench mortars keeping the German machine gunners' heads down.

The following day the battalion was pulled out of the front line and moved back to intermediate lines in front of Beaucamp. Here they provided anti-aircraft defence for the divisional artillery. For the next few days, the battalion was split between Havrincourt Wood and Vallulart Farm. From here the battalion was fully engaged in working parties helping to strengthen the British lines. The frost had returned, making the ground easier to move over but harder to work on. Digging was back-breaking and slow work. On 17 January the battalion was again in the support lines in Ribecourt. Two US officers were attached to the battalion for instruction in trench warfare.

On 21 January the battalion was to start its last period of front-line trench duty of the war. The British Army, having assumed the brunt of offensive operations on the Western Front since May 1917, had fought itself to a standstill by the end of the Battle of Cambrai. The number of reinforcements that would become available in 1918 to replace the very severe casualties sustained at Ypres, Cambrai, Vimy, Arras and Messines looked likely to fall way below what Haig and his generals were planning – about a quarter of a million fewer men by the spring, rising to nearly half a million by the autumn. Even though it was now almost inevitable that the British and French forces would have to rest on the defensive for the early part of 1918, unless these losses could be made up, it would be necessary in addition to drastically reorganize the BEF. Infantry units would need to be broken up, and divisions reduced so that their establishments could be brought up to full fighting strength. The British and French would have to await the arrival of large numbers of US forces before they could think of attacking again. And since the exit of Russia from the war in November 1917, the Germans could now concentrate their superior number of troops on the Western Front, posing a very real risk to the Allies.

On 18 January, Haig had decided how to manage the shortfall in manpower. He would reduce each division (apart from the Guards and the Royal Naval Division) from twelve battalions to nine. In total, 115 battalions out of the total of 806 in France would have to be disbanded. In the case of the 19th Division, the decision was taken to disband all of the battalions in 56 Brigade.

This decision was not communicated to the 7th King's Own until 25 January, when the GOC of the division told Major Bromlow the news. Bromlow had earlier been given an assurance by the divisional commanding officer that the 7th

King's Own would not be disbanded. It was army orders that required him to disband the whole brigade. This information was not shared with the other officers until several days later. In the mean time, the battalion's last tour of front-line duty went incredibly peacefully. They spent 21–23 January improving the condition of their trenches which were in a poor condition because of the terrible weather. Their front-line positions, a scattered line of shell holes, were in-accessible during the day and so work on them had to be done under cover of darkness. There were no casualties during these final few days. On 23 January they were relieved by the 9th Welch Fusiliers. The men travelled back to their rest camp by light railway although there was a big delay at the Trescault rail-head. The men were billeted in Nissan huts in Havrincourt Wood.

On 26 January, the corps commander, Lieutenant-General Fanshawe, visited the battalion. He was saying farewell to the men and their officers. On 28 January the battalion moved up into support positions at Wood Support in the lines around Ribecourt where they would stay without incident until 4 February. It was here that the men would learn the news of their demise as a battalion.

There was a frantic last-minute effort made in London to save the battalion. Major Wingrove, a former battalion CO, met the Secretary of State for War Lord Derby and the Lancashire Members of Parliament. He petitioned the King as colonel in chief of the regiment. It was to no avail. The die was cast.

On 4 February, the battalion travelled by light railway to Ytres, two miles to the south-east of Havrincourt Wood. There they marched for the last time as a battalion along a quiet country lane to the nearby village of Lechelles and into billets at Grazing Camp. The last day of the battalion was 5 February. Each man was presented with a tin of salmon or herrings, a bottle of beer, a packet of biscuits and some candles. Captains Overton and Simpson, five other officers and 205 men left to join the 4th King's Own who were stationed nearby. Captain Hunt, four officers and 162 men left to join the 5th King's Own.

It was a quiet and sad end for the battalion. Nothing is recorded of what was said on that cold wet morning in February when the battalion paraded for the last time. There would have been some of those on parade who had joined the colours in Barrow, Ulverston, Millom and Dalton in the heady days of August 1914. There could be no doubt that the thirty months they had spent in France had changed them all. They were hardened veterans now of the horrors of trench warfare. None of the glamour and excitement of August 1914 could have remained on display on that miserable February morning in Lechelles. Hundreds had fought and died in the service of the 7th Battalion, and for these survivors, the fighting would still last another nine gruelling months.

For the men, there would have been the inevitable sadness associated with the ending of their time together. But for them the war would still go on. The fighting had not ended. Far from it: the war itself was about to enter its most intensive phase. For the 7th Battalion, however, the fighting was over. It had been involved in some of the most significant actions of the war and had conducted itself with distinction and bravery throughout. But now its record of service and sacrifice had come to an end. We can only speculate what would have been in the minds of those men as they went their separate ways on 5 February 1918. There would be no triumphant homecoming for the 7th Battalion. It simply disappeared from sight in the mist and drizzle at Lechelles.

Chapter 4

The 8th Battalion

The first few months

The 8th Battalion was formed at Lancaster in early September 1914. It was attached to the newly formed 76 Brigade of 25th Division, which began to be formed on Salisbury Plain later that same month. The division was made up of battalions from Cheshire, Lancashire, Cumberland, Wales and Shropshire. Alongside the 8th Battalion in 76 Brigade were battalions of the Royal Welch Fusiliers, the King's Liverpool Regiment and the King's Shropshire Light Infantry. In November, the battalion moved into camp on Boscombe Down.

During the early months of the war, the 8th King's Own suffered all of the same privations as its newly constituted sister battalions. There was little in the way of equipment. There were no khaki uniforms for its proud new recruits to wear. In fact many of the men had to make do with a number of old army issue red coats. They paraded in these unusual jackets along with their civvy street hats and trousers. But in the same way as others before it, the battalion overcame these indignities and got on with the hard job of training, and improving their physical fitness levels. There was a lot of marching and drilling. The raw recruits were slowly but surely being turned into soldiers and fighters.

The problem with inadequate equipment in particular dogged the 8th King's Own – like all the Kitchener battalions – for many months. They were issued with some of the old long-barrelled Lee Enfields so they could at least begin to develop their skills at musketry. But their war service short magazine Lee Enfields were not issued to the men until August 1915, nearly a year after their formation and only a few weeks before they left for active service on the Western Front. This hardly gave the men enough time to become familiar with their principal weapon. And for many months the battalion had to train using wooden replica machine guns. The genuine article did not become available until the late spring of 1915.

The battalion moved to Odiham near Aldershot for its final training on 14 May 1915. On 12 August, Lord Kitchener himself inspected the division – this was the only one of the service battalions of the King's Own to encounter him. The battalion was led onto the parade ground by its commanding officer, Lieutenant-Colonel A D Thorne.

Overseas service begins

Such inspections were always a precursor to service overseas. Sure enough, the battalion received its orders to move within a few weeks. It was being sent to the Western Front. On 26 September, more than a year after it had been formed, the battalion advanced party of 3 officers and 108 men, commanded by Major Williams, left Aldershot by train bound for Southampton. The SS *Blackwell* crossed without incident the following night to Le Havre. The men camped at No. 5 camp just outside the town. On 27 September, the rest of the battalion – 26 officers and 833 men – took two trains to Folkestone and crossed over to Boulogne on the SS *Duchess of Argyle*. They spent the night under canvas on the outskirts of the city. Their war too had now begun.

The next day the Boulogne party travelled by train to Pont de Briques and then on to Ceastre where they picked up members of the advanced party. From there they marched to Merris where they spent the night. The next day they marched again to Lampernisse and were attached to the 1st Canadian Infantry Brigade for instruction in trench warfare. The battalion would be pitched straight into it. On 3 October, A Company was the first to experience trench conditions. They spent the whole day as guests of the Canadians in the support lines. Each of the other companies followed suit, spending twenty-four hours in the line. No one fired their weapon in anger. It was a quiet and peaceful introduction to living and working in the trenches.

On 7 October, the whole battalion took over a section of the front line at Ploegsteert Wood, where they spent six days in the trenches. The battalion recorded its first battle casualty. One man was wounded when a rifle grenade prematurely exploded after being launched at an enemy sniper. The battalion's induction to the fighting had been almost immediate. Within ten days of landing, they were firing their weapons in anger. They had had barely time to draw breath before being pitched almost straight into the action. But the battalion was still a novice in trench warfare. They had a lot to learn. On 13 October, the trenches held by the 8th Battalion were subject to heavy shrapnel shelling in the afternoon. The fire lasted for four hours. One man was killed and four men were wounded. The battalion returned machine gun fire on the German positions. At 9 pm that evening they were relieved by the 10th King's Own Yorkshire Light Infantry. In the early hours of 14 October, the men marched to billets at the Piggeries, two miles behind the front line. They arrived at 5 am. The Piggeries were a group of houses along a minor road lying in the shelter of Hill 63, a prominent landmark used by the British as an observation post over the German lines running north towards Messines and Wytschaete.

In the afternoon, the battalion marched to Bailleul. That day 76 Brigade of 25th Division was transferred to the 3rd Division, one of the regular army units that had formed part of the original BEF. The brigade was reorganized so as to form two new army battalions, the 8th King's Own and the 10th Royal Welch Fusiliers, and two regular army battalions, the 1st Gordon Highlanders and the 2nd

Suffolks. The two other new army battalions of the original 76 Brigade, the 10th Cheshires and the 8th Loyal North Lancashires remained with the 25th Division in the newly reconstituted 7 Brigade which transferred from 3rd Division on the same day. The high command had decided that, wherever possible, the new army divisions should have at least some regular army battalions serving alongside them to provide extra experience and battle discipline. The new comrades in arms of the 8th King's Own would serve with them for the rest of the war.

On 15 October, the battalion marched with the rest of the brigade to Poperinghe, a rest area for the British troops seven miles to the west of Ypres. On arrival, C and D Companies were attached to the 1st Northumberland Fusiliers and 1st Lincolns of 9 Brigade for training and spent the next few days in the trenches at Sanctuary Wood, on the Ypres front south of Hooge. It was a bitter experience. The trenches were heavily shelled throughout their time in the line. Five men were killed and three wounded. On 18 October, A and B Companies relieved C and D Companies and spent the next two days in the trenches. These men had a better time of it. There were no reported casualties. During the day, the trenches would normally be lightly held by sentries. The rest of the men would be sheltering underground in dugouts, sleeping and resting. At night, the trenches would come alive with men doing trench repair work, carrying up stores and equipment and getting ready for night patrols in no man's land.

For the next few weeks the battalion took part in intensive weapons and battle training with their new sister battalions in 76 Brigade. On 21 October they had marched to Eecke, ten miles to the south-west of Poperinghe. Captain Colebrook formed part of a composite brigade unit, which was inspected by the King at Renninghelst. The strength of the battalion at this time was 30 officers and 911 men.

The battalion remained at Eecke until 22 November. Heavy rainfall in the first few days meant their campsite was a foot deep in mud for most of the time. Then in November the freezing weather turned the mud into an ice rink. The weather took its toll on the men. Among the growing sick list was the battalion CO, Colonel Thorne. His war was at an end and he would not return to the battalion. On 22 November, he was replaced by Major Williams

On 27 November, the battalion was back in the front line again. The battalion was holding a position along the Ypres–Comines canal southwest of Verbrandenmolen at a place known by the Tommies as The Bluff. Two miles south of Ypres, the canal took a sharp turn to the east and passed at right angles through the British and German front lines. It formed a formidable obstacle, being approximately 40 yards wide in a deep cutting. When the canal had been constructed the spoil from the excavation had been built up on either side in a terraced fashion. The northern bank ended in an artificial hill about 30 feet above local ground level, which was just behind the British front lines. This was The Bluff and it provided excellent observation over the German lines. Both sides were anxious to hold The Bluff and it had been the scene of bitter fighting since the autumn of 1914, with heavy mining operations under way on both sides.

At this section of the line, no man's land was a narrow strip of territory about 150 yards wide near the canal, gradually reducing to no more than 40 yards a little further to the north at a salient into the British lines known as The Bean. German mines exploded in the winter of 1915 and then later in January 1916 had created a heavily cratered landscape about 150 yards north of the canal and the British front line ran along the easterly facing lip of these craters.

The battalion would spend the next few weeks in and out of the line at The Bluff. On 2 December, the battalion launched a rifle grenade attack on the German positions on as part of the policy of maintaining an 'aggressive spirit' along the British front. About 10 am Major Williams was wounded by a German rifle grenade. He died about 5 pm at the regimental aid post at Reninghelst, a few miles to the rear. Major West assumed temporary command of the battalion. One other man was killed and four others wounded during the day. Late in the evening of 3 December, the battalion was relieved by the 1st Gordons and went to billets at Reninghelst. They were back again in the front line on 9 December. The battalion's snipers claimed nine German victims over the next three days. This tour of duty lasted until 15 December when they returned to Reninghelst. The battalion strength was now down to 27 officers and 784 men. On 19 December, Major Smith from the 4th Gordon Highlanders took over the command of the battalion.

For the next few weeks this pattern repeated itself on a regular basis. The men enjoyed their first Christmas in France out of the line at Reninghelst and managed at least the semblance of a traditional Christmas dinner and festivities.

1916: the beginning of heavy fighting

On 5 January, they were back again in the front line at The Bluff. They relieved the 1st Gordon Highlanders during the night. One man was killed by shellfire during the relief. The next two days were very quiet, with no enemy action reported. On 8 January, the men fired rifle grenades at a German working party in no man's land. The following day the artillery of both sides was very active. Over 120 of the new Newton Pippin rifle grenades were fired at the enemy lines on 10 January. The grenade had a range of over 400 yards and was proving to be very popular with the men. Slowly, the British were beginning to have at their disposal some of the weapons they would need if they were to start matching the Germans blow for blow in the bitter theatre of trench warfare. But the new rifle grenades were not always very user friendly. On 11 January, one man was severely wounded by one of these grenades exploding as it was fired at the enemy.

On 12 January the 1st Gordons replaced the 8th King's Own in the front line and the battalion moved back to Reninghelst. On 17 January fifty replacements arrived. Two days later the battalion was back in the front line again at The Bean.

On 22 January, the Germans exploded a large mine at 1.55 am under the 2nd Suffolks on the right of the King's Own. The battalion immediately 'stood to' and mounted rapid rifle fire on the enemy lines, but no infantry attack was mounted by the Germans. One man was killed and three others wounded. All of the wounded men were accidentally injured by faulty rifle grenades.

The German artillery was active throughout the morning and afternoon of 23 January. Five men were killed and five men wounded during the day. One sergeant had his life saved when a shell fragment was deflected from his head by the newly issued steel helmets. Over the next few days, an unusual peace descended on the front line. The battalion was relieved by the 1st Gordons and returned to Reninghelst for some well earned rest. On 29 January, 20 more replacements from the regimental depot arrived to strengthen the battalion.

On 2 February the battalion was once again back in the front line at The Bean. Sniping and rifle grenade fire was the extent of hostile action – the by now normal attrition of trench warfare. On 5 February, both sides launched artillery and trench mortar fire on each other. One man was killed and three wounded when a German shell scored a direct hit in the front-line trenches. On 7 February, the 3rd Division was replaced in the line at The Bluff by the 17th Division and the men travelled by train to St Omer and then marched on to Hellebruuk where they arrived at 10 pm on 18 February. It was to prove a fortuitous relief.

The Germans had been planning a major attack on the French lines at Verdun in what was to be a decisive engagement that would break the French Armies and bring the war to a speedy conclusion. The attack was originally planned to begin on 12 February. The German Armies were therefore ordered to create a series of diversionary attacks on both the British and French lines in the run-up to the main offensive. Wherever possible these attacks should also help to improve the line they held. The attack at Verdun was postponed until 21 February. But in the period between 8 and 19 February, the Germans mounted a series of attacks at various places around the Ypres salient. One of these was directed against The Bluff.

52 Brigade of the 17th Division had responsibility for holding The Bluff on 14 February when the Germans launched their surprise attack. Only a single platoon of the 10th Lancashire Fusiliers held The Bluff defences, the most important part of the line. During the morning of the 14th, the line on the north of the canal was heavily shelled several times. The single platoon of the Lancs Fusiliers took shelter in The Tunnel, a former German mine gallery which led from the canal bank to The Bluff. All the signs began pointing to a likely attack as trench mortars joined the bombardment of the British lines. At 5.45 pm, the Germans exploded a small mine under The Bluff which completely buried the platoon of Lancashire Fusiliers – only three men were to escape – and two more further to the right near The Bean. The German infantry then launched an attack on a half-mile front. They captured The Bluff and pushed a salient into the British lines at The Bean. There was an unfortunate delay in launching the British counter-attacks.

As a result, reinforcements were sent in piecemeal and an ineffective series of small local counter-attacks made no impression on the newly consolidated German positions. By 7.30 am on 15 February, the Germans were strongly in possession of The Bluff and most of the former British front line for a length of 500 yards to the north. Fresh counter-attacks that day were a failure. The Germans had now had time to strengthen their defences and it was clear that dislodging them would require careful preparation and stronger forces.

The V Corps Commander, Lieutenant-General Fanshawe decided that the job of recapturing The Bluff should be entrusted to the troops who knew the ground. On 15 February, therefore, 76 Brigade was put on notice to return to The Bluff and relieve 52 Brigade. At 3 pm, the machine gun and small arms limbers were ordered to go by train from St Omer, with their teams proceeding by road to the front. At 3.40 the battalion was ordered to join trains at Watten and left at 7 pm. At 11.30 pm the battalion arrived at Poperinghe and marched to camp on the Ouderdum–Vlamertinghe road. Here the battalion was to remain until 1 March. Every day it practised the planned assault, sometimes with the other battalions to be employed – the 1st Gordons and the 2nd Suffolks – over an exact representation of the German positions. On 21 February, Captain Hollins joined the battalion.

New assembly and communication trenches needed to be dug and stores of ammunition had to be moved up nearer the front line. Enemy artillery made all of these essential preparations very difficult to complete. This was compounded by the heavy snow falls after 27 February, which showed up the new trenches being dug to enemy air observation.

There were obvious dangers to the troops created by these changed circumstances. The normal plans for an infantry advance would have involved a lengthy artillery bombardment prior to the assault going in. But this would also have exposed the troops in the newly dug and now exposed assembly and communication trenches to concentrated enemy artillery fire in return. The assault was being planned for dusk. This would have meant moving the men up to the assembly trenches some fifteen to eighteen hours prior to the assault. The risk of heavy casualties before the attack had even started was clearly unacceptable. It was therefore decided to carry out an artillery bombardment up till the original time of the infantry assault at dusk, cease fire, bring the infantry into position under the cover of darkness and then launch the attack after a hurricane 90 minute bombardment at dawn on 2 March. It was hoped that these tactics would help confuse the enemy about British intentions, minimize casualties and maximize the chance of a complete success.

These plans went through a number of variations before the final details were settled. General Plumer, commanding Second Army, felt that success would be more likely without any preliminary bombardment at all. It was eventually settled that on the evening of 1 March a bombardment would begin at 5 pm and last for 45 minutes with a subsequent series of lifts but then should stop suddenly. This was designed to give the impression that an attack had been planned but had failed to materialize. After a complete pause, the local commanders would decide whether a follow-up bombardment should take place or not, depending on whether or not the Germans had begun to repair the damage done to the trenches. In addition and in order to confuse the enemy, a battery of 60-pounders would fire a regular series of salvoes on the German front line. The pattern of shelling would be regular enough to convince the defenders that they should remain in their shelters when the firing started. During the gaps in this shelling the British would launch their attack, hopefully finding the front line lightly manned and therefore easier to assault successfully.

The British bombardment on 1 March was a complete success. Thirty-five heavy guns were used to complete the demolition of the German front line. Twenty-seven trench mortars were used to attack those parts of the line the howitzers could not reach. The guns kept up a slow rate of fire on the night of 1/2 March to prevent trench repairs and wire being put up. There was little enemy retaliation during the night. Early in the morning of 2 March it was decided that the attack would go in without the planned 20 minute preliminary bombardment. By 3.45 am, the 8th King's Own was in position opposite The Bean, in the centre of the ground to be attacked. The strength of the battalion going into the line was 24 officers and 790 men.

At 4.30 am the attack began. It was a complete success. The 8th King's Own overran its objectives. It found no Germans at all in the first two lines attacked. It reached the third line and began to consolidate. Some patrols went even further without finding any German infantry. Later, a party of some 60 Germans who must have been sheltering underground as the King's Own passed over them began firing on the men from behind. They were soon compelled to surrender. In total, 5 officers and nearly 250 men were taken prisoners.

Three companies of the 8th Battalion had 'gone over the top'. Within two minutes, the Germans opened up rifle and shrapnel fire on their attackers. The battalion trench mortar battery kept up a heavy fire on the German lines throughout their advance, hoping to suppress as much enemy fire as possible. There was no hand-to-hand fighting in the initial assault, although the trenches on either side were cleared by bayonet and bomb. German infantry of the 123rd Grenadiers began a counter-attack at midday. It was quickly dispersed by machine gun fire. This was the only attempted assault over the open. Some bombing attacks were mounted by the Germans against the left of the new line held by the British in the evening. The Germans launched their attacks up a number of communication trenches. These were easily repelled. For once it seemed the British had ample supplies of Mills bombs. Over 52,000 had been assembled for use by the brigade in the attack.

The battalion sustained a heavy toll of casualties in the enemy shrapnel barrage that met the initial assault and in the heavy enemy artillery fire that continued all day. There were many casualties at the regimental aid post, which suffered a number of direct hits. On 3 March, a number of men were killed by British guns firing short. In total, three officers were killed, including Captain Hollins, who had only joined the battalion a fortnight earlier. Seven other officers were wounded. Fifty-five men were killed and over 200 were wounded. Another sixty-five men were missing; most of them would never be found. The

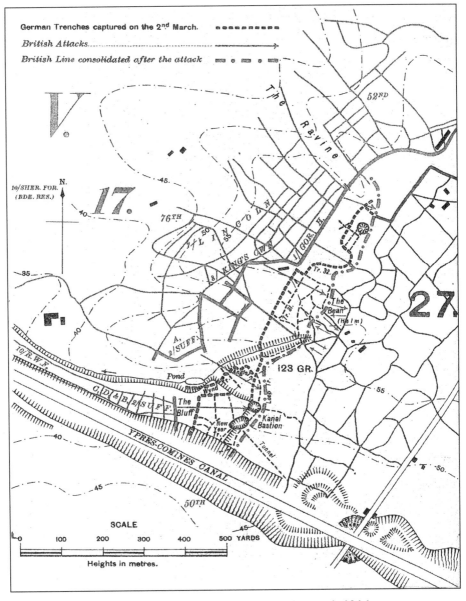

Ground over which the 8th Battalion attacked on 2 March 1916.

machine gun teams had suffered particularly heavily. Overall, nearly half of those who had attacked were either dead, injured or missing. The 76 Brigade as a whole incurred nearly 1,000 casualties between 1 and 4 March, by which time the men had been relieved by 8 Brigade.

The action had been a great success. All of the objectives had been taken and successfully held against counter-attack. For the 8th Battalion, this was their first major engagement of the war and, despite the heavy loss of life, they had emerged victorious. They had gone into action with regular army units on both their flanks and had shown themselves to be as good as them in combat. Although triumphant, the attack on 2 March had been no walkover. Careful preparation and the element of surprise created by the absence of a preliminary bombardment had seen them through on the day. But many of these men would never see home again. Amongst these were Privates Lawrence Wilkinson from Carnforth, Isaac Brockbank from Coniston and Robert James from Barrow.

On 4 March, the men reached their rest camp behind Ypres in an exhausted state. The next day, General Plumer visited the battalion to pass on his personal congratulations for their first major action. Lieutenant Pollock and Second Lieutenants Harvey and Heaton were awarded the Military Cross for their bravery in leading their platoons into the attack. Sergeants Charles Avery, A W Holgate and T Withers, Corporal Philip Haith, Lance-Corporal Hill were all awarded the DCM.

For the next three days, the men were allowed some rest. On 8 March, Major Deakin joined the 8th Battalion from the 7th King's Own. The rest and recuperation did not last very long. On 10 March they were back in the trenches at The Bluff. On their way up the line, the men had marched for the first time through the ghostly city of Ypres, leaving by the Lille Gate. The city had been heavily shelled for most of the war and must have presented a dreadful image of death and destruction. But this was now the grim reality for the men of the 8th King's Own. This was their new world. As they marched through the Lille Gate, the battalion looked like a shadow of its former self. Only 12 officers and 384 men marched into the front line on 10 March – a fraction of its strength just a few days earlier.

The trenches were incredibly wet. Conditions were thoroughly miserable. Many of their own dead comrades still lay on the ground in front of them. There were precious few dry dugouts. The continuing wet weather made it difficult to effect any worthwhile repairs. For the next three days, the men did as much as they could. Three were killed by German snipers. On 13 March, they were relieved by the 1st Gordons and went into support lines along the canal. Here they were joined by four new subalterns, Lieutenants Cook, Moorcroft, Katz and Taylor. On 14 March they were back in rest camp. On the evening of 17 March they were once again on the move back into the front line where they took over the trenches at The Bluff in the early morning of the 18th. This time the trenches were much improved. They had been drained and were much drier and comfortable for their new occupants. New trenches with proper frames and revetted with corrugated iron were being prepared.

The front was now much quieter, although there was regular sniping and inter-mittent shelling. On 21 March, a draft of 85 replacements arrived to strengthen the battalion in the line.

On 24 March, the battalion returned to camp at Reninghelst. Twenty-seven other ranks arrived. On 28 March, A and B Companies went to new billets at Dikebusch. C and D Companies went into dugouts at Scottish Wood, half a mile to the west of Voormezeele. The men were engaged in working parties throughout this period. On 29 March, another 29 men arrived as replacements, bringing the strength of the battalion to just over 500 men.

General Plumer, whilst planning to recover The Bluff by assault, had also decided that there must be a retaliatory strike against another section of the German line. The Germans had hit the British hard at several parts of the line held by Second Army in the run-up to their big attack at Verdun and Plumer was keen to respond in kind. He selected the St Eloi sector, a mile to the west of The Bluff, to make his demonstration. The Germans had held since 14 March 1915 a salient 600 yards wide and 100 yards deep at St Eloi. Unlike The Bluff, the salient at St Eloi did not command significant observation over the British positions, but it did contain The Mound, an artificial bank of earth which was about 30 feet high. Shelling had reduced it somewhat, but it was still a significant feature of some tactical importance in the otherwise flat ground of Flanders. Plumer consid-ered it worth fighting for. However it was in turn overlooked by the high ground to the rear – ground held by the enemy. Even assuming it could be successfully assaulted, holding it could prove to be very difficult indeed.

This section of the line in Flanders, like The Bluff, had been the scene of a great deal of tunnelling and mining. It would be in these tunnels that the seeds of success would be sown.

On 23 February, Plumer had informed the 3rd Division commander, Major-General Haldane, that his division would be used for the St Eloi operation.. It was hoped to launch the attack, which would have strictly limited objectives, as soon after 10 March as possible. By that date it was hoped that new, deeper mines under The Mound and the German front-line trenches would be ready. Because of operations at The Bluff, where both 76 and 8 Brigades were heavily engaged, only 9 Brigade was available. It was selected to make the attack, which would be a surprise assault without an artillery bombardment. The assault would start 30 seconds after the mines were exploded. The objective was the third German line, about 200 yards beyond the craters the mines would create. The craters would be left unmanned and act as a magnet for German artillery fire. The infantry would assault from the flanks, avoid the craters and converging behind them, would make their attack on the German lines. No assembly or jumping off trenches were dug in order to avoid preparations for the attack being spotted.

The attack was eventually launched at dawn on 27 March by the 1st

Northumberland Fusiliers and 4th Royal Fusiliers, in freezing snow and sleet. In total, six mines were successfully detonated under the German lines, causing considerable damage. One small mine had been detonated on each flank to help the troops forward, and four much larger mines had exploded in the centre of the line being attacked. At once, the artillery put down their barrage. The 1st Northumberland Fusiliers, attacking on the right, reached all of their objectives with virtually no casualties at all. The Royal Fusiliers were less fortunate. They suffered severely from machine gun fire and shelling. They failed to secure their objectives. There was considerable confusion about the exact whereabouts of the attacking troops and whether they had succeeded in joining up the newly won ground. It eventually became clear that the attack had only been partially successful on the left. The conditions were appalling. The mines had destroyed the drainage system and the captured trenches began to fill up with water. Things were so bad that the men rapidly became exhausted. Although they were tired from the fighting at The Bluff, it became imperative for 76 Brigade to be put into the front line to relieve the men of 8 Brigade. On 28/29 March, two battalions of 76 Brigade, the 2nd Suffolks and the 10th Royal Welch Fusiliers went into the newly won front line at St Eloi.

On 30 March, arrangements were made for a fresh attack designed to capture the objectives on the left, which had not been secured in the original assault. It was a makeshift body of men drawn from the 1st Gordons, the 12th West Yorks and the 3rd Division Bombing School. The attack was postponed because of in-accurate intelligence about the enemy's whereabouts. It became clear that the Germans had taken possession of Crater 5. General Haldane, who had made a personal inspection of the front, decided that the enemy would have to be expelled from this crater and so complete the original purposes of the assault on 27 March. This task fell on the 8th King's Own, as by now all of the battalions of 76 Brigade had been deployed and were in no fit state to carry out any further major operations. It was decided to attack in the early hours of 3 April.

Zero hour was fixed at 2 am and was preceded by an intense 30 minute bombardment. The night was dark and misty. Conditions were extremely diffi-cult, with mud and the heavily cratered ground making rapid progress almost impossible. Two companies led the assault, attacking in two lines each. They were followed by two parties of sixteen bombers and with one platoon from A Company to mop up behind the attackers. They blackened their faces. The enemy suspected that an attack was imminent, and there was already some rifle and machine gun fire before the men had even left their shell holes. Smoke from the British barrage further impaired their visibility.

Despite all of these obstacles, the attack of the 8th King's Own was a total success. Most of the defenders were in a thoroughly demoralized and exhausted state. Only in Crater 5 was there any real resistance. The brigade major, Billy Congreve VC, an outstanding young officer who was to die in action on the Somme a few weeks later, went up with an officer and four men of the 8th

Battalion and invited the Germans to surrender as they were effectively surrounded. Five officers and 77 men duly handed themselves over. The 8th King's Own had been ordered only to take prisoners if they 'voluntarily disarm and give themselves up'. Any resistance would have meant certain death and the Germans knew it.

Three officers were killed in the attack: Captains Barnes and Bridson and Second Lieutenant Williams. Sixteen men were killed, forty-five wounded and one man was missing presumed dead. One of the dead men was Private George Curwen from Cartmel who had enlisted in Ulverston at the beginning of the war. It was another significant triumph for the battalion. They had again succeeded where others had failed. But they were now at the limit of their physical endurance. In the early hours of the following morning, after they had done what they could to consolidate their gains, the men were relieved by the Canadians.

Despite the heroic efforts of the 3rd Division, the ground gained at St Eloi proved impossible to hold on to. On 5 April, it was recaptured by the Germans after a heavy barrage aimed at the craters. Repeated counter-attacks by the Canadians failed to recover it. In the end, and with the Battle of the Somme rapidly approaching, it was decided not to attempt any fresh assault by infantry. These were certain to prove too costly and unlikely to succeed. The fighting descended into a series of artillery exchanges, which changed nothing very much at all. The ground, now totally devastated, remained in German possession. The action at St Eloi, designed as it was to teach the Germans a lesson, proved to be a fruitless and painful operation for the British.

On 4 April, the battalion was moved by bus to Poperinghe and then on by train to Eecke. They would spend the next three weeks here, resting, reinforcing and re-equipping. The battalion had endured an extremely trying period in the front line, but had established a reputation as a hard fighting unit. It was now very much under strength. A total of just fewer than 160 new men arrived to strengthen the battalion. On 13 April, Brigadier-General Kentish, the newly appointed officer commanding 76 Brigade inspected the battalion. The following day Major West took over command of the battalion as Lieutenant-Colonel Smith went on leave to London. On 17 April officers and NCOs were given a lecture on bayonet fighting in the cinema hall at Eecke by a supposed expert, Major Campbell. The reactions of the men were not recorded.

By 22 April, the men were being employed on digging new trenches under the supervision of the Royal Engineers. A further nineteen men arrived as replacements that day. On 24 April, Colonel Smith returned from leave and took over command of the battalion. On 29 April, the battalion marched from Eecke to Locre. They were to stay there, a few miles to the south-west of Ypres, until 6 May. They continued to provide the manpower for various working and carrying parties. The new recruits were brought up to scratch. But most importantly, the men were getting regular hot food, could keep themselves clean and were out of the range of enemy artillery.

The next month would be spent out of the front line itself, but not entirely out of harm's way. For most of this time the battalion would either be in the reserve or support trenches around Mont Kemmel. The battalion was gradually being built back up again, as were many other battalions. Preparations were well under way for the Somme offensive, in which the battalion would feature in a series of extremely difficult and costly engagements.

On the evening of 6 May, the battalion went into support trenches at Mont Kemmel. These positions were under fairly regular fire from machine guns as well as heavy artillery. Over the next few days, three men were killed and three wounded by this harassing fire. At night, the men were employed on working parties strengthening their positions and the wire in front of the trenches. On 13 May, they were relieved by the 1st Gordons. Between 14 and 19 May, the battalion was in brigade reserve at Kemmel Shelters. During this time another eighty-eight recruits joined the battalion. Lieutenants Knox and Neville arrived for duty. On 20 May, they were back in the support lines again. One man was killed by machine gun fire on the 22nd, probably a random bullet fired at long range. On the same day, five new replacement officers joined the battalion – Lieutenants Samson, Roberts, Millbank, Taylor and Holland. On 23 May, a further 32 replacements arrived. In just over a month, the battalion had doubled in size.

The enemy shelled the battalion's trenches with trench mortar and artillery fire intermittently over the next couple of days. Four men were wounded. On 27 May they were relieved by the Gordon's and marched back to camp at Eecke. The battalion was being taken out of the line for intensive battle training.

On 3 June another 19 men arrived to serve with the King's Own. By 7 June the battalion was back in fresh billets at Locre, where for the next few days it performed a number of labouring duties, laying new signal cables, and working on the supply routes up to the front line. On 11 June the battalion marched to Bailleul and then travelled by train to St Omer, where they occupied some former cavalry barracks. On 13 June they marched again to Westrove, a small village six miles north-west of St Omer, where they were to spend the next four days. Here they practised attack in open warfare conditions. A daily routine quickly became established. The men would get up early in the morning, and rehearse over and over again their assault methods. In the afternoon they would take part in route marches to build up their strength and fitness. In the evening there would be lectures and classes. The men stayed here for the rest of the month.

On 1 July, the opening day of the Battle of the Somme, the 3rd Division began its move to its new theatre of operations. The battalion marched to St Omer, where they got on a train at 7.30 am. The heavy traffic on the railway made for a long slow journey to Doullens, where they arrived at six the following morning. Doullens is only forty miles from St Omer. Cramped into cattle wagons, it was an uncomfortable, hot journey. But it was probably better than marching in the hot sunshine. On 2 July, the battalion marched eight miles to billets in the village of Autheux, south-west of Doullens. Over the next two days they marched to Franvillers, seven miles south-west of Albert on the Amiens road. All through this period, the battalion would have been continuing to train and to keep as fit as possible for the trials that lay ahead of it.

Between 9 and 12 July, the battalion was stationed at camps near Bronfay Farm, on the road from Maricourt to Bray. On 13 July, the battalion marched to Carnoy and into support trenches in divisional reserve behind Montauban Ridge. The 3rd Division was to join in the dawn attack on the German second line on Bazentin Ridge. 76 Brigade would be in reserve. The assault would be made by 8 and 9 Brigades, attacking in the centre of the line. Their task was to capture and secure the village of Bazentin le Grand.

These brigades had moved into position on the Montauban Ridge between 7 and 8 July. They had established a night outpost line nearly 1,000 yards ahead along a sunken track, which ran about 250 yards from and parallel to the German front line. From this position, active patrolling of no man's land had been carried out. The Germans were clearly expecting further attacks on their trenches following the capture of Mametz Wood. The wire in front of the German second position was being strengthened each night and the long grass in no man's land made it quite difficult for patrols to establish clear observation over the enemy lines.

Communication trenches were dug in Caterpillar Valley during the nights of the 11 and 12 July. This lay just to the east of Mametz Wood. The ground here was protected from direct German observation and was used by the field artillery as well as the Royal Engineers.

The troops would assembly in conditions of total silence and secrecy on the night of 13 July. Troops from 8 and 9 Brigades were assembled in lines of platoons up the slope from the sunken track and were in position by 1.45 am. A hurricane artillery and heavy machine gun bombardment fell on the German trenches at 3.20 am and five minutes later, the troops of the 3rd Division advanced towards the enemy. At the same time, the 8th King's Own was moved forward to Caterpillar Valley to provide close support to the two assaulting brigades. Here they dug in for extra protection from German shelling.

The soldiers of the 8th East Yorkshires and 7th Shropshires of 8 Brigade found the enemy wire largely undamaged by the barrage. The attack was held up until Major Congreve, the brigade major, led a company of the 2nd Royal Scots into the German trenches on the left and started to bomb his way along the German front-line trench towards the held-up troops. The troops pinned down outside the wire were then able to break through and capture their objectives. The 13th King's Liverpools and the 12th West Yorkshires from 9 Brigade found the wire on their front almost entirely destroyed by the barrage and quickly entered the German front line. Desperate hand-to-hand fighting ensued, with the Germans putting up fierce resistance. The trench mortar teams were brought up and the village was eventually secured. Two of the four battalion COs were killed and the other two seriously wounded in the fighting. Within a few hours the whole of the German position had been taken and the work of consolidation began. And by 10 am, all fighting had effectively stopped. Over 1,400 prisoners were captured and the German dead lay thick on the ground and in the trenches. The dawn attack had been a huge success, although the Germans had managed to hold on to parts of the village of Longueval and Delville Wood on the right.

The success at Bazentin was not immediately pressed home by a further advance up to the strategically important High Wood, a mile and a half away and the highest point on this section of the Somme front. Commanders were anxious not to move the infantry beyond the reach of artillery protection. Both the 7th and 3rd Divisions were ready and willing to push on with the advance. The day was fine and clear. The ground ahead, undamaged by shellfire or laden with heavy mud, leant itself to rapid movement. General Potter, commanding 9 Brigade, in fact walked up to High Wood himself and found no evidence of any German defensive works or troops at all. Not a single shot was fired at him. The troops were ordered to hold fast to their positions on the ridge. The high command planned to use the cavalry to make the next stage of the advance to High Wood but it was not in position to do this until later in the evening. The cavalry charge, bravely though it was carried out, was a predictable failure. The moment had simply slipped away. The Germans had by now had several hours to reinforce the wood and its approaches. Horses proved, once again, as vulnerable to machine gun fire as the infantry. It would take many weeks of bitter fighting before High Wood could be captured – fighting in which the 7th Battalion King's Own would soon become embroiled.

The 8th Battalion spent the next two days were spent away from the front line. But they were not out of danger. On 15 and 16 July their trenches in Caterpillar Valley came under regular German shellfire. On 16 July one man was killed and fourteen were wounded.

General Rawlinson, commanding operations of the Fourth Army on the Somme, ordered his forces on the evening of 14 July to complete the capture of their objectives, including Longueval and Delville Wood. British forces, including the South Africans, were in possession of the southern half of the village. Their job would be to complete their occupation and push the line beyond the boundaries of the wood itself. An attack by the 12th Royal Scots of 7th Division in the morning of 15 July had failed to make much impression. They made another attempt in the evening, which also failed. The remains of the South African Brigade were ordered to take Deville Wood 'at all costs' and they moved up in the morning of 15 July to make further attacks. In heavy fighting, they managed to capture large parts, although the Germans held out in the north-western sector. Fighting continued all day and night and the area was subjected to heavy shelling and machine gun fire. Casualties rose significantly. The wood was now a tangled mass of fallen tree trunks, exposed roots and, above all, thousands of dead soldiers – both German and British. Digging effective trenches and any other form of protection from the remorseless shellfire was practically impossible. At best, the men could dig down to waist height. And in these miserable conditions, they fought and died in some of the most terrible conditions imaginable.

Further attacks on the northern part of the village and on the north-western part of the wood were launched on 16 July. Both failed in the face of intense machine gun fire. Fighting continued all day long. The British commanders decided that further infantry attacks were unlikely to succeed unless the German positions were subjected to heavy artillery fire. This began in the early hours of 17 July. The German bombardment on the tenuous British positions went on at the same time. Fresh infantry attacks began at 2 am on 17 July. By noon it was clear that these attacks had also failed. The barrage had not succeeded in destroying the concealed German machine guns. The British forward positions in the wood and village were subjected to heavy shelling as well – involving gas, shrapnel and high explosive. Gun fire also fell on Caterpillar Valley and Montauban.

After these horrendous engagements, the corps commander decided that the 9th Division and the heroic South Africans should be relieved as soon as possible. The attacks would, however, have to continue as the whole advance depended on clearing the wood and village. Lieutenant-General Congreve planned to use the

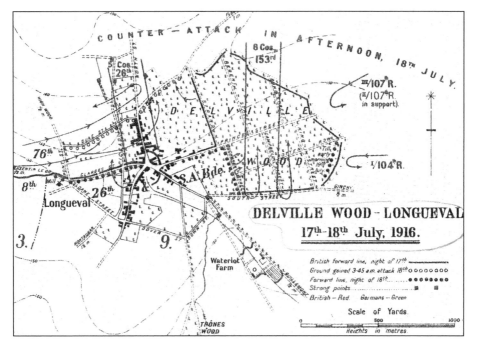

The attack of the 8th Battalion at Delville Wood, where the battalion managed to advance into the orchard before being forced to retire under heavy fire.

3rd Division in a renewed offensive. In turn, the 3rd Division commander, Major-General Haldane, decided to use 76 Brigade in a fresh attack against Longueval village and Delville Wood from the west on the morning of 18 July. It would now be the turn of the 8th King's Own to enter this fearful cauldron. And the 8th Battalion would be employed at the very moment that the Germans themselves were making their own attempts to seize back control of the wood and the village. The 8th King's Own were informed of their role in the attack in the morning of 17 July and during the early hours of the next day they moved up into their attack positions.

The attack would be launched by one battalion – the 1st Gordons – with two companies of the 8th King's Own in support. The intense German gun fire slackened off by 3.45 am on 18 July, when the attack was launched. It was delivered after a British barrage that lasted for an hour and became intensive in the five minutes before the men went over the top. The attack was mounted from trenches near to the Windmill.

The two companies of the 8th King's Own joined the fighting at around 5.30 am, when they were ordered up to support the Gordon's in Longueval village. B Company, under Captain Lyons, dug in on a line through the orchards on the western side of the wood. As soon as they entered the orchards they came under heavy machine gun fire from the wood. Captain Lyons was killed here leading his men forward. Several other men were killed alongside him as they tried to consolidate their positions. One of these men was Private Joseph Murray from Barrow. The suvivors were forced to withdraw almost immediately under this withering and murderous fire. A second attempt was made to carry the orchard but it met with a similar fate. Both A and B Companies were ordered to entrench themselves in the northern end of the village. This was done between 6 and 9 am. For the next six hours the men endured very heavy German artillery fire. Very soon the ruins of the village were completely ablaze whilst heavy clouds of thick dark smoke poured out of the wood. From about 2.45 to 3.50 the enemy barrage intensified. Survival in these conditions was impossible. The scene was one of utter chaos and destruction.

The enemy barrage was accompanied by a renewed infantry assault on the wood from the direction of Ginchy in the east. Others attacked from the north. The Germans pressed the few remaining South Africans in the wood back into the village. Here the enemy forces met the combined rifle and machine gun fire of the Gordons and the King's Own. Bitter fighting continued into the evening. Only after heroic resistance from British forces in the village, including reinforcements in the early evening from troops of the 9th Division on the right of 76 Brigade, was some semblance of order restored. The British had managed to hold on to a line through the centre of the village, but they had been removed from the wood.

In the evening, A and B Companies were withdrawn to trenches west of the Windmill. C and D Companies were brought up from Caterpillar Valley to replace them in the front line. Here the battalion remained for the whole of 19 July until they were relieved in the early hours of 20 July. The battalion's casualties for 18–19 July were very heavy. In total ten officers and 342 men were dead, injured or missing.

The 3rd Division continued to be heavily involved in the fighting for Delville Wood and Longueval over the next few days. In the early hours of 20 July, another attempt was made by 76 Brigade to capture the wood and village. The remaining two battalions of the brigade attacked from the Windmill area at 3.35 am. The two leading companies of the 2nd Suffolks were almost entirely wiped out in the attack. The 10th Royal Welch were late in launching their assault as they had got lost during the way up to the starting lines. A guide had taken them in the wrong direction. Because of this delay, they ran into the British machine gun barrage, losing all their officers before they could even properly form up. Although the fighting continued, the attack now stood no chance of any real success. Casualties were once again horrific. Amongst them was Private Percy Airey from Grange over Sands, who had joined the battalion in Ulverston.

On 22 July, the battalion was again ordered up to the front line at the Windmill to provide support to an attack this time by 9 Brigade, led by 1st Northumberland Fusiliers and 12th West Yorkshires. The orders for this attack were received very late and the men were unfamiliar with the ground over which they were to advance. The British barrage was not very accurate or effective. Advancing at 3.40 am on 23 July, they were hit once again by extremely heavy machine gun fire to their left and centre. Despite these obstacles, some initial gains were made, although the men were eventually forced to retire under the effects of another very heavy enemy barrage. At 6 am the 8th King's Own were ordered to send up reinforcements to help push the attack on further. Two companies were sent up the line into the village. The trenches by this time were heavily congested by the dead and injured. They could not get through. To leave the trenches and attempt to advance over the open would have been suicidal and a pointless waste of life. The men were withdrawn to their original trenches. Here they were heavily shelled all day but their misery would soon be over.

On 24 July, the battalion were ordered back to Montauban Alley to reinforce the line in case of an enemy counter-attack. Once again, they were heavily shelled all day. But at least in the trenches the former German support lines captured on the first day of the battle provided good protective cover for the men. A company was sent up to the wood via Waterlot Farm. They were caught in an enemy barrage going through Trones Wood and suffered severely. One of the men to die that day was Private Joe Western from Warton near Silverdale. In a letter home to his parents, Joe's platoon commander, Second Lieutenant Jay, who was to die himself at Arras, wrote: 'Throughout the heavy bombardment they were subjected to he behaved like a soldier and a man.'

On the night of 25 July, the 3rd Division was replaced in the line by the 2nd Division and the men marched back to Bois des Tailles, via Carnoy, and Happy

Valley, arriving at 5 pm. Casualties between 20 and 25 July were two officers wounded, fourteen men killed, sixty-two wounded and eight men missing – none of these men were ever found alive.

These small-scale attacks on heavily defended positions offered little chance of progress. The enemy artillery could focus exclusively on the small area being attacked. And conditions on the ground did not lend themselves to rapid movement. Only the prospect of a much broader, well-coordinated attack stood any real chance of succeeding in clearing the Germans out of the wood and village. But such an attack was neither conceived nor delivered. The consequences for the 8th King's Own were appalling. The same was true for the 3rd Division as a whole. For the period between 11 and 27 July, casualties in the division were 248 officers and 5,854 men. These losses were amongst the highest sustained by any division during the Battle of the Somme and are the clearest testimony to the bitter fighting endured by the men. By this time, the battalion's losses were catastrophic. The battalion could muster less than 200 fit men and a handful of officers. Delville Wood was not cleared of the enemy until 24 August and the Germans briefly succeeded in regaining part of the eastern section of the wood on the 31st. It would take more than a week of hard fighting to remove them and for the British to push their front line beyond the wood towards Flers and Ginchy. The fighting at Delville Wood, more than perhaps anywhere else on the Somme, came to typify the popular historical image of the battle – that of painfully slow advances, secured only by enormous loss of life and with little obvious tactical advantage.

The men enjoyed a few days rest at Bois des Tailles, which runs along the side of the valley south of Meaulte across the Morlancourt to Bray road. On 28 July they moved to Maricourt, a couple of miles behind the original British front line of 1 July. Here they were joined by the first of a steady stream of new recruits. In the next couple of days, 31 men joined the battalion at Maricourt. Over the next ten days, the battalion's strength was boosted by another 182 men. It was being prepared for another attempt to break the German line. It would however enjoy a brief respite in the glorious summer weather. The battalion continued to rest, train and recover at Maricourt until 11 August when it began moving back up the line. In a few days, the battalion would be back in the thick of things.

All was not well between the Allied commanders. The French were getting increasingly frustrated with the incremental nature of the British campaign. A seemingly endless series of local attacks by the British Fourth Army was making little progress against stubborn German defenders. Haig and his generals were however rightly concerned about a repeat of the first day of the battle when nearly 60,000 British soldiers had become casualties – the worst losses in a single day in the entire history of the Army. The British had been seeking to exploit their initial gains in the southern end of the battle front by employing smaller, more localized attacks on weak points in the German line. But there were no really weak points any more. After the first shock wave of 1 July, the Germans had poured men and materiel into the Somme. The defences were being strengthened continuously whenever circumstances allowed.

From the end of July, with little real or substantial progress in the battle, Joffre had become increasingly impatient. He wanted a resumption of the grand attacks on a broader front, with the British and French combining operations in a way that would put the German defence under much greater pressure and weaken the power of its artillery in particular.

On 11 August, Joffre wrote to Haig setting out details of a plan designed to capture the line Thiepval–High Wood–Ginchy–Combles–Somme in three large-scale attacks beginning on 22 August. A follow-on attack on or around 1 September would push the whole front back even further. It was a grandiose scheme designed to end the stalemate on the Somme and provide further relief to the French defenders at Verdun. The precise details of this plan did not find much favour with Haig, particularly as he was not confident that British forces were in a position yet to take the stronghold at Thiepval, which remained very firmly in German hands. Haig however did agree with the basic assumptions that lay behind Joffre's ideas. He too was becoming increasingly unhappy with the meandering nature of Rawlinson's battle tactics and wanted to see bigger and bolder advances. Haig put forward his own alternative. As a first step, he proposed that the French and British should jointly attack and seize a line from the River Somme to High Wood, for which he promised the British could be ready by 18 August.

The British and French strategy came together over the following days. The French would attack along the whole of their front north of the Somme while the British would seek to advance their line around Guillemont and Delville Wood. The combined French and British attack would take place on 18 August and would be preceded by a local operation on the 16th. Further combined attacks were planned for 22 August.

The preliminary operation planned for 16 August would once again involve the 3rd Division and the 8th King's Own. The plan involved a simultaneous attack by French forces on Angle Wood and an attack by the 3rd Division on the spur to the south of Guillemont. The British would advance in two stages: first to the Hardecourt–Guillemont road and then hopefully several hundred yards further to make contact with the French at the northern edge of Angle Wood. On the night of 14/15 August the 3rd Division replaced the 55th Division in the front line. The 8th King's Own would be in the first wave.

By 4 pm on 15 August, the men were in position. B and C Companies would go over the top in the initial attack. Their objective was Lonely Trench, a strongly held German position 500 yards to the south of Guillemont on top of the spur. The men would face an anxious wait of over twenty-four hours before their attack was to be made.

Zero hour was fixed at 5.40 pm on 16 August. The afternoon was sunny and hot. The British artillery fire increased in tempo and for the three minutes before zero reached a peak of intensity. On the extreme right of the advance, the 2nd Suffolks made good progress and succeeded in reaching their objectives on the Guillemont–Hardecourt road. However the 8th King's Own on the left of the line suffered very heavily. Lonely Trench was too close to the British front line to be subjected to the artillery barrage and the battalion's trench mortars had failed to do much damage. As soon as the men went over the top they were met by heavy machine gun and rifle fire. It was Delville Wood all over again. The men made repeated attempts to get forward. But their situation was completely hopeless. All of the officers and NCOs of the two attacking companies became casualties and the men were left leaderless and unable to press on. Those who had managed to get forward took cover amongst the hundreds of craters that littered the ground they were fighting over. Lonely Trench could not be successfully attacked by infantry unless all of the enemy machine guns could be subdued prior to the men moving forward. This was simply beyond the ability of the British gunners to deliver. At night and under cover of darkness the survivors eventually crawled back to their original lines. The French troops of the 153rd Division suffered a similar fate in their attack on Angle Wood. Privates John Quinney aged 20, from Walney Road, Hindpool and Frank Jenkinson from Barrow died in this attack as did Private Felix Mallon from Ulverston.

On 17 August the battalion was relieved by the 10 Welch Fusiliers who had orders to resume the attack that evening. D Company of the 8th King's Own would act as support. During the afternoon and under fire from the enemy, men from the King's Own helped lay out tapes in no man's land to guide the 10th Welch to their objectives. The British front line was cleared before the attack to enable a heavy bombardment of Lonely Trench by British howitzers. The barrage finished at 8 pm and two hours later, the infantry assault went in. It too was a complete failure. The attack was conceived as a surprise infantry assault. The Germans were far from surprised and repulsed the invaders without any diffi-culty at all. No British soldier managed to enter the German lines that evening.

General Haldane was not prepared to give up. On the evening of 17 August he ordered a fresh attack for the following morning at 4 am. This time it was the fate of D Company again. It supported an attack by one company of the 2nd Suffolks over the same ground. This attack fared no better than the others. All of the officers of D Company became casualties. In the afternoon, further attacks by the 1st Gordon's and 10th Royal Welch Fusiliers, although making modest gains, were forced back to their original start lines because troops on their left failed to keep up with them. Taken in enfilade, they were forced to retreat. Later that day the battalion was relieved from front-line duties and made its way – shattered and exhausted by three days of combat – back to the reserve lines at Carnoy. The fighting for Guillemont would continue for three more weeks.

The battalion's casualties for the period 16–18 August were extreme. Five officers were dead and one was missing presumed dead. One of the dead officers was Second Lieutenant Samson from Barrow who had only joined the battalion on 22 May. He was the son of a local Barrow GP who had premises in Chatsworth Terrace. Five other officers were wounded, including Lieutenant-Colonel Smith, the battalion CO. Thirty-one men were killed, 81 were missing – most of them dead – and 149 were wounded. This amounted to over half the trench strength of the battalion. The losses amongst the officers were so serious that Sergeant Holgate, who had won the DCM at St Eloi, was given an immediate field commission and taken on as a Second Lieutenant – the only time this happened in the whole time the 8th Battalion served on the Western Front.

On 19 August, the battalion moved to Happy Valley, a sheltered hollow behind the original front line near Bray. The following day seven new subalterns joined the battalion, including Lieutenant Schneider, a member of a prominent Barrow family. On 21 August, the men moved back to huts in Morlancourt, a village on the D42 road between Albert and Sailly Laurette, where they could rest and recover. Second Lieutenant Flewett and 51 other ranks joined the battalion. The next day another 79 other ranks joined. Fifty-four of these men were bantams from the 11th Battalion, King's Own, which had itself only just come out to France. The battalion and the whole division was in fact being withdrawn from the Somme battle altogether for a while. Over the period 11 July to 19/20 August, the division had suffered nearly 8,000 casualties – amongst the heaviest of any division. It was not in a fit state to continue active operations. It would, however, make one last appearance on the Somme in November. On 23 August the battalion marched to Mericourt, went by train to Candas and marched on to Autheux. The battalion then marched via Crepy, Siracourt, Fortel and Ruitz to Mazingarbe near Loos – a march of over 40 miles. The newly arrived bantams marched as a separate company. Loos was now a quiet stretch of the front line. Here the men would hopefully be able to get a measure of rest and rediscover some of their pre-Somme capabilities as a fighting unit.

On 1 September, some specialist units including the signallers, bombers, snipers and machine gunners moved up to the front line in the morning to take over duties from 10th Loyal North Lancashires of the 37th Division. Brigadier-General Kentish, commanding 76 Brigade, visited the battalion in the early afternoon. By 2 pm the rest of the battalion was on the way up to the line. The relief was complete by 6 pm. The evening was spent working on strengthening and improving the trenches, which were in a generally good condition. The trenches were dry and well drained. The men had good protection from shelling and machine gun fire in the deep trenches that had been dug into the chalky soil. During the night and the following morning, the men were largely undisturbed by the enemy. Later in the day and into the evening, the Germans fired a number of trench mortars but without any of the men being killed or wounded. The wire in front of the trenches was improved in the evening.

On 3 September the level of hostile machine gun fire increased substantially. There was also some light shelling from trench mortars. Two men were killed and three others wounded.

The next two days were much quieter. Some working parties were sent off to work under the supervision of the Royal Engineers to make dugouts. There was very little enemy activity. The same pattern repeated itself for the final two days of front-line duty. On 8 September they were relieved by the 1st Gordons and moved back into brigade reserve at Mazingarbe.

For the next five days the battalion trained in the peace and quiet of a glorious late summer, out of the range of enemy guns. The focus of their training was on open warfare tactics. They were being prepared for a return to the Somme where the fighting still raged on inconclusively. But the men were given some opportunity to relax and enjoy themselves. On 14 September they visited the cinema at Noeux-les-Mines and watched Charlie Chaplin films.

On 16 September Major-General Deverell, the new commanding officer of the 3rd Division paid a visit to the battalion to express his thanks for their service on the Somme. Undoubtedly, he would also have given the officers a sense of their likely new role in the further offensives planned for the next few weeks. In the afternoon, the battalion was back in the same section of the Loos front line, relieving the 1st Gordons. It was extremely quiet during the night. The battalion's Lewis guns were deployed to fire on the gaps that had been created in the German wire by artillery fire. Suspecting an infantry attack, the Germans retaliated by artillery fire of their own. Hostile shell and machine gun fire lasted all morning on 18 September. The battalion trench mortars and machine guns kept up their fire on the gaps – preventing any repair work being done. This fire continued overnight.

By 19 September, German nerves had calmed down. Both sides stopped firing at each other. It began to pour with rain and the conditions in the trenches began to deteriorate sharply. The parapets started to collapse. Dugouts became flooded. The bottoms of the trenches filled with heavy mud. At night, patrols went out into no man's land, but there was no trace of the enemy. He was more concerned about fighting the weather than the British.

The atrocious weather continued the next day. The men battled against the elements in their efforts to keep the trenches habitable. Fire was again brought to bear against the gaps in the German wire. In the evening three brief bursts of intensive artillery fire on the enemy line, with every rifle joining in, brought no response from the Germans. It was if there were no enemy troops opposite them at all. The night was quiet again. There was little to report the following day either. The men worked on their trenches.

After another quiet day on 22 September, the battalion was relieved in the evening by the 14th Argyle and Sutherland Highlanders of the 40th Division, and marched to Noeux-les-Mines where they billeted for the night.

On 23 September they marched to Allouagne, six miles west of Bethune, en route to their new training area at Flechin, a small village fourteen miles southwest of Hazebrouk, where they arrived the following day after a march of over thirteen miles kilometres. The battalion remained there until 7 October. For all of this time the battalion trained intensively in the art of open warfare – rehearsing rapid advances over open ground, storming and seizing strong points and machine gun nests, and advancing under the protection of creeping barrages. As a preparation for their return to the Somme battlefield, the 3rd Division was transferred to the command of the Reserve Army under General Sir Hubert Gough, which on 4 July had taken over responsibility for the northern half of the Somme battlefront from Rawlinson's Fourth Army. The 3rd Division now formed part of Lieutenant-General Fanshawe's V Corps.

On 7 October the battalion marched at 5.30 am to St Pol a few miles to the west of Arras where they boarded trains to Acheux, ten miles to the north of Albert, a distance of about 50 miles. The train left St Pol at 9.30 am but did not arrive at Acheux until 11 pm. The line was crammed with trains either taking men and materiel up the line or wounded men and worn-out troops back to safety and out of harm's way. The men were crammed into the infamous cattle wagons. It was anything but a pleasant journey, but it was undoubtedly better than marching. On arrival at Acheux, the men marched a further four miles west to Raincheval, twelve miles north-west of Albert, where they billeted for the night. It poured with rain. The men were soaked through when they arrived at 3 am.

At 1 pm the following day they marched east again to Bertrancourt, arriving three hours later. This was a tiny village south-west of Courcelles au Bois and was within a few miles of the front line. The battalion was now acting as the divisional reserve. At night the men were formed into working parties carrying supplies up to the forward positions, and digging dugouts and other positions under the command of the Royal Engineers. During the day they continued to practice for open warfare. On the 10 October the battalion practised an attack over a flagged course replicating the ground at Serre over which they would eventually be ordered to fight.

Serre lay a mile or so to the north of Beaumont Hamel on the top of the Redan Ridge. Serre had been due to be taken as one of the first day's objectives on 1 July. It was still in German hands. A disastrous attack uphill, over 200 yards of exposed ground by the 31st Division, containing many of the Pals Battalions from Yorkshire and the North-East had seen one of the greatest calamities of the first day of the battle. Thousands of men had become casualties. Whole battalions were effectively destroyed on their first serious engagement of the war. After two years of training and preparation these battalions took not a single inch of German ground.

By October, the ground resembled a lunar landscape, heavily cratered with the ground cut up into a loose powder by the incessant shelling from both sides' heavy guns. Heavy and persistent rain had also made the battlefield a quagmire. If anything, the German positions were even more strongly held in the autumn than they had been in July. The enemy had no intention of giving an inch of ground to the British as the position on the ridge was vital to the defence of the northern sector of the front, commanding observation and fire positions over a wide area.

There had been no attempt by the British to attack Serre by infantry assault since 1 July. All this was now to change.

Haig had come to the view in October that the Allies should continue the Somme offensive without intermission. He was confident that, if the momentum could be maintained, there was the prospect of a far-reaching success that would 'afford full compensation for all that has been done to attain it'. Gough, Rawlinson and Haig accordingly decided that the Fourth and Reserve Armies should mount simultaneous attacks on both sides of the River Ancre, pushing the Germans back in a north-easterly direction on a four-mile front. V Corps would attack north of the river and take the line Beaucourt–Beaumont Hamel–Serre.

The original plan was to attack towards the end of October, but conditions on the ground and in the air were extremely unfavourable and the attack had to be postponed several times. Simply existing in the front line at all at this time required a major effort of endurance and willpower on the part of the men. Heavy mist and rain for much of the time made it impossible for the Royal Flying Corps to offer much assistance. They could barely see anything. Counter-battery work suffered as a result and British shells were constantly falling short due to inaccurate observation. The guns themselves were becoming worn out and increasingly inaccurate through constant use.

No man's land at Serre was a vast ocean of mud. It was impossible for the infantry to mount an attack in conditions like these. Haig was clear that no attack should be attempted until the ground had sufficiently dried out and where it looked reasonably clear that there would be the prospect of fair weather for at least a couple of days. Late on 8 November, General Gough, after conferring with Fanshawe, decided that, providing no further rain fell, the attack should be launched on 13 November.

In the mean time, and in preparation for the main attack, the British kept up a steady rate of fire on the German positions. A heavy gas attack was launched by the Special Brigade, Royal Engineers, against Beaumont Hamel on 28 October. That night phosgene bombs were also fired at the German lines at Serre. Active patrolling took place at night. On 1 November, patrols entered the German front line at Serre and penetrated as far as the support lines. Confidence was high. It seemed that there was a real prospect of moving the line forward at last.

Whilst all of these plans were being laid, the 8th King's Own continued to train for their part in the proposed attacks. Between 11 and 14 October, they trained in skirmishing and assault techniques. At night they provided the manpower for working parties. On Sunday 15 October most of the men attended a divine service in Bertrancourt in the morning. In the afternoon the men carried out equipment checks. Officers and NCOs went up to the front line to reconnoitre the ground. At night 400 men were out on working parties.

On 16 October four men were killed and sixteen were wounded while taking part in night-time working parties. On 17 October they moved from Bertrancourt to Louvencourt. Another day was spent in training.

On 19 October they went into the front-line trenches for the first time at Serre where they relieved the 1st Northumberland Fusiliers of 9 Brigade. The battalion came under heavy shellfire. The weather continued to be appalling with torrential rain for most of the day. It was quieter at night, although the British guns were busy into the early hours.

The men came under heavy enemy trench mortar and shellfire again on 20 October that badly damaged the front line. At night the British artillery directed their fire at the wire in front of the German trenches.

On 21 October the battalion was relieved in the early hours of the morning by the 14th Yorks and Lancs of 31st Division. By 11.30 am the relief was complete and the men marched back to Courcelles tired and dirty. The rest of the day was spent cleaning up. In the evening, 10 officers and over 500 men – practically the whole battalion – were out on working parties. For the next three days, the battalion continued to train for their attack on Serre. At night they worked into the small hours on working and carrying parties. On 24 October Major Hunt of the King's Dragoon Guards took over the command of the battalion from Lieutenant-Colonel Smith who was sent to command a base camp at Rouens.

The 25th saw the battalion back again in the front line at Serre. The Germans greeted them with a heavy barrage of high explosive shell. The cook house of D Company received a direct hit, killing the sergeant and four other men. One of the dead soldiers was Private James Leck of Lowick. Another soldier was killed and six men were wounded during the relief. The next day was the same. The battalion came under heavy shellfire all day. Battalion stores in Observation Wood were blown up, but this time there were no casualties. The conditions in the front line were now so bad that the men could only complete short tours of duty. They were relieved in the early hours of 27 October by the 1st Gordons and moved back to Courcelles. On the 29 October they marched to billets in huts at Bus en Artois. Here they were at least out of the range of German guns. And at Bus they would complete their training for the attack. They stayed there until 11 November. On that day they marched to Courcelles again and from there they went into the trenches opposite Serre on 12 November.

Up until 10 November, the generals were still divided as to the timing of the attack along the Ancre. There had been no rain since 8 November. The weather had also got much colder, making the ground easier to move over. On the 11th, Gough made his decision. He would attack on 13 November. Haig continued to express doubts. On the afternoon of 12 November, Haig visited Gough at Army Headquarters. By this time the preliminary bombardment had already begun. Although Haig wanted a victory, he did not want to run the risk of further heavy casualties. Gough persuaded him that the attack should go ahead as planned and Haig agreed. It literally was now or never as far as Gough was concerned.

The British attack was effectively an attempt to reduce or hopefully eliminate the German salient that now jutted out into the British lines from the Albert–Bapaume road to Serre itself. The British advances south of the Albert road had created this salient. Removing it would straighten the British line. The objectives were therefore strictly limited. Success would give the British a useful platform from which they could make later advances and would further wear down the German defenders. It was not conceived as a decisive blow against the Germans.

The main attack would go in north of the Ancre. The V Corps had the 3rd, 63rd, 2nd and 51st Divisions in the front line. The operation was divided into three stages. In the first stage, the troops would advance an average of 800 yards. Three trench lines had to be subdued. The line to be carried extended up the Beaumont Hamel valley, round behind the village, then across the Redan Ridge and the slope in front of Serre. Having taken this line, the next movement forward would take the British another 600–1,000 yards further on and would involve the capture of Serre village itself. The final objective was Beaucourt village.

For the men of the 8th King's Own, the waiting and the training was finally over. Their mission was to support the 2nd Suffolks on the left of the brigade front to be attacked. Once the Suffolk's had taken the first objective, Serre Trench which lay across the forward slope of the ridge some 200 yards from the nearest point to the village, the King's Own would pass through them and carry the village itself. Zero was set for 5.45 am. The night was dark and cold and the whole battlefield was covered with a heavy wet mist. Visibility was down to about 30 yards. The Germans held this sector of their line with two battalions of the 169th Regiment in the line.

The conditions in front of 76 Brigade were as bad as it is possible to imagine. There was no prospect of a rapid advance across no man's land. The ground was a muddy morass. The official history simply records that the division 'lost the battle in the mud'.

The 2nd Suffolks started in good order once the barrage lifted, but the men struggled to keep going in the thick mud. The barrage had failed to clear a path through the German wire. The attack miscarried almost immediately and by 6.15 most of the Suffolk's were back in their trenches. A few managed to get into the German support lines. Here they were quickly isolated and either killed or captured. A heavy enemy barrage that came down in no man's land made it almost impossible for the King's Own to make any progress at all. D Company made a brave but futile attempt to come to the rescue of the trapped and isolated Suffolk's. Their efforts came to nothing. The German lines were just too strongly held for them to have any chance of success. Captain Dickinson, in charge of the company, ordered the survivors to withdraw to their original positions. Some of the men were trapped in shell holes and had to wait until dark before they could brave an attempt to return to the safety of their own lines. B and C Companies then joined the remnants of D Company in the front line where they were all subjected to very heavy enemy shelling for several hours. The whole attack was a complete and total failure. Serre had held out against the British again, and in the process many more men had lost their lives. This attack probably represented the very nadir of the battalion's experiences of the war so far. They had been asked to do something that the local conditions had rendered impossible to achieve.

Major-General Deverell, aware that the troops on both his left and right were making some progress, was keen to renew the attack. At 7.30 am he ordered his brigades to prepare for another attack without delay. The continued German artillery fire made any such effort completely impossible without further horrific losses. At 12.45 pm the division informed Fanshawe at Corps HQ that there was no prospect of any further success in front of Serre. Deverell continued to look at the possibility of renewing the attack if the conditions improved. He even suggested a fresh attack at 10 pm. Under instructions from Army HQ at 4.30 pm, V Corps cancelled all further operations. To continue would be simply to invite disaster. Privates Charles Turner and Robert Kinnish from Ulverston both died in the knee-high mud that morning, as did Private John Fuge from Millom.

General Gough continued to hold the view that the attack could be renewed and that V Corps had a real chance of taking its objectives if they attacked again on the 14 November. Orders issued that night confirmed this intention. The renewed attack would not however involve 3rd Division. At least on this sector, the consensus continued to hold. The battalion continued to hold the front line until 19 November, and moved back to rest billets at Bus. By now operations on the Somme had been called off for the winter.

Here the men would stay for the next week, recovering from their ordeal of mud and death. Five officers and 99 other ranks had become casualties during the period 13–19 November. Private Robert Kinnish of 58 Ainslie Street was another of those killed on the 13th. His body was never found and his name is recorded on the Thiepval Memorial to the missing. He was a boy of 17.

By 1 December, the battalion was back in billets at Courcelles in brigade reserve. In the evening they relieved the 1st Gordons in the front line north of Serre. It was completed at 8.20 pm. There was little enemy action. At night, a hard frost descended over the trenches and the men struggled to keep warm.

The following days things began to heat up. The Germans laid down heavy artillery fire on the trenches around Serre all day and there was continuous sniper fire. The men attempted to improve their living arrangements as best they could. One man was wounded during the day. At night, patrols in no man's land found the enemy wire to be very strong. On 3 December, a heavy mist offered some protection from the enemy sniping, although another man was slightly wounded by shellfire. At night, wiring parties went out to strengthen the British defences. The same pattern repeated itself on 4 December. German aircraft flew high overhead, making observations over the British lines. Two men were wounded.

On the night of 5 December the battalion was relieved by the 12th West Yorkshires and returned to billets at Bus, arriving at 2 am. They were greeted by hot soup. A mixture of sleet and snow fell throughout the night. Here they would spend the next eight days. Colonel Hunt went off to assume temporary command of the brigade and was replaced by Major Cowper. During the day the battalion provided working parties at night. During the day they continued to train.

On 13 December the men moved back up to Courcelles and took over huts from the 12th West Yorkshires. They remained at Courcelles until 17 December when they went back into the front line at Serre around John Copse and Chasseurs Hedge. The trenches were once again in a wretched state, thanks to the combination of the appalling weather and the incessant German artillery. The following day, Major West took over command of the battalion. The following morning, three men were killed instantly and three others seriously wounded when a shell landed in one of the dugouts. In the early hours of 21 December, they were relieved again by the West Yorkshires and went back to Bus. Here the men would enjoy a peaceful Christmas out of the line and out of danger. They were warm. They had plenty of hot food. They received a delivery of parcels and mail from their loved ones. In the evening on Christmas Day they enjoyed an extra ration of beer. The battalion band played carols and hymns. For a moment at least, the war seemed far away.

On 29 December they moved back to Courcelles and were joined by 94 new recruits. They stayed here in brigade reserve until 31 December.

Arras and Ypres

Between 1 and 4 January 1917, the men were holding the front line at John Copse in front of Serre. It was fairly quiet. One man was killed while on attachment to a working party under Royal Engineers orders at the railway near Getorix. On 4 January a huge party of 153 replacements arrived at Courcelles to strengthen the battalion. The battalion remained at Courcelles overnight. The new recruits were hurriedly assigned to their platoons and companies. The next day they were back in the front line. For the next two days the front remained exceptionally quiet. There were no casualties amongst the men.

On 7 January the battalion left the Somme front. The battle had been a bitter experience for them, as it had been for all of the British Army. They had been involved in some of the heaviest fighting of the campaign in July and August, where their bravery and sacrifice had borne little fruit. And at the end of the battle, the final muddy, desperate and doomed struggle for Serre was a depressing note on which to end their contribution to the 'big push'.

They marched that day to Courcelles for the last time and were issued with gum boots and hot soup. They marched on again to Bertrancourt, where at 1 am they were picked up by lorries and driven to Puchvillers. In the afternoon of 9 January they arrived at Halloy via Val de Maison, Talmas, Haureas and Canaples, a slow, circular route west and then north of about fifty miles. But at least they were not marching or carrying their packs. Halloy was a small village about four miles east of Doullens. Two companies went into billets and two companies into huts. They remained here until 28 January, training and preparing for their next engagement. That day they moved into billets at Amplier, a few miles away. On 29 January they were on the move again, this time to Barly about twelve miles north. The next day they moved on to Sibiville, about ten miles to the north-west. And then on to Villers Brulin, twelve miles north-east of Arras. Here the battalion would spend another week, training and rehearsing their attack and assault techniques. They would be needed again soon.

At Chantilly, after the conclusion of the Somme battle, Haig had issued his plans for the coming year. The British would continue to press the Germans at every opportunity throughout the winter so far as the weather and the state of the troops permitted. They would also prepare a major new offensive in the central part of the British front, somewhere in the vicinity of Arras and Vimy. These plans were to be materially affected by both the major French offensive planned by General Nivelle for the Aisne and the retreat by the Germans to the Hindenburg Line, which began in the middle of February. In order to allow the French to concentrate their resources for the Nivelle offensive, the British had agreed to extend the length of their front by several miles further south. This meant that it would be difficult for the Fourth Army to continue with major offensive operations on the Somme front. They would have to close with the enemy first, and would be operating in front of a wasteland of ruined communications created by the Germans as they retreated to their new defensive positions. However, the retreat to the Hindenburg Line did now facilitate the transfer of more troops to the proposed active front around Arras. The Third Army under General Allenby would now have 18 divisions with which to pursue a slightly amended plan to advance along both banks of the River Scarpe. Its objectives would now be to break the German line running from Arras to St Quentin and then to push on in the direction of Cambrai. The First Army would protect its northern flank by capturing the Vimy Ridge.

However, the German defensive positions were strong and deep around Arras. The trenches had been carefully sited and were solidly constructed. There were three and sometimes four lines of trenches between 75 and 150 yards apart and these were served by communication trenches every hundred yards or so. Behind these lines stood the support line which was itself joined to the Hindenburg Line curving up from the south-east. Strong fortress-like positions were built around Feuchy Chapel along the Arras–Cambrai road and at Monchy le Preux, a commanding hilltop village four miles east of Arras. An equally strong reserve line 3 miles behind the front line, known as the Wancourt–Feuchy Line completed the German position at Arras.

The final British plans were simple enough. The Third Army would break through at Arras; capture the Hindenburg Line by attacking it in flank and rear and advance on Cambrai. The infantry had four separate lines to reach, which in total would have amounted to an advance of over four miles from their start lines.

If all went to plan, Monchy le Preux would be in British hands by nightfall. Z Day, the day of the attack, would be preceded by a bombardment lasting four days. Some of the necessary wire cutting would be done unobtrusively before this bombardment started. The 8th King's Own and the 3rd Division would attack in the centre on the VI Corps front. The cavalry corps would be used to exploit any success. Following their successful deployment on the Somme, the attack would be supported by forty tanks. Over 1,700 guns would be available to support the infantry attack. The artillery would fire a bombardment of lethal gas shells just prior to the infantry going in. This, it was hoped, would help suppress much of the German artillery. The attack was scheduled to begin on 8 April, but was eventually delayed until the 9th, on news that the Nivelle offensive on the Aisne would not take place on the date previously planned.

In the mean time, the battalion kept up its training regime for the Arras offensive. It remained at Villers Brulin until 7 February. On the 8th, it moved to Wanquetin into very poor and insufficient billets, which resulted in serious overcrowding. Here they continued to train and rehearse for the battle ahead.

On 16 February they moved into Arras itself. HQ was located in 4 Rue des Trois Pommettes. The men stayed in the enormous caves that lay underneath the city where they were safe from German shelling. For the next twelve days the battalion stayed in Arras, providing large numbers of men for working parties digging assembly trenches, dumps, strong points and signalling for the attack. On the 19 February, virtually the whole battalion was employed – over 660 men. On 20 February the battalion rations were brought up by supply column into the Fish Market and were distributed to the men there. On the evening of 28 February, the battalion left Arras for Wanquetin again, leaving the city in companies at 200 yard intervals – the standard precaution against artillery fire. They arrived back in their old billets at midnight.

For the next fortnight they remained at Wanquetin. There was no rest for the men however. Working parties were continuous and in between they had to maintain their focus on training for the forthcoming attack. Field-Marshall Haig inspected the battalion on 8 March. On 16 March the battalion moved to billets at Liencourt and Denier, about a mile away. The battalion continued to train here for the next two weeks on specially prepared ground resembling the area to be assaulted on the 9 April. On 29 March, they marched back to Wanquetin in pouring rain. The men were absolutely soaked through. On arrival, they made hastily improvised braziers from oil cans to get warm and dry.

The next day they were back in Arras by 11 pm and found billets in the cellars of the ruined town houses in Rue Gambetta and the Rue des Bardets. The preliminary bombardment began as planned on 4 April. For the next few days the men continued to provide the hard labour required for any major attack. They carried ammunition and material up to the front lines. They dug trenches and dugouts. The Germans made no serious attempt to disrupt preparations for the attack. The city came under sporadic artillery fire. On the evening of 6 April tear gas shells were fired into the city centre. None of this represented any serious difficulty to the British.

On the front allotted to 76 Brigade, the 1st Gordons and the 10th Royal Welch would both attack the German front line and capture Devil's Wood. The King's Own would act as brigade reserve. 9 Brigade would then pass through and capture the second objective, the Blue Line. In turn, 8 Brigade would then pass through and seize its allotted section of the Wancourt–Feuchy Line, a total distance of about 3,500 yards.

On 8 April there was a Holy Communion service at battalion HQ with a large attendance. It was clear to everybody that the offensive would be a major operation and that heavy battle casualties could be expected. In the afternoon, the battalion moved up into advanced positions alongside the Cambrai road and relieved the 1st Royal Scots. At 10 pm they moved into their assembly trenches further forward. The Gordons moved up to the assault lines, taking B Company with them to provide extra support. Two young officers of B Company were killed as they took their men forward under gun fire – Lieutenant Fielder and Second Lieutenant Sparks. B Company sustained heavy losses at this point. Two other officers were wounded, four men were killed and over twenty men wounded. The night was spent putting bridges and ladders into position and in cutting gaps in the wire in front of the British lines.

Zero hour was set for 5.30 am. It was preceded by a hurricane bombardment of Stokes mortars and heavy machine guns. The 1st Gordons took the first three trenches of the German defensive lines within the time scheduled. The 10th Royal Welch Fusiliers passed through and by 7.45 am, captured Devil's Wood and reached the Black Line. All these objectives were captured without serious difficulty or heavy losses. The Germans were simply overwhelmed by the ferocity of the barrage and the speed of the infantry advance. A Company was sent forward to act as a carrying party for the troops in the newly won trenches.

9 Brigade passed through at 7.30 am. They began their attack at 8.15 am, assaulting The Harp, a strong point in the German front lines, and the village of Tilloy. Both were taken. The advance was however slightly held up by the non-arrival of most of the expected tanks, which had got trapped in muddy ground on the way up to the starting line. Without the fire power and protection of the tanks, the men experienced some very hard fighting.

The rest of the battalion remained in their assembly trenches until noon. They were then ordered forward to the western edge of The Harp to consolidate the gains and to construct a roadway over which the cavalry could move up to exploit the breach of the German lines. It was another wasted expenditure of manpower. The cavalry were never deployed.

The advance to the third objective, the Brown Line was not going so well. The infantry could not overcome the fortress of Feuchy Chapel, which had a commanding field of fire. From here, the defenders could pour machine gun fire into the flanks of the advancing troops. The Wancourt–Feuchy Line was holding out. At 6.35 pm, the battalion, still in The Harp and in reserve to 8 Brigade, was ordered forward to assault the Wancourt–Feuchy Line. The attack was to begin at 7 pm. There was no way the men could get into the position in time. They were over a mile and a quarter from the point of attack. The Gordons were also ordered to make the same attack. They were 900 yards further forward than the King's Own, and they attacked on time, but on their own. Their attack was a failure and they sustained heavy casualties. Colonel Hunt led his men forward in artillery formation and under shrapnel fire. Colonel Lumsden of the 2nd Royal Scots met the battalion on its way up the line. He reported that there were scattered units of 8 Brigade about 100 yards further up but that the King's Own were needed to fill a gap in the earlier advance caused by his battalion drifting to the right. The battalion eventually found the positions they were supposed to reach and dug in. There was no point in trying to press on with any attack. A protective barrage could not now be organized and the Germans were expecting further attacks and were ready for them. To attack in these circumstances would have been a pointless waste of life. The first day of the Arras battle had ended with the British scoring a significant success. They had not reached all of their objectives. Monchy had not fallen and the Wancourt–Feuchy Line south of the River Scarpe was still in German hands. But they had landed one of the heaviest blows against the enemy since the start of the war. Over 5,000 prisoners were taken and 36 artillery pieces were captured. They had smashed through a section of the most strongly defended part of the Western Front and advanced over 3,000 yards in a single day. Private Willie Clarke of Dalton, Private William Hoggarth from Lindal, Private Isaac Hudson from Kirkby and Tom Rogerson from Ulverston all died on this first day of the Battle of Arras. But the battle was far from over.

The men dug all night, making a good, deep trench from which an assault could be launched the following day if needed. Just before dawn on 10 April, the battalion withdrew back to The Harp, handing over their position to 8 Brigade. The battalion would continue to act as close support to the brigade with 1st Gordons in reserve. If the victory won on the first day of the battle was to be fully exploited, the Wancourt–Feuchy Line had to be secured as rapidly as possible. The army commander therefore issued new orders on the evening of 9 April for the attack to be resumed on the 10th. All four battalions of 8 Brigade would be employed. It was a complete success. The King's Own were not called to support 8 Brigade's attack. The front of VI Corps had moved forward another mile. The battalion stayed at The Harp all day, trying to get some rest. In the afternoon, they were transferred back to 76 Brigade.

On 11 April there was the last serious and sustained attempt by the British to press home their first day's triumph. Allenby was anxious to avoid the battle becoming another series of costly and limited local engagements. He felt that the Germans had been defeated and the battle should now become a pursuit in which risks should be taken. He wanted all three corps under his command to push forward simultaneously. Although it is true that a powerful blow had been landed,

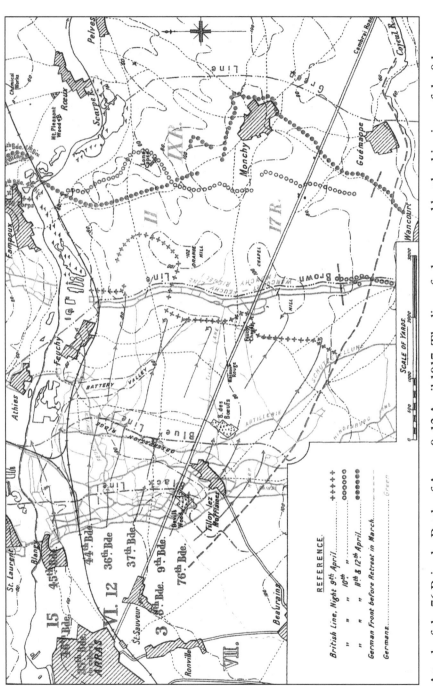

Attack of the 76 Brigade, Battle of Arras, 9–12 April 1917. The line of advance and battle objectives of the 8th Battalion appear south of the Arras–Cambrai Road.

the Germans had now had two days in which to bring up reinforcements. They had lost the first two days fighting, but they were far from being routed.

The 3rd Division was ordered to attack and seize the village of Guemappe, about a mile to the south of Monchy, which was to be assaulted by troops of the 15th and 37th Divisions. Lieutenant-Colonel Hunt left the battalion's trenches at 3.30 am on the 11 April to get his final orders at a brigade conference at the Feuchy cross-roads. The battalion moved forward at 4.30 am in artillery formation to the Wancourt–Feuchy Line, arriving in their allotted positions just before dawn. The enemy had time to observe this movement and within minutes had called down heavy artillery fire. The CO himself was wounded at this point, three men were killed and six men wounded. The battalion MO, Captain Wallace, performed an emergency leg amputation on one of these wounded men in the trench. The attack on Guemappe began at 7 am. The men moved quickly forward, but as soon as they reached the crest of a hill in front of the village, they were hit by heavy rifle and machine gun fire both from the village itself and from Wancourt to the south. It was impossible to get any further forward. The men sought shelter in shell holes where they remained for the rest of the day. Any movement drew lethal fire. Snipers were also active. Communication with companies was also severely disrupted by the constant damage being done to signal cables.

A second effort was made later in the day. The 1st Gordons joined in and this time extra artillery had been brought forward to provide better protection. The second attack also failed. The barrage failed to hit any of the machine gun nests. Two officers were killed and eleven wounded during the course of the day.

The attack on Monchy, however, was one of the most spectacular achievements of the battle and was achieved by successful cooperation between infantry and the tanks.

After the failure of this second attack on Guemappe the men were totally exhausted and were relieved at 1 am on the morning of 12 April by the 10th West Yorkshires. They retired that night to dugouts at The Harp, arriving at 5 am. They were met with a hot breakfast and rum. They spent the day resting. On 13 April they moved back to Arras in the evening and went into cellars near the main square. They went to sleep warm and comfortable. Battalion HQ was located at 33 Rue d'Amiens. On the night of 13 April, the division was replaced in the line by the 29th Division.

The battalion's casualties for the period 8–11 April were heavy. Five officers were dead and eleven wounded. Thirty-eight men were reported killed, twenty-eight were missing and 164 were wounded.

The battalion remained in Arras for the next few days. They continued to train for fresh assaults on the old racecourse north of Rue d'Amiens. They reverted to the 'old' methods of advancing in short rushes, rather than in straight lines. Because of the casualties, the battalion was reorganized into companies of three platoons.

Haig and his commanders, looking to continue the pressure on the Germans, decided that, rather than continue with local operations at Arras, they would try and coordinate a much bigger series of actions against the enemy. At a conference of the commanders of the First, Third and Fifth Armies at St Pol on 16 April, Haig had decided that the First Army would attack on 20 April at Oppy and capture Gavrelle. The Third Army would attack north and south of the Scarpe, pushing the Germans beyond the Sensee. The Fifth Army would attack the Hindenburg Line around Bullecourt and break through to capture Riencourt and Hendecourt. The operation was eventually postponed to 23 April to accommodate the wishes of local commanders. On 16 April the French had launched their major attack on the Aisne, but this would not mean any change in the attack planned for the 23rd. For the British there would be no let up. This time, however, there would be no chance of exploiting any element of surprise. And fewer tanks would be available as production was not yet at the level required to replace the high wastage rate of these new weapons on the battlefield. The Germans had by now significantly reinforced their lines and had many new batteries in place, ready to meet any renewed operations by the British. This second phase of the Arras battle held out the prospect of hard fighting.

The 3rd Division would not however be directly involved in the fighting of 23 April, which turned out to be some of the hardest of the war so far. South of the Scarpe, the British made some progress. On the front of the VII Corps, the British advanced another 1,500 yards or so in the centre. The ground was not given up lightly. If they lost ground, the Germans would immediately counter-attack in strength. The accuracy and ferocity of German gun fire inflicted heavy losses on the British troops. The fighting ebbed and flowed. Confusion reigned over the exact whereabouts of the troops. It was a battle fought and directed principally by company and platoon commanders. Around Monchy the fighting was particularly obscure, although a little ground was gained to the north of the village. Guemappe was entered by British troops. North of the Scarpe, the XVII Corps captured Gavrelle.

On 23 April the battalion left Arras at 5 pm for trenches in the north-west corner of The Harp. It had been decided that the 3rd Division would replace the exhausted soldiers of the 29th Division around Monchy and Guemappe on the night of 24 April. The battalion spent the night here. They moved up the following morning to the Wancourt–Feuchy Line near the Cambrai road. They were shelled during this movement. Four men were killed and five wounded. By 9.30 pm they had relieved the Border Regiment east of Monchy in the front line. The front of the 3rd Division would be held by 76 Brigade alone, with 8 and 9 Brigades in support.

The relief was extremely difficult because of the state of the ground, the heaviness of the enemy gun fire and the confused state of the position. Three companies went into the front line. There was intermittent shelling all through the night. Lieutenant Jay was killed. Movement in the open was suicidal and communication with battalion and brigade virtually impossible. But one thing was clear. The Germans were desperate to recover the ground they had lost at Monchy.

On 25 and 26 April the men worked hard to consolidate their new positions. On the night of 26 April the enemy mounted an infantry assault on the right of the battalion's trenches. C Company repulsed this attack with rifle and Lewis gun fire. The men 'stood to' all night fearing another attack. The situation at Monchy was far from ideal. The village was under heavy and constant shellfire. Getting supplies up to the men was very hazardous. And the King's Own could not establish contact with the battalion on their left. It was a grim and harrowing night. Private Joseph Williams of Dalton was killed on the 26th. He was 19 years old and before the war had been a barman at the Majestic Hotel in Barrow.

The men were shelled heavily all day on 27 April. The opposing front lines were very close, with the Germans occupying shell holes for cover. Another counter-attack was repulsed at dusk. The next two days were much quieter, and on 1 May the battalion was relieved by the 13th King's. They moved back to trenches at Tilloy. The brigade had suffered 464 casualties during its time at Monchy. One of those was Private Frank McGuire from Barrow. He was only 18 years old and had only been in France for three weeks before he was killed. He was an apprentice riveter in the shipyard in Barrow and had been a pupil at Sacred Heart School.

On 2 May they moved further back to trenches near the Bois des Boeufs. On 4 May they were back in the Wancourt line near the Cambrai road. Here they would stay until 10 May, during which time they were employed on carrying and working parties. They would regularly go up to Monchy to help with the endless digging and consolidating. On 5 May, Private John France from Barrow died at Etaples from wounds he had received earlier in the fighting at Monchy.

On the evening of 10 April they were back again in the front line at Monchy. Haig was carrying on with operations at Arras in order to assist General Nivelle and until the outcome of the French offensive on the Aisne had become clear. In truth, this had by now largely fizzled out and would end with modest territorial gains but huge casualties to the French. It would finish with the sacking of Nivelle and large-scale mutiny in the French Army. In the mean time, the British were determined to make good their commitments to the French and remained heavily committed to the battle. But Haig was also determined to complete his other principal operation of 1917 – the capture of the Messines Ridge and the advance through Flanders to clear the Belgian coast of the German submarine bases. The challenge for Haig was to extricate himself carefully from the Arras battle without risking a reverse of the hard-won gains. He planned a series of local operations along the whole front.

Attacks were launched on 28 April and 3 May which, although producing some useful minor territorial gains, did not create the conditions for a major review of tactics. Towards the end of April, Haig had also learnt of the imminent departure of Nivelle and the very real prospect of the French breaking off major offensive operations. If this happened, Haig planned to maintain a good defensive line at Arras, and carry out some surprise attacks in the hope of pinning down the enemy on this front whilst he prepared to mount his fresh attack in Flanders. The Paris Conference on 3 and 4 May ended any uncertainty. The job now of the Third Army in particular was to maintain some form of offensive operations on the Arras front, but with no fresh troops and with a dwindling number of guns. Reserves of fresh troops and all other materials would now be directed north to Flanders.

For the men of the 8th King's Own none of these tactical considerations would have seemed important or relevant. They were occupying trenches that were still being bitterly contested. On 11 May Monchy was again heavily shelled. At night machine gun fire raked the parapets. During the next day, things were much calmer. In order to secure their positions at Monchy, 76 Brigade would however attack the enemy front line with three battalions in the early evening. At 6 pm, the British guns opened a three-minute hurricane bombardment of Devils Trench. Three companies attacked under this barrage. They were immediately met by heavy rifle and machine gun fire from three sides. The attack completely failed, with none of the troops entering the enemy lines. At night, the survivors crawled back to their own trenches. Five officers and ninety-three men became casualties that night. Twenty-six men were killed, and twelve were missing after the attack. Fifty-two men were wounded. Two of the men to die in this attack were Privates Cuthbert Whalley and James Swindlehurst. James was 39 years old. Both men were from Barrow. Neither body was ever found.

The enemy's artillery retaliated on 13 May. Shells landed on the trenches at Monchy all through the day and night. The 14th saw a similar pattern. The battalion was relieved that night by 1st King's Own Scottish Borderers of 86 Brigade. The battalion collected itself on the Cambrai road near Tilloy. The battalion cookers were brought up. The men had bacon sandwiches, hot tea and rum for breakfast. They marched to Arras station where they were picked up by buses and driven to huts at Duisans, fifteen kilometres to the north-west. To all intents and purposes, the main operations stage of the Battle of Arras was now over. Ten men of the King's Own were to be awarded Military Medals for the action at Monchy,

The battalion stayed at Duisans for the next two days. They were issued with new clothes and cleaned up. On the morning of 17 May they moved to nearby Habarq via Agnez and Laresset. Their billets were considered to be very poor. The next day they marched a few miles to Ambrines into much better billets. Here they would stay for the next fortnight, relaxing, resting and bathing. Major-General Deverell came to inspect the battalion.

On 2 June, the battalion moved by bus back to Arras, leaving their billets at 8 am and arriving in the Rue de Lille at 12.30 pm. They were moved to very poor and exposed billets in the Levis Barracks for the next couple of days. On 5 June they were moved into much better and safer billets in cellars in the Rue des

Capuchins. For the next week the battalion dug new trenches in the old no man's land in front of Arras and furnished endless working parties for other jobs that needed doing. On 12 June they returned to the support lines around at Monchy. Things were generally quieter now, although both sides were constantly seeking to improve their tactical positions wherever they could. The fighting was far from over. On 14 June the battalion acted in support of a 76 Brigade attack on a gently sloping hill to the north of Monchy known as Infantry Hill. Here the Germans enjoyed a good fire position over the British in front of Monchy. The British had made several unsuccessful attempts to seize this high ground. That day they succeeded in reaching the crest of the hill for the first time. The battalion provided carrying parties for the attack. One man was killed and nine others wounded. On 15 and 16 June enemy artillery fire was constant and heavy as they tried to recover the lost ground. Another man was killed and 16 wounded over these two days.

On 17 June the battalion took over the front line from the 1st Gordons. Three companies were in the firing line. At dawn the following day, the Germans launched another counter-attack to recover Infantry Hill. It was preceded by a heavy barrage that fell on the battalion, which lasted for two hours. The enemy counter-attack was repulsed all along the brigade front. The British guns provided excellent covering fire and the men poured rifle and machine gun fire into the advancing troops. Eighteen men were killed, seventeen were missing and thirty-nine were wounded in this attack. One of the dead was Private Joe Bennett from Barrow. Joe was 22 and had joined up in 1914. The next day was quiet and peaceful.

36 Brigade of 12th Division relieved 76 Brigade the following day. They had spent their last tour of duty at Arras. The battalion marched by companies into Arras and was billeted in St Sacrament Convent. Later in the afternoon the battalion was moved by bus to Halloy. Here they would stay for the rest of the month, training and resting in the warm sunny weather. Lieutenant-General Haldane, the corps commander, visited the battalion on 29 June to present the medals won at Monchy. One of those to receive the Military Medal was Private John Tyson of Holker Street, Barrow. When in charge of a bombing party he successfully held on to a captured German post and resisted several strong counter-attacks.

The next two months would be one of the quietest periods the battalion had enjoyed since arriving in France. On 1 July they marched to Doullens where they caught the light railway to Achiet le Grand. From there the men marched again to Bihicourt, where they went into bivouacs south of the village. On the evening of 3 July they marched via Bapaume and Fremicourt to the reserve area at la Bucqueriere. Three companies stayed in tents south of the village while C Company were found huts and HQ was put into the village itself. They spent the week here, training and drilling. On 10 July the battalion moved up to the front line around Bullecourt, about five miles away. The front line here was merely a series of outposts, big enough for about 30 men each, separated by about 200–300 yards. The men were stationed around the villages of Louveral and Boursies.

The following week was very quiet indeed. The fighting had been intense here three months earlier, but the front seemed now to have settled down into a routine of 'live and let live'. The men worked on improving their outposts and patrolling no man's land. At dawn on 17 July, the enemy fired a barrage on the British front-line posts and enemy infantry mounted a raid on one of the outposts. This was driven back without loss. At midnight the following day the battalion was relieved by a battalion of the Shropshires. No casualties were reported for the whole week they spent in the line at Bullecourt.

The next week was spent in huts at Fremicourt. A routine of training, drilling and working parties became established. On 24 July they moved back into the front line for another week of duty. Once again, they were to experience a very quiet time. One of the outposts received a direct hit from a trench mortar, causing casualties. A wiring party in no man's land came across an enemy patrol and was fired on. Two men were killed and three others wounded. On 30 July the enemy raided one of the outposts on the left. They were seen crawling through the long grass between 6.45 and 7 am. The Germans threw some bombs at the post which all fell short. Lewis gun fire was opened on them and four men were seen to fall, although only two bodies were later recovered. No enemy action was reported for 31 July.

The battalion was relieved on 1 August and moved back to Fremicourt. Another week was to go by in a familiar routine of training and working parties for the front-line units. The men had regular hot food and access to the divisional baths. On 8 August they were back in the front line. They spent the next few days working to join up the various outposts into a proper defensive line. Again, there were no reported casualties. On 17 August they moved back to Fremicourt. This time there was time for sports. The officers beat the sergeants and corporals at rounders. On 25 August the battalion moved up again to the front line. There was a little intermittent shelling but, once again, no casualties were recorded in the war diary.

On 2 September, the battalion was relieved by the 10th Royal Welch. They stayed at Fremicourt until 5 September, when they moved to Barastre, two miles away to the south and about five miles south-east of Bapaume. Here the battalion began to train seriously for a fresh operation. The division had been given an important role to play in the developing battle at Ypres, where the Second Army was trying to push the Germans off the high ground around the city. In particular, General Plumer was tasked with capturing the Gheluvelt Plateau to the south-east of Ypres. He planned to do this in a series of stages, separated by six days so that supplies and guns could be moved forward. The first of these assaults would occur on 20 September.

The 3rd Division, having been effectively 'rested' for two months, would form part of the second stage of the battle, providing protection for the left flank of the main attack, which would be mounted by I Anzac Corps. The first stage of the operations on 20 September were successful and the British front moved forward by about 1,600 yards. It was primarily an artillery battle and the British had assembled a huge array of guns on a narrow concentrated front. Infantry tactics were changed. Skirmishing parties would go forward first. These small fighting groups would deal with strong points and machine gun nests, paving the way for the main assault parties to move up. They in turn would be followed by mopping up units who would deal with stragglers and garrison the captured strong points as soon as they were cleared.

These were the new tactics the King's Own began to train for at Barastre. In fact they were not dissimilar to the way they had fought at Arras. The men would stay at Barastre until 18 September. They began their ten-kilometre march to Bapaume at 2 am. They got on trains to Watou, twenty kilometres east of Ypres, at 5 am. One hundred and fifty men and three officers joined the battalion just before it left Barastre, helping to bring it up to full fighting strength.

Their new camp at Watou was five kilometres west of the town and was in a poor state when they arrived. They spent 19 September making it habitable. They continued to train for their role in the Gheluvelt operations until the 22 September. They moved then to Brandhoek, arriving in their new camp in the early evening. They continued to practise their assault techniques. On 24 September they relieved the 13th King's in the support lines. Battalion HQ was sited in a captured German strong point won on the 20 September. They were heavily shelled on the way up, and there were many casualties from high explosive and shrapnel shells. They were in their final assembly positions at 12.45 am on 26 September. Here they would have to stay until zero hour at 5.50 am. Given the circumstances of their advance, the conditions they found themselves in and the reputation that Ypres enjoyed amongst the British Army, they must have been some of the longest five hours of the war.

The Germans, expecting another British attack at Gheluvelt, had launched a major counter-attack of their own in the early morning of 25 September between the Menin Road and Polygon Wood. The heavy shelling the battalion encountered on their way up the line was connected with this attempt to disrupt British planning. It failed. The attacks were repulsed with heavy losses to the attackers. The attack scheduled for 26 September would go ahead as planned.

A heavy bombardment preceded the advance of 76 Brigade. The King's Own attacked with the 1st Gordons on their left on a front of about 750 yards. The brigade was supporting the northern flank of the main attack by the Australians. By 7.10 am reports began to arrive at battalion HQ indicating that the men had secured their objectives. The brigade began to consolidate a position south of the railway up to the western outskirts of Zonnebeke, just short of its objectives. To their immediate left, 8 Brigade almost succeeded in reaching their objective, Hill 40, but was caught by heavy machine gun fire 600 yards short of their final line.

The German forward line was, in truth, only thinly held. The real danger came from counter-attacks and from enemy artillery fire. By noon, the sun had broken through the mist and haze caused by the intense British barrage. The notorious Ypres mud had dried out by September and the barrage had caused a dense cloud of dust and debris over the battlefield in the early hours of the attack. Visibility noticeably improved by midday. The danger was obvious. The Germans began to move up large forces against the whole front of the attack. The positions won by the King's Own and Gordons began to be heavily shelled with shrapnel, high explosives and gas shells. Under the incessant pressure of this barrage, A Company sought permission in the afternoon to withdraw, but was ordered by battalion HQ to 'hold on at all costs'. By 4 pm it was reported that only 15 men were left in B Company. By 5 pm, enemy infantry could be seen to assemble in front of 76 Brigade. It was completely destroyed by the British artillery. But still the punishment continued. The CO of B Company was reported to be unfit for duty because of shell shock. The condition of his men must have beggared description. The shelling continued without break for the next forty-eight hours. Private Timothy Benson from Newton in Cartmel died on 26 September from shellfire. His body was never found and his death is recorded on the Tyne Cot memorial to the missing. He was 27.

The men held onto their newly won positions until they were relieved just before midnight on 29 September by Australians of the 34th Battalion. The battle had been largely an artillery affair. Enemy counter-attacks were repeatedly broken up by accurate gun fire. But the infantry too were heavily involved in the fighting. German infantry advancing down the slopes of the Broodseinde Ridge presented numerous and excellent targets for the men in the front lines. Casualties were high on both sides. The 8th Battalion arrived at camp south of Ypres in the early hours of 30 September. The second stage of the Gheluvelt operation had been a success. The front had moved forward as planned. But the casualties were very high.

The 3rd Division had the highest casualties of all of the units employed on 26 September. Thirty-four officers were killed, 100 were wounded and 3 were reported missing; 463 men were dead, 2,573 wounded and 859 were missing – a total of over 4,000 men. There are no precise casualty figures for the 8th King's Own, but they must have been in the hundreds.

On 30 September they left their new camp at 5 pm in buses for Winnizeele. where they arrived at 9.45 pm. Fifty new men and five officers arrived as replacements. The battalion played cricket against the 10th Royal Welch Fusiliers and won by 30 runs. The battalion stayed here until 4 October, when they marched to billets at Arques. On 6 October they marched to Wizernes at 7.30 in the morning, where they caught a train to Bapaume at 10.30 am. They arrived in Bapaume nine hours later and marched to their old camp at Barastres, arriving at about 9.30 pm. The battalion remained in this camp until 11 October. It rained heavily the whole time they were there. The huts were anything but weather-proof. It was a major effort to keep themselves dry and warm. On 11 October they were taken by bus to Mory and at 6 pm paraded for the trenches. They were back in the line near Bullecourt by midnight.

The next eight days in the front line were very quiet indeed. No casualties or any hostile enemy action of any kind were reported. Major-General Deverell and the army commander General Allenby both visited the men in the front line on 16 October to express their appreciation for the battalion's efforts at Gheluvelt. They were relieved in the evening by the 10th Royal Welch and travelled by light railway from Ecoust to Mory, arriving early in the morning.

The next week was spent training and in fitness work. The weather remained very wet. On 27 October they in turn relieved the Royal Welch Fusiliers at Bullecourt. One soldier was killed by shell fire on 28 October. The next day there was some sniping from the German lines and some light shelling. The next two days were very quiet. Between 2 and 4 November the battalion launched a number of trench raids and fighting patrols in no man's land. The patrols made no contact with the enemy. The trench raids were not entirely successful. On 3 November a small patrol of one officer and three men passed through a gap in the enemy wire and entered the enemy's trenches. Second Lieutenant McClean shot and wounded one enemy soldier in the trench but could not bring him back as a prisoner because he was too heavy to carry and could not be lifted out of the German trenches, which were 12 feet deep. The raiding party eventually retired. The Germans threw bombs at the retreating men. All of them were slightly wounded. On 4 November a much bigger raiding party of 30 men under Lieutenant Hodson tried to enter the enemy trenches to capture prisoners and gain identification and intelligence but failed to do so. The enemy were very much on the alert after the previous night's activities. Five men were wounded and one was reported missing. That night they were relieved by the 10th Royal Welch and returned to camp at Mory.

From 5 to 12 November they remained at Mory. The heavy rain continued. Most of the activities planned for the men were washed out and cancelled. Their principal job was to keep dry.

On 13 November they were back in the front line, this time for just four days. It was very quiet. On 17 November they returned to Mory where they would spend a fortnight training and providing working parties. On 23 November they were entertained by a concert party in the Theatre Barn in the village. On the night of the 30 November they returned to the front line and would stay there until 4 December. Neither side was active.

On 5 December they were back in camp at Mory. The following day they moved to Ecoust and into the support line trenches where they worked hard at improving the defences until 11 December. All through this time the men were employed on carrying and working parties. Their next spell in the front line from 11 to 16 December at Bullecourt would be much more lively.

On 12 December the dawn was greeted by a heavy enemy barrage on the front line followed by an infantry assault. It was successfully repulsed without the Germans entering the British trenches. The enemy sustained numerous casualties. The men were shelled on and off throughout the day. Three men were killed, one was missing and fourteen were wounded. Further raids were anticipated. On 13 December the guns on both sides were active again. Four men were killed and eighteen wounded, but there was no repeat of the previous day's attack. The 14th saw a similar high level of artillery fire, but this time the casualties were much fewer – only two men were wounded. The next day was much quieter and the battalion was finally relieved by the 10th Royal Welch on 16 December.

The battalion was at Mory until 22 December. At 9 pm that day they returned to the trenches at Bullecourt. This tour was much quieter than the last. There was little enemy action. On Christmas Day the Germans attempted to fraternize but were met by rifle and machine gun fire from the British lines. At 8 pm the officers of the battalion enjoyed a Christmas dinner together in one of the large dugouts constructed by the 10th Royal Welch. The men had their dinner in the trenches. On 26 and 27 December there was some desultory shelling, but there were no casualties amongst the men. On 27 December they were relieved by the 12th Suffolks and marched back to Mory.

The weather became extremely cold over this period and a hard frost set in. On 29 December they marched to No. 4 Camp between Hendecourt and Blaireville, back to the Arras front.

The final campaign

The men were to remain at this camp until 27 January 1918. On New Year's Day the men were treated to a special pork dinner. The officers had clubbed together to buy 246lbs of pork in the market at Arras, which was then roasted in the company cookers. Plum pudding and nuts completed the feast. For the next three and half weeks the men trained and exercised. The corps commander Lieutenant-General Haldane visited on 10 January. The wretched weather continued. It rained continuously and the huts were always wet.

On 27 January the battalion left for Blaireville where it was picked up by buses and moved on to Mercatel. From there they marched into brigade support at Wancourt, relieving the 1st Northumberland Fusiliers at 7 pm. The night was very quiet. The men went up to the front line as carrying and working parties. The front line had not moved since the men were last here in June. The fighting had broadly died down, with each side strengthening their lines and waiting. The British were expecting a renewed German assault on the Western Front now that the war in the east had concluded with exit of the Russians and the signing of the Treaty of Brest Litovsk. Substantial enemy troops were moving west. The only question on the mind of every British soldier was where the strike would land.

For the next two days the battalion continued in brigade support. On 30 January they relieved the 2nd Suffolks in the front line at Guemappe. There was very little enemy activity for the next few days the men spent in the front line. The occasional trench mortar round was fired at them. No casualties were recorded.

On 3 February they were relieved by the 2nd Suffolks and went into brigade support again. On 5 February the CO went off to inspect a draft of six officers and 221 men from the newly disbanded 11th King's Own, a bantam unit of the 40th Division. These men would prove to be doughty fighters. The 11th Battalion also donated their brass band to the 8th King's Own as a gift. It was gratefully received. During the morning of 6 February, these new recruits arrived in the battalion's trenches at Wancourt and were dispersed amongst the different companies. In the evening the battalion, together with its new recruits, relieved the 1st Gordons in the front line at Guemappe. The next day was quiet. However on 8 February the enemy launched a large raid on the battalion on the right of the King's Own. To support their raid, the enemy fired a heavy barrage on the battalion's positions. Four men were killed and five wounded. This was the only serious action during this spell in the front line. On 12 February they were relieved by the 2nd Suffolks and went into brigade support at Wancourt.

For the next three days the battalion was engaged in the normal carrying and working party duties. On 15 February they were back in the front line. At dawn the following day the enemy launched another big attack on the battalion on their right. It was preceded by heavy gun fire aimed at the positions held by the King's Own. It was all over in three-quarters of an hour. There were no casualties amongst the men. The next three days were very quiet.

The quiet was punctuated abruptly on 19 February when at 2 am Lieutenant Smith (one of the new arrivals from the 11th King's Own) and five men went out on a routine patrol of no man's land. They came across an enemy patrol of ten men. Leaping across a disused trench in front of them, they took two of the enemy party prisoner. They were attacked by stick bombs but escaped unharmed with their valuable prizes. The men were immediately rewarded with a fortnight's home leave. In retaliation, the enemy fired gas shells at the battalion lines, wounding four men.

On 21 February the battalion moved back to brigade support trenches at Wancourt. On 24 February it was their turn to man the front lines again. They remained here until 2 March without any serious incident being reported.

On that same day, an intelligence statement prepared for an army commanders conference indicated that there was no indication of any imminent offensive on a large scale between the River Lys and the River Scarpe, but that there was evidence of an attack being prepared on the Third and Fifth Army fronts, with the object of cutting off the Cambrai salient and drawing in the British reserves. On 10 March, the Weekly Summary of Intelligence reported that an imminent offensive on the Arras–St Quentin front had been confirmed by information gained from prisoners and by aerial intelligence, which revealed the construction of large ammunition dumps and light railways. There was, however, no hard or reliable intelligence as to when this attack would be launched. There was no doubt however about one thing – that the German forces on the Western Front had been greatly strengthened by the transfer of divisions from the east. The Germans had at least 185 divisions available to them in early March, giving them a significant advantage over the French and British forces. The British for example had fifty-five divisions in the front line in March 1918, with eight divisions in reserve to man their front line of 126 miles. The British had about 100,000 fewer men in France in 1918 than they had in 1917. The French had ninety-nine divisions available to them.

The Third Army front, on which it was expected that some of the blows would land, was strongly held. On a front of twenty-eight miles, there were fourteen divisions under the command of the new army commander, General Byng. Over 1,000 guns, of which over 400 were heavy guns and howitzers, were also available – approximately forty guns to the mile. Unfortunately, it was estimated that the Germans had probably twice this number. For the first time since 1915, the British had to prepare for a defensive battle. The basic plan was simple enough. A Forward Zone, usually organized in three lines, would generally be lightly held. These lines might not even be held continuously. Outposts would be sited so as to provide arcs of covering machine gun and rifle fire. The Forward Zone defences would simply delay the advance of the enemy. The main line of resistance would be the Battle Zone further to the rear. This too would consist of three lines – front, intermediate and rear. Special posts were prepared for all-round fire. Roughly two-thirds of the troops would normally be deployed in the Battle Zone lines.

VI Corps, in which the 3rd Division was serving, was defending a front of about 13,000 yards. The division had all three of its brigades (now made up of only three battalions each) in line, with four battalions in the Forward Zone and the remainder in the front part of the Battle Zone. General Byng's instructions to his corps commanders was that a stout fight should be made in the Forward Zone, but if an attack was made in great force, the main defence should be made in the Battle Zone.

On 2 March, the battalion moved to a new camp near Beurains where they would spend the next five days. They trained and drilled and were briefed about the latest intelligence reports. At dusk on 7 March, they moved up into brigade support at Wancourt. On 8 March, Lieutenant-Colonel Hunt relinquished command of the battalion to Lieutenant-Colonel James. Hunt had commanded the battalion for seventeen months and was moving on to a staff post at divisional HQ. For the next three days, the battalion worked tirelessly on improving the defences in and around Wancourt, Monchy and Guemappe. On 12 March they moved up to the front line. They were expecting an attack at any time. The men took up two days rations and were on special alert at all times. Extra sentries were mounted. The British guns were actively seeking targets behind the German lines. The 13th and 14th were very quiet days. Numerous night-time patrols failed to find any sight or sound of the enemy. On 16–17 March enemy artillery fire began to increase steadily. No casualties were reported amongst the battalion. On 17 March the men were relieved at dusk by the 2nd Suffolks. The battalion remained in close support, not far behind the front lines. There was some shelling overnight. Battalion HQ was positioned in cellars near to Wancourt church.

The new OC, Lieutenant-Colonel James, was rightly anxious to glean as much intelligence as possible. A party of 45 men volunteered and began to prepare for a trench raid as soon as possible to capture prisoners. Meanwhile, the shelling was increasing in tempo all the time. Before the raid could be launched, the Germans launched a massive offensive on 21 March. A huge artillery bombardment on the front of the Fifth Army around St Quentin obliterated most of the Forward Zone and led to a major breach in the British lines that threatened to separate the British and French Armies from each other.

On the front of the Third Army, the main blow was launched against IV and VI Corps by the German Seventeenth Army under General von Bülow. The main infantry assault began at 9.40 am after a punishing artillery barrage that inflicted enormous damage on the Forward Zone positions. On the VI Corps front, the main attack came up against the 59th Division holding the line around Bullecourt. By noon, the enemy was in complete possession of the Forward Zone and was beginning to press on against the rear defences. The four battalions holding the front line had practically ceased to exist. Mory, Longatte and Noreuil were all lost, along with many guns. By early afternoon, after heavy fighting and the loss of the whole of 178 Brigade, the Germans began to attack the rear trenches of the Battle Zone. A serious breach of the line looked inevitable. However, scratch units made up of transport units, pioneers, engineers and officers' servants hurriedly dispatched from HQ succeeded in holding the line. The Germans had advanced so quickly that they were now operating without the cover of their own artillery. It had been a desperately close call.

Further to the north, and on the immediate right of the 3rd Division, the 34th Division had fared slightly better than the 59th Division. It had managed to hold on to the left section of its Forward Zone and its Battle Zone, although penetrated in parts, remained nonetheless intact.

There was no serious fighting on the front held by the 3rd Division until later in the afternoon. The German bombardment here had landed on the rear areas and on the gun batteries. A series of small-scale attacks on the Forward Zone had been effectively repulsed. After a much heavier bombardment in the afternoon, the Germans launched a heavy infantry attack on the junction of the 3rd and 34th Divisions along the Sensee valley. Despite taking large casualties, the Germans managed to break through the outpost line along the front of 9 Brigade and advanced about 1,000 yards near the Cojeul. The enemy was held however at the support line.

The enemy shelling continued the following day on the front of the 3rd Division and on the 8th King's Own trenches. By the evening, the battalion was withdrawn a few hundred yards to trenches behind Wancourt, in order to conform to the withdrawal of the division on its right, which had continued to face heavy German pressure during the day. This withdrawal was completed by 4 am the following morning. A couple of hours later, the enemy opened up a heavy barrage on the recently evacuated line. By 8 am, enemy infantry were in contact with the new defensive line. Heavy losses were inflicted on the Germans with rifle and machine gun fire. The attacks against 3rd Division troops are described in the following terms by the historian of one of the attacking German divisions.

> The advance was made against strong wired trenches in which the brave defenders, unshaken and not disheartened, were standing firm. There were more heavy losses and the attack came to a standstill.

For most of the rest of the day and night, the men worked flat out on improving their new positions, converting them into as strong a defensive line as they could. The fighting was anything but finished.

On the next day, there were further infantry attacks on their line. The battalion's Lewis gunners took a heavy toll on the enemy. Two officers, Lieutenants Bailey and Hewitson, were killed whilst directing this fire. Another officer, Captain Kent, who had just joined from the 11th Battalion was also killed on 24 March. He had rushed the enemy over the open ground, throwing bombs and firing his revolver. The brunt of the German attacks fell on 8 Brigade holding the right of the 3rd Division line, where the Germans were attempting to seize the high ground at Neuville Vitasse. From here it would be possible for the enemy to threaten the front of XVII Corps in front of Arras itself. On 24 March the division held its ground.

Over the previous three days the Third Army had managed to hold on reasonably well in the face of enormous pressure. V Corps in the south had been severely shaken and had been pushed back nearly seventeen miles. But further north, in the area defended by the 3rd Division, little ground had been lost at all and Byng felt confident about maintaining his front.

The enemy shelling continued to be heavy on 25 March, but there were no more infantry assaults on the front line. The men took as much advantage as they could of this to strengthen their positions. Wire was put up. Trenches were deepened. On the night of 25 March the Third Army began another withdrawal to the south, but not on the front of the 3rd Division, which continued to hold its ground. The next two days were generally quiet for the 8th King's Own. No attacks were made against the front held by the 3rd Division. All was to change in the morning of 28 March.

At 3 am an enormous artillery barrage fell on the front held by the 3rd Division. The new offensive, codenamed 'Mars' by the Germans, was designed to break through on both sides of the Scarpe in front of Arras at the junctions of the Third and First Armies. The barrage was carefully and brilliantly executed. First, the artillery batteries were gassed. Then communication lines were shelled with long-range heavy artillery. Front and support lines were bombarded at about 4 am before a final murderous trench mortar bombardment of the front line began.

On the front of the 3rd Division, the infantry attacks were launched initially against 8 and 9 Brigades at about 5.50 am. At 6.45 am, 76 Brigade was attacked. The first waves of attackers were met by heavy fire from the British trenches. The machine guns had been kept deep underground during the artillery bombardment and now came into action to inflict grievous casualties amongst the German troops. The King's Own held its ground firmly and resolutely. But soon after 7 am, the situation began to deteriorate rapidly. Enemy infantry were seen moving up the Arras–Cambrai road in force. German soldiers began to appear behind the trenches held by 44 Brigade of the 15th Division on the left of 76 Brigade. The troops of 44 Brigade were seen to withdraw. Simultaneously, on the right of the King's Own, the left battalion of 9 Brigade was swept away by the ferocity and numerical weight of the German assault. The position of the battalion was now becoming impossible as both its right and left flanks had been breached. Enemy troops began to work around behind their front-line positions. The two companies of the King's Own in the front line were given permission to withdraw to the support lines and rejoin the two other companies in a new defensive line, which represented the rear line of the original Battle Zone. By 10 am the fighting became intense but also extremely confused. Small parties of German troops would often penetrate into parts of the front line only to be driven out again by grenades. It was impossible for the artillery to help out as no one knew exactly where the front line was at any given moment. Parties of the 1st Northumberland Fusiliers from 9 Brigade joined up with the King's Own men in trenches that were heavily congested with the dead and the dying. The enemy gradually began to envelop their right flank.

Lieutenant-Colonel James moved up to the front line to take personal command. He ordered the front line to be thinned out and a new defensive flank on the right to be formed along one of the old communication trenches. Lieutenants Allison and Brierly were placed in charge of this trench. At noon, Colonel James was killed instantly by an exploding shell that landed on his headquarters and command passed to Major Morgan. At 1 pm, the right flank began to withdraw to new positions just to the north of battalion HQ. Trench blocks were established here. As the left flank of the 2nd Suffolk's (on the left of the King's Own) was also beginning to give way, the men were ordered to retire in small groups of six men at a time over the open ground to the Neuville Vitasse Switch Line running along the eastern outskirts of the village. The withdrawal of the men was covered by Lewis gun teams, rifle fire and grenades. There were very few casualties in this manoeuvre. Second Lieutenant Adams was in charge of the rear guards.

The Neuville Vitasse Switch Line was the rear line of the Battle Zone. On arrival, the King's Own men were placed on the right of the brigade between the centre of the Cojeul valley and the village itself. The majority of the men were in front of the village. The King's Own defended their lines stoutly, repulsing repeated attacks by German troops. At 4.30 pm, a heavy artillery barrage landed on the village. The position became completely untenable. A new line of outposts was established just to the west of the village. Parties of the King's Own remained in these posts overnight.

On 29 March the heavy artillery firing continued. The enemy made repeated attempts to push through at Neuville Vitasse and other points in the line. All of these attacks were repulsed. The losses on both sides were high. By nightfall, the King's Own were still firmly in place. They were relieved that night by the Canadian 21st Battalion. The relief was complete by 4.30 am on 30 March. The men moved to billets at Riviere, about seven miles to the south-west of Arras. The men were simply dead on their feet.

The battalion casualties for the period 21–29 March were 16 officers and 480 men, a 70 per cent casualty rate. Private Edward Hoskin from Haverigg died in the initial German attack on the 28 March as did Private William Langstreth from Flookburgh. On 29 March, Private Tom Silver from Barrow was seriously wounded and died a few hours later. He was 24 years old. His platoon sergeant, writing to his parents, described him as 'a fearless and willing soldier'. Before the war, Tom had worked as a labourer at Askam Brickworks. He was also a well-known local footballer with Barrow North End FC. Acting Corporal John Brockbank from Ulverston died the same day.

On 30 March, they marched to Warluzel, a further six miles away, where they rested and cleaned up. On 1 April they marched to Liencourt and then caught buses to Dieval near Bethune, about twenty-five miles to the north. The next four days were spent reorganizing and recovering from their ordeal. At Dieval they were joined by 250 new recruits and a new commanding officer, Lieutenant-Colonel Likeman. On 7 April they marched to a new camp nearby at Marqueffles Farm where another 40 men arrived as replacements. They provided working parties for the front line and on 9 April even had time to practise making an attack through woods. With hindsight, such training must have been done largely for morale purposes as the British Army was still in the middle of the biggest defensive battle of the war. And it was not going well. The Fifth Army in the south had been driven back to Montdidier. The ground won at such cost on the Somme had all been captured by the Germans.

Worse still, the German offensive continued to gather pace. A major German attack had been launched against the British line between La Bassee Canal and Armentieres and had succeeded in driving parts of the front line back several miles. The 3rd Division would be called on to reinforce the line against further German advances. On 11 April they began marching towards Bruay en route to Bethune and the front line to the north and east of the town. The orders were cancelled while the battalion was on the road north. They were now ordered to march towards Mont Bernenchon. They marched to Petit Sains where they caught buses to the Hinges area. 9 Brigade had already been sent to the front line and came under the orders of the 55th Division, which had been successfully defending the line around Givenchy. The rest of the 3rd Division was also now transferred to XI Corps.

On 12 April 76 Brigade was ordered to move up to positions around the village of Le Hamel and the Avelette bridgehead at the junction of the line held by the 51st and 55th Divisions, about two miles to the north of Bethune. The Germans were continuing to apply serious pressure to this part of the line in the hope that it would result in a fracture of the British positions north of La Bassee Canal. The battalion was informed that it was not known whether or not there would be any troops in position for the battalion to relieve or not. If no troops were found to be occupying their designated positions on arrival, they were ordered to make good a defensive position and to hold on at all costs. When they arrived at about 6 am on 12 April no trenches or troops were found, only a few scattered half-dug posts. The line here had been held earlier by troops of 8 Brigade who had been ordered during the night to relieve the exhausted 154 Brigade of the 51st Division which had borne the brunt of the fighting over the previous three days. The men were not sure what troops, if any, were between them and the enemy, whose where-abouts were not entirely clear.

The men began to dig in and wait.

From the British perspective, the prospects for the battle ahead were bleak indeed. The Germans had made some significant advances since the attack in Flanders began on 9 April. The front line by the close of 11 April was nine miles behind the British front line of 9 April. Further movement forward could result in the separation of the First and Second Armies and the possible capture of the Channel ports. This would mean defeat and the end of the war for the British Armies in France. Thirteen divisions had already been deployed by the Germans in their Flanders attack. Intelligence reports indicated that they had as many as fourteen still in reserve ready to join the battle. The British, in contrast, had precious few additional resources to commit to the battle and such troops as were potentially available, such as the 39th Division, had already suffered terribly in the earlier fighting in March. Meagre French reinforcements (four divisions from the Somme front) were on their way north. But these troops were not being deployed in the area of the main German attacks and the French Army had not yet fully recovered from the disaster of the Nivelle offensive in April 1917 and the mutinies that followed.

The situation was therefore extremely perilous. Part of the area around Dunkirk was flooded on 12 April to try and stem the German advance. On the same day that the 8th King's Own arrived at the Flanders front, Haig issued his famous Special Order of the Day, which, whilst summarizing the general situation, contained these words of exhortation:

Many amongst us are now tired. To those I would say that victory will belong to the side which holds out the longest.

There is no course open to us but to fight it out. Every position must be held to the last man; there must be no retirement. With our backs to the wall and believing in the justice of our cause each one of us must fight to the end. The safety of our homes and the freedom of mankind alike depend upon the conduct of each one of us at this critical moment.

To many, this would have been the first intimation about how serious the situation had become. For others, it probably had some effect in helping to boost morale. But one thing was absolutely clear; 12 April was going to be one of the critical days of the war.

The line occupied by the 8th King's Own was heavily shelled at 10 am and German infantry began to press forward. Further to the north, the enemy penetrated another 2,000 yards through the lines of the 51st Division and reached as far as Robecq, capturing the entire brigade HQ of 152 Brigade. This sudden advance threatened the whole British line and the right flank of the 3rd Division in particular. The news of this breakthrough did not reach the King's Own until 11 am. The situation in front of them was far from clear. Small patrols were sent out to try and establish contact with either the enemy or British forces. Earlier, the battalion had sent two companies under Major Morgan forward to fill what was thought to be a gap in the British lines on the left, where the Germans had already penetrated. If a gap was found to exist, the two companies were to fill it and establish contact with the 51st Division. At 11.30 am, a heavy enemy barrage landed on both the front and support lines.

By 2 pm it was clear that things were not going well. Troops of the 1st Royal Scots and 2nd Royal Scots Fusiliers appeared in front of the trenches held by the King's Own. They were retreating in some disorder but dug in about 400 yards in front of the support lines held by the 8th Battalion. Trench mortar battery personnel, along with assorted Royal Engineers and soldiers of the brigade machine gun company were put under the command of Colonel Likeman and helped to extend the lines on the left, where the main threat was emerging. The two companies under Major Morgan had been deployed about 2,000 yards ahead and, together with some stragglers, had been ordered to dig in. He commanded them to hold on if they could until dark and then to withdraw back to the canal at Pont Levis.

The British retirement continued during the evening as they sought to establish a new and stronger defensible line. By midnight, the remaining companies of the King's Own, together with their newly attached comrades, were stretched out in their new lines from the Avelette bridgehead to the Locon road, forming a defensive line barring the progress of the advancing German forces, who did not attempt to exploit their successes earlier in the day. Somehow, the British lines, although forced back, had managed to remain intact. At no time on 12 April, however, did the battalion engage with enemy infantry. Major Morgan's men returned during the early hours of the morning.

On 13 April the enemy made no further successful advances. They switched their main efforts further north where they had taken ground around the Ypres salient. The King's Own lines had been reinforced by three Lewis gun teams which had been detached from tank duties. When the mist lifted during the day, enemy troops could be seen moving in front, but there was no infantry contact until later in the day. With the growing belief that the German advance had been halted, three platoons of the King's Own were sent out in full battle order in the morning to make contact with the enemy. Under Lieutenant Goddard, they advanced about 2,000 yards towards their left front and eventually made contact with soldiers from the 51st Division. But at this point they came under very heavy machine gun and rifle fire from concealed German positions along the numerous hedgerows that littered the flat countryside. They were ordered to stand firm and hold their ground. There was to be no withdrawal.

The men held on grimly in their very exposed positions. Lieutenant Goddard was seriously wounded, command passing to Sergeant Rivett. Here they stayed until about 4 pm when Sergeant Rivett was ordered to try and get his few remaining men out. They had become virtually surrounded, but managed to fight their way back to the lines. The men began arriving under cover of darkness. Only eleven men returned out of a party of over a hundred. The total casualties in the battalion on 13 April were one officer and 155 men. One of these was Private Isaac Thursfield from Barrow.

The battalion remained in the front line until the evening of the following day when they began to be relieved by soldiers of the 4th Division. They went into the brigade support lines around Sevelingue where they were to remain until 23 April. Nine men were wounded on 21 April when a German shell landed on battalion HQ. They moved up to the divisional reserve lines near Annezin and Vendin during the evening of 23 April. Here they were subjected to intermittent fire from gas and high explosive shells. Three men became casualties on 24 April. On the 26th they were back in their old positions around Hinges. By now the force of the German advance had focused on the capture of Mont Kemmel to the north. Around Hinges, things were much quieter.

The King's Own held the front line until 4 May. For much of that time they came under artillery fire, but it was sporadic rather than persistent. In the early hours of 2 May, a raiding party of 24 men under Second Lieutenant Ashley attacked enemy outposts on the eastern side of the canal near Hingette Bridge. The enemy sentries spotted the attack and the men came under heavy machine gun fire from two guns. There were many casualties. The men made two attempts to capture their objectives but both failed under impossibly heavy fire. Lieutenant Ashley's body was never found. One of the men killed was Sergeant James Warriner of C Company. James was 28 years old and came from Barrow. On 4

May at 2.30 am the line moved forward about 150 yards over the canal after a successful attack by the 1st Gordon Highlanders further to the left. One German officer and forty-four men were taken prisoner. In retaliation, the Germans subjected the men to continuous gun fire all day. But they made no attempt to recover the lost positions.

Early in the morning of 5 May, the men were relieved and marched back to reserve trenches near Chocques. For the next few days the men worked on digging new trenches and dugouts. They had the luxury of visiting the YMCA baths nearby.

On 8 May they were once again in the front line around Locon on the right of the brigade front. It would be a very quiet tour of duty and they were eventually relieved on 12 May by the 2nd Suffolks. The great German spring offensive was effectively over. Enormous casualties, problems over supply and heroic resistance by the British forces had brought it to an end. Over the next few weeks, the initiative would gradually return to the Allies.

In the mean time, the battalion would spend the next three months holding this section of the line. It would be a largely uneventful time. The German artillery kept up a harassing fire on the British, frequently using gas shells, but there were no further major actions on this section of the front. When the battalion was not in the front line around Locon or Hinges, it was employed on endless carrying and working parties. Divisional baths at Lapugny were keenly looked forward to and the men took whatever rest they could. They organized football and boxing competitions. When they were not in the front line, the battalion would either be in divisional reserve at Chocques or in brigade reserve and support lines near the canal at Hinges.

On 2 June, the battalion provided the men for a trench raiding party near Locon. Preceded by an effective artillery barrage, the men rushed the 40 yards of no man's land and entered the German trenches. There was no wire in front of the German lines except for a single strand of telephone wire, stretched tight about 18 inches above the ground. It was easily cut. Two prisoners were taken. The party came under machine gun fire, which wounded eight men and killed another. It was silenced by Lewis guns. It was all over in half an hour.

On 3 June, Colonel Likeman went on leave to England and command of the battalion passed to Major Perry of the 2nd Royal Scots. Major Perry would take the battalion through to the end of the war.

On 10 July, a fighting patrol of ten men under Sergeant White left the front line trenches at Hinges and crept forward alongside a track through a corn field in no man's land as far as an enemy machine gun post. The gun had been causing a serious nuisance to the men for several days. They found the post unoccupied. However they spotted several other machine gun nests nearby and Sergeant White decided to attack these instead. Under cover of Lewis gun and rifle fire, four men including Sergeant White rushed the nearest post. It was full of Germans. Two prisoners were taken and the rest disposed of by grenades. White himself was seriously wounded in this attack and was carried back to his own lines under heavy fire. He died later of his wounds.

At the beginning of August, the battalion was in divisional reserve at Chocques. They were employed laying new signal cables and training for the new offensive operations being planned by Haig and his army commanders. The tide of the war was about to change decisively in favour of the Allies. On 8 August, the British at Amiens had won a decisive victory over the Germans, forcing the enemy back several miles. Ludendorff labelled 8 August the 'black day' of the German Army in the war. The French had also begun the Second Battle of the Marne, which had forced the Germans to retreat at Chateau Thierry. Large American forces were beginning to assemble and had enjoyed considerable success against the Germans in the St Mihiel salient south of Verdun.

To follow up the success at Amiens, Haig and Foch, the new Allied Supreme Commander, planned to launch a major offensive against the Germans around Albert and to the south. The French Tenth Army, holding the line to the south, would join in a large-scale offensive with the British Fourth and Third Armies that would maintain the pressure on the Germans, forcing them to give up the ground they had fought so hard to reclaim from the British in the spring offensive.

The 3rd Division began to move south to take part in these operations on 4 August, when the 8th King's Own marched to Lozinghem and was found billets in huts in the grounds of the Chateau. On 6 August they marched in the afternoon to Ames. The division became part of Haig's GHQ Reserve.

On 10 August the King visited the area and the men lined up along the Bellamy–Erfay road to cheer him as he passed by. They continued to train for their role in the new attack. But they were still able to put the impending operations out of their minds for short periods of time. On 11 August the men took part in a battalion boxing competition.

On 14 August they moved again to Pernes where they caught the light railway to Warlincourt. The men then marched to a new camp at Beaudricourt. The weather was hot and fine. On 16 August they were inspected by both Major-General Deverell and Brigadier-General Porter, commanding 76 Brigade. On the same day, the division was transferred into VI Corps Reserve, and their training intensified. On 19 August they moved to Berles au Bois where they camped out in the orchards. The trees would have been heavy with the late summer fruit. The next day they moved into their assembly positions for the attack, which was due to go in the next day at dawn. The initial assault would be launched by the Guards and the 2nd Division. The 3rd Division would pass through the troops of the 2nd Division, once they had secured the first-line objectives, and seize the line of the Albert–Arras railway. The infantry would be supported by tanks, field guns and long-range heavy guns firing from the north.

A thick fog descended on the battlefield as zero hour – set for 4.55 am – approached. The tanks lost their way and few arrived to support the infantry. None were seen by the soldiers of the 3rd Division during the battle. The advance at 4.55 am was entirely successful. Resistance only came from a few machine guns and they were quickly dealt with. The real difficulty for the men was to maintain direction amidst the fog and smoke of the battlefield.

The 8th King's Own were acting in support to 8 Brigade and the 1st Royal Scots Fusiliers. Their objective was the railway embankment at Courcelles. The battalion assembled near Adinfer Wood and at 5 am moved from there to Ayette. The battalion advanced behind the Royal Scots Fusiliers and a crushing artillery barrage and reached their objective on the railway embankment at 08.30 where they began to dig in. Patrols pushed out to the east of the railway line, but no further major advance was attempted that day. Their new line came under increasingly heavy artillery fire as the day continued and the fog lifted. Twelve men were killed in this attack and eighty-five were wounded. The battalion took thirty prisoners and thirty machine guns. By nightfall, the battalion was pulled out of the front line and moved back into trenches behind Courcelles.

The 22nd was another hot day. This time there was no fog. The Third Army was ordered to stand fast, while the Fourth Army to its right completed its capture of the salient between the Somme and the Ancre and the town of Albert itself. German counter-attacks on the front held by 8 Brigade were repulsed with heavy enemy losses. The battalion's Church of England padre, Captain Lendrum, was killed by artillery fire while trying to bring in the bodies of those killed at Courcelles.

The next day, the Third Army resumed offensive operations. Overall, the seven divisions employed advanced up to 4,000 yards on an eleven-mile front, capturing a number of villages. However, the centre of the front opposite the Third Army around Achiet le Grand was strongly held by the Germans. Further prospects for maintaining the advance depended on breaking the resistance of the enemy at this point. A frontal attack was deemed to be too risky. Casualties would be too high. Therefore V Corps on the right and VI Corps on the left would attack it in flank by breaking through the German lines on either side of it. The 3rd Division was selected to capture the village of Gomiecourt two miles to the north of Achiet le Grand and on the high ground overlooking the village. Having captured the village, the division was ordered to move on to Sapignies–Ervillers. The greatest importance was attached to the capture of Gomiecourt. Once it had been captured, the 2nd Division was to pass through the 3rd and move on Ervillers.

Zero was set for 4 am. Under a powerful creeping barrage of shrapnel and high explosive, supported by forty machine guns, 76 Brigade moved forward to Gomiecourt. Twelve tanks provided close support to the infantry, and although they arrived too late to support the initial attack, provided useful help in mopping up. The 8th King's Own and 2nd Suffolks led the attack over 1,000 yards of open, flat countryside. A and D Companies were in the first line of the attack, with C and B in support. It was completely successful and was made with few casualties. One officer and five men were killed, along with twenty-nine other casualties. Three hundred prisoners were taken, along with seventy machine guns, two heavy trench mortars and five field guns.

At 11.30 am, the Highland Light Infantry of the 2nd Division passed through the newly captured village and launched their attack on Ervillers. By 1 pm, the village had been taken, after stiff resistance had been overcome. Heavy German machine gun fire checked any further advance from Ervillers. In fact this was the pattern of the day's fighting. The main resistance was provided by German machine gun crews. Their infantry put up little fight at all and quickly surrendered when they had the chance to do so.

Achiet le Grand was captured on 23 August and the German main line of resistance, the railway line itself, had been overrun. The British line had moved forward another 2,000–3,000 yards along a broad front of 6 miles. Over 5,000 prisoners were taken by Third Army.

The fighting continued over the next few days as the British continued to force the Germans to retreat further. By 27 August the troops had advanced the line another three to four miles to the outskirts of Bapaume and the village of Vaux Vraucourt to the north.

The 8th Battalion held the line at Gomiecourt until the evening of 24 August when they were withdrawn to the area around Ayette and went into corps reserve. On 26 August they moved up to trenches east of Hamlincourt to support the 1st Guards Brigade who were seeking to take St Leger Wood. In fact the Germans had already retired from their positions in the wood and so the Guards were able to move up in the afternoon without any opposition and take up positions on its eastern edge. The Guards made further progress on 27 August, although not as much as on previous days. The battalion, still tasked with providing close support to the Guards, moved up to Mory on 27 August and by dusk on 28 August had relieved the Coldstream and Irish Guards in the front line west of the village of Ecoust. The scorching hot weather of the previous few days had become cold and wet.

Information received by captured prisoners revealed that the enemy was about to evacuate Bapaume. If these rumours turned out to be untrue, then another attack would have to be prepared. During the night of 28–29 August the Germans did in fact move back behind Bapaume, retreating two to three miles. North of Bapaume, the Germans still manned their defences in strength.

On 29 August patrols of the 8th King's Own pushed into Ecoust itself, and one patrol of ten men moved close to the southern edge of Langatte. The enemy trenches were strongly held. Five men were wounded and two were missing after the patrol came under heavy small arms fire. However, the battalion was able to move up another 2,000 yards, and spent the rest of the evening and night consolidating its new trench line. It came under heavy artillery fire from the direction of Noreuil. One officer and two men were killed and twenty men wounded. The following morning, the 2nd Suffolks and 1st Gordons launched a combined attack designed to clear the enemy out of Langatte and Ecoust. At 5 am, under a heavy barrage, the troops captured their objectives, but were later forced to retire in the afternoon under pressure from an effective German counter-attack. D Company was sent up to support the Gordons and fill a gap in the line that had opened up between them and the 2nd Suffolks. The rest of the battalion was withdrawn that evening to support lines around Mory. On the following day, D Company joined the Gordons in a second and this time successful attack on Ecoust. No casualties were recorded and later that night, the men rejoined the rest of the battalion, which was preparing to attack Noreuil the following morning.

The battalion launched a pre-dawn raid on 1 September against the German trenches at Noreuil, capturing the line to the west of the village, and taking over 30 prisoners along with a number of machine guns. Later patrols pushed into the village itself, gathering further useful intelligence. On 2 September the men consolidated their new positions under sporadic but not very effective artillery fire. On the same day, 8 Brigade pushed on ahead and took Ecoust and the approaches to Lagnicocurt. German resistance was much more determined. That day the German lines were threatened by significant success achieved by the Canadians to the north and the Australians to the south who succeeded in capturing Peronne. The fighting on the Third Army front intensified as a result, as the enemy fought to hold on to an effective line of defence. Their position had however become impossible. On the night of 2/3 September, the Germans pulled back to the line of the Canal du Nord, some six miles in the rear. The persistent pressure of the Allies was now beginning to yield results.

Whilst this retreat was under way, the 8th King's Own were pulled out of the front line. At midnight on 2 September they withdrew to support trenches at Moyenville, arriving at dawn on the 3rd. They were now part of corps reserve and could enjoy a few days rest and recuperation. On 6 September, after a four-hour march in the hot sunshine, they arrived at new billets in La Bezique Wood near Humbercamp. The huts were small and overcrowded. The men spent the following day improving their new homes. The weather turned. The night was heavy with thunderstorms and rain. The battalion remained at Humbercamp until 12 September when they moved into support trenches at Behagnies. They were still in corps reserve. They continued to train for open warfare. On 15 September they moved again to Fremicourt, to old huts and dugouts south-east of the village. They were bombed during the night by enemy aircraft without any casualties.

The following day, they replaced 1st King's Royal Rifle Corps in divisional reserve in Beaumetz. Battalion HQ was in the catacombs under the village church. For the next ten days, the men stayed at Beaumetz, training and providing working and carrying parties.

On 26 September the battalion moved up to assembly positions to the north of Havrincourt. It had been decided that, in order to exploit the new situation brought about by the retreat of the Germans over August and September, the French, British and American Armies should launch a series of coordinated offensives. The exhaustion of the German soldiers displayed over the previous two months and their clear shortage of reserves held out the prospect of a decisive action, which could bring about the end of hostilities. The French and American Armies would commence this new phase of operations with a major attack between the Meuse and Reims in the south on 26 September. Operations would then be taken up by the British Third and First Armies on 27 September. Operations on each of the next two days would also begin in Flanders and on the Somme. The British Armies under Haig were to break through the Hindenburg Position on the St Quentin–Cambrai front.

VI Corp's task was to capture the Flesquieres Ridge and clear the Hindenburg support lines, which ran across its front of advance. 76 Brigade had the job of securing the division's second objective, which included the village of Flesquieres itself and a central section of the Hindenburg Line beyond it. It would pass through the first objectives, which were to be secured by 8 and 9 Brigade. Overall, the division was given the job of advancing nearly 3,000 yards against strongly held German positions.

The attack of 8 and 9 Brigades began at 5.20 am on 27 September and, although both met heavy resistance, succeeded in crossing the Canal du Nord and taking the first line of objectives. At zero hour, the 8th King's Own moved up in artillery formation to within 400 yards of the British front line. It did so under heavy machine gun fire. The battalion passed through 8 Brigade at about 7 am. After some very hard fighting and with the help of several tanks, it succeeded in passing over the Hindenburg support line and through to the eastern side of Flesquieres village. Here the men came under heavy fire from artillery over open sites at close range as well as small arms fire from a shattered sugar factory on its left flank. There were many critical moments in the advance when it looked like the men would have to retire under the weight of enemy fire. But they managed to hold on in bitter close-quarters combat, where the actions of individual section, platoon and company commanders were to be crucial. During the attack, the men came up against a string of heavily reinforced concrete machine gun nests that ran through the village. Most of the officers had become casualties. The initiative passed on to the non-commissioned officers of the battalion to press on the attack.

One of these men was Corporal Thomas Neely of 15 Platoon, D Company. Neely was one of the bantams from 11th King's Own, which had transferred to the 8th Battalion in February. He was 21 years old and came from the Wirral. Before the war he had worked at Bibby's Mills, cattle food manufacturers. He had originally joined the bantam battalion of the Cheshire Regiment in September 1914, but had been transferred to the King's Own later in the war. He was an inspiring soldier. He had won the Military Medal in July 1918 for his part in the trench raid led by Sergeant White. He had been given home leave to England and had only returned to the battalion on 26 August.

Neely, on his own initiative and under point-blank fire from machine guns, dashed out with two other men and rushed the enemy posts. He killed the occupants and captured three machine guns, which had been holding up the advance. Thomas had only just started. Not content with this act of extraordinary bravery, before the day was out, he had rushed two other strong points single-handed, killing or capturing all of the defenders. He was immediately promoted to the rank of lance-sergeant. He was tragically killed three days later, leading another attack at Rumilly. He is buried at Masnieres Cemetery near Cambrai. For his bravery, Thomas was awarded a posthumous Victoria Cross. His medal was presented to his parents at a private reception at Buckingham Palace in February 1920. Thomas's VC was the only one awarded to the battalion during its service in France.

Sergeant George Inman and Private John Ireland from Ulverston were both killed in the fighting on 27 September. So was Private Thomas Smith from Barrow.

Later, the 62nd Division passed through the lines of 76 Brigade and pressed home an attack on Ribecourt. Eventually, Bourlon Ridge was taken, along with 800 prisoners, 200 machine guns and a number of guns and trench mortars. Three officers of the battalion were killed and five wounded. No mention is made in the war diary of losses to the men, but they must have been very heavy indeed, probably in the order of around 200.

On 27 September, the battalion was relieved by the 2nd Suffolks in the evening and moved back to Havrincourt to rest and reorganize. The following day, VI Corps and the Third Army continued to advance. By the end of the day they had moved forward between 2,000 and 5,000 yards, reaching as far as the Schelde Canal. A breach six miles deep and twelve miles wide had been forced in the German defences over the previous forty-eight hours – in lines that had been considered so strong they could be held indefinitely. The position was so bleak that by the end of the day Ludendorff had informed Hindenburg that Germany would have to sue for peace. The German Army was at breaking point. Allied tactics of maintaining maximum pressure all along the front were beginning to pay off.

On 30 September the battalion returned to the support lines east of Ribecourt. On 1 October, the battalion attacked Rumilly and the ground east of the village. The men left their positions at Ribecourt at 2.15 am and finally reached their assembly positions at 6.02 am. The guides had taken them to the wrong place by mistake. The barrage opened just as the men were getting into position. C and D Companies were in the front line. By 9.15 am, the village and all the other objectives had been taken. It had been a hard fight. Having taken the southern end of the village, the men had come under very heavy fire and had to make a partial withdrawal so that the village could be bombarded again by the British guns. German troops had managed to penetrate into the narrow streets and houses as soon as the original British barrage had passed over. It was only later in the evening that the village was secured. Four officers had been wounded and over

130 men were casualties. One of the dead men was Corporal G Holmes from Barrow. George had won the Military Medal with the 11th Battalion at Cambrai in the fighting for Bourlon Wood the previous November. He was originally from Troutbeck, but had lived in Barrow for several years, working for the Barrow Carting and Trading Company. Also amongst the dead that day was Private John Willshaw of Holly Terrace, Windermere. He had joined the King's Own in September 1914 – one of the original Kitchener's Men. Private David Round from Barrow also died in the attack of 1 October. He was 22 years old. In the evening the battalion was relieved by the 2nd Suffolks.

Over the next few days, there was little movement on the front of the Third Army, as the Germans held on strongly to their positions on the Schelde Canal. Progress by the Fourth Army to the south on 3 October, however, forced the Germans to retire behind the canal and the Hindenburg support line on 5 October. That evening, the battalion returned to the trenches at Rumilly, in divisional reserve, where they were under orders to move at short notice to support 9 Brigade.

At dawn on 8 October the division attacked alongside the 2nd Division and sought to advance two miles into the German lines, taking the villages of Seranvillers, La Targette and Forenville. The 3rd Division's attach was led by 9 Brigade, with 76 Brigade and the 8th King's Own in close support. The advance met with initial success, but the enemy was determined to regain any ground lost. Counter-attacks forced the British back. Bitter fighting ensued. In the evening, the 8th King's Own entered the fight. After a fresh 30 minute barrage, the men went forward in the fading light with the 1st Gordons and took the village of Seranvillers. All of the other objectives were taken. The British were successfully wearing down the German rear guards as the enemy continued its retreat to the east.

On 9 October, the battalion moved back into corps reserve at Havrincourt, where they enjoyed hot food and baths. On 12 October a draft of 240 men arrived to strengthen the battalion. Most of these men were under 19. On 14 October the battalion marched via Ribecourt to Marcoing where they billeted in houses and cellars. For the next five days, as the Third Army continued its steady advance, the battalion was engaged in battlefield clearance work, salvaging equipment and stores for reuse in future operations. They helped bury the dead of both sides. On 19 October they moved eastwards themselves, in pursuit of the retreating German Army. They were gearing up for their last major action of the war. On 20 October the battalion was stationed at Quievy. It was wet and cold. They remained here until the 22nd.

VI Corps was to move forward another three miles and take the villages of Romeries and Escarmain and get as far across the St Georges stream as possible. Zero hour was set for 3.20 am. The attack was a complete success. The German defenders were caught by surprise and the men of the 1st Gordons leading the attack of 76 Brigade succeeded in entering Romeries. At 12.10 pm, the 8th King's

Own pressed on the attack, passing through the village and carrying the advance across the stream on the east side of Escarmain. At 3 pm, 9 Brigade passed through 76 Brigade and took the final objective unopposed. The battalion finally dug in on the line Escarmain–Beaudignies. Seven officers and 103 men had been wounded, seventeen men killed and one person was missing. In the evening they were relieved by soldiers from 9 Brigade.

This action at Romeries would prove to be the last serious action in which the battalion was engaged in the Great War. They stayed in and around Romeries and Escarmain until 27 October, when they took over front-line outposts beyond Ruesnes. There was no action for the twenty-four hours they were there and they moved back again to reserve trenches at Cattenieres, where they stayed until 3 November. On 4 November they were back in Romeries, where they had lectures, sports and training duties to perform. On 8 November they moved up to Frasnoy and were put to work on improving the lines of communication. They laboured on the roads. They helped lay new signal cables. On 10 November they moved up to the village of La Longueville, three miles east of Bavais, arriving just as it was getting dark.

The next morning, the Armistice was signed. The band of the battalion, using the instruments given them by the 11th Battalion, played a concert in the village square at 11 am and again in the afternoon from 2 till 4 pm. The men continued to work on the road network for the next few days. They were allowed to play football and other sports in the afternoons. The band continued to put on performances in the village square. On 12 November the officers met for a celebration dinner in the mess at battalion HQ. Their commanding officers, Deverell and Potter paid them visits on the 13th. The war had ended quietly for the 8th King's Own.

For the next three weeks, the battalion moved steadily towards the German border. It was to form part of the army of occupation. On 11 December it entered Germany and spent the night at Krombach. Over the next few days it marched into billets at Turnich-Balkhausen, where it would spend the next three months. The battalion marched into every German town and village it passed with bayonets fixed and flags flying. The men performed guard and sentry duties, but no incident of any importance is recorded in the war diary for this period.

On 6 February, the first men left for demobilization. By the end of the month, 130 men had begun their journey back to England. By March, the battalion had moved into billets in Cologne. On 10 March, 22 officers and over 300 men were transferred to the 16th Lancashire Fusiliers. By the end of March, another 80 men had gone home.

By April, the battalion, now just a small cadre, had moved to Brauweiler. More men were returning home every day. The final moments of the battalion are not recorded. For this battalion, just like the 7th, there would also be no triumphant homecoming, no march through the streets of Barrow with bands playing and people cheering. When the end came, the battalion quietly faded from sight. It had been raised with the sole purpose of fighting the Germans. With the job done, the survivors came home quietly in dribs and drabs, to the delight of their families and friends. They returned with extraordinary stories to tell, and with the knowledge that they had played their part in the greatest victory of British arms in our nation's history.

Chapter 5

The 11th Battalion

The bantams take shape

Kitchener's initial appeal for men to enlist in his new army had brought forth an explosion in recruitment. In the last five months of 1914, nearly 1,200,000 men came forward to join the colours. Four new service battalions of the King's Own had been formed to accommodate this surge of new recruits from north Lancashire. These four new battalions joined the two territorial and two regular battalions on active service.

In fact so many men had volunteered that the physical standards each recruit had to meet before he could join up had been raised as early as 10 September 1914. Quite simply, there were not enough arms, accommodation or uniforms to go around. In October, the height restrictions were reduced to 5 foot 5 inches and then in November to 5 foot 3. The heavy losses amongst the regular army in 1914 and then the further losses in spring 1915 had resulted in increased pressure for fresh manpower. The army was desperate for more men.

Recruitment was, however, beginning to stagnate. News of the terrible fighting, and the onset of trench warfare had reduced the flow of new recruits. Between November 1914 and June 1915, an average of 125,000 men enlisted in the army and territorial force each month. But recruitment varied from month to month. In February, only 87,000 men came forward. Kitchener's appeal in May 1915 for an extra 300,000 men fell largely on deaf ears. The May figures were 10,000 above the average, but in June they fell 10,000 below. The mood of August and September 1914 had long past.

The government's initial response was the National Registration Act, which required every man and woman between the ages of 15 and 65 to register their trade with local boards. This information was then passed on to the recruiting offices in each district. Certain trades, known as 'reserved occupations', were created which exempted those from any military enlistment. The Act was not an exclusively military measure, but it was in truth a halfway stage to full conscription, which was to come into effect in March 1916. The Act certainly helped the local recruiting offices to be more systematic in their efforts as they had proper and reliable information on the pool of possible new recruits. It was supplemented by the 'Derby Scheme' which the newly appointed Director General of

Recruiting, Lord Derby, instigated in October 1915. Under this scheme, men were enabled to attest for military service and became liable for subsequent call-up if the need arose. Between October and December over 2 million men attested for military service in this way.

In the Furness area, like everywhere else, recruitment had certainly slowed down during the spring of 1915. In June, for example, only eleven new recruits joined the King's Own. But it was to pick up again as the result of the establishment of the so-called bantam battalions in the early months of 1915. Arthur Bigland, the MP for Birkenhead, had been impressed by the efforts of four Durham miners to enlist in the Cheshire Regiment in December 1914. They had travelled across the north of England trying to enlist in any regiment that would take them. They had failed to meet the standard height requirement, and had therefore been rejected, but in all other respects were considered fit and healthy. Bigland, who chaired the local Birkenhead Recruiting Committee, felt that this was a waste of manpower and lobbied the War Office for permission to recruit a battalion of under-sized men. Bigland was summoned to see Sir Henry MacKinnon, the GOC of Western Command, who told him that Kitchener was interested in his idea and that he should consider raising a special battalion of the Cheshires, made up of men who did not meet the Army's minimum height requirement. Recruitment began shortly thereafter. The 35th Division, known as the first bantam division, quickly came into being in the early summer of 1915, made up entirely of these small, stocky soldiers. Most of these men came from the industrial heartlands of Britain.

Plans for a second bantam division soon came into fruition. As part of these plans, recruitment for a bantam battalion of the King's Own began in the summer of 1915. Adverts began appearing in the local newspapers in July 1915, addressed to the 'loyal men of Lancashire'. A new battalion of the King's Own was being raised, to be known as the 11th Battalion. Applicants had to be at least 5 feet tall, have a chest measurement of 33 inches, fully expanded, and be between the ages of 19 and 40. Ex-soldiers would also be accepted up to the age of 45. The new recruits were promised they would be kept together and trained at Lancaster. Notices appeared right across the regiment's traditional recruiting grounds of Barrow, Ulverston, Lancaster, Fleetwood, Morecambe, Millom, Garstang and Dalton.

Over July and August, the new battalion began to take shape. There are no surviving records to indicate how many of these new recruits to the regiment came from the Furness area, but it is probable that at least two hundred or more would have done so. The flock of new recruits from the Furness area were originally looked after by a local retired officer from Lancaster, Major F V Churchill, until the arrival of its first commanding officer, Lieutenant-Colonel Priestley. Every effort was made to keep the men comfortable in a collection of huts and tents in Coulston Road field behind the regimental depot. One of the first recruits to join the new battalion was Harry Stansfield.

In an interview given many years later, Harry recalled those first few days.

The place was bedlam. Groups of soldiers and civilians mixed together were being drilled on every patch of open space inside and out. They were so mixed up, I was given two medicals and two sets of uniforms. We were well received by the regulars at the depot who worked hard enough on our training that we won the regimental prize cup for general smartness at our passing out parade eight weeks later. Our drill sergeant was a Liverpool Irishman, an amusing character who said we would never be sent abroad as we wouldn't be able to see over the parapet. How wrong he was.

In September, this second bantam division, the 40th, started to assemble at Aldershot. It was made up of bantam battalions from Scotland, England and Wales. By this time in the war, the uniform shortages of last summer had been addressed. The men at least looked like soldiers. But there were other real difficulties facing these new recruits. As the division began its training programme, problems soon emerged. By the New Year, it was clear that drastic action would be needed if the division were ever to be ready for overseas service. 119 Brigade was made up of Welsh soldiers who were generally considered to be fit for active service. However, in the battalions making up 120 and 121 Brigades, it was a very different story. The general officer commanding the division, Major-General Ruggles-Brise, took the view that many of the soldiers in these two brigades were not even fit enough to be trained, let alone fight. They were undoubtedly brave and committed men. But their bodies were just not strong enough. He therefore instigated a radical programme to weed out those men who were simply not going to make the grade.

The 11th King's Own was one of the battalions of 120 Brigade. It was in a better state than the others. Two of the battalions in 120 Brigade which had joined the division at Aldershot were disbanded: the 13th Cameronians and the 12th South Lancashires. The fit men from this latter battalion were transferred to the 11th King's Own and two new battalions – which were not bantam units – joined the brigade, bringing it up to its full fighting strength. The other bantam battalion in the brigade was the 14th Highland Light Infantry (HLI). The two new battalions were the 13th East Surreys and the 14th Argyle and Sutherland Highlanders. The same pattern repeated itself with 121 Brigade. Only two of its original battalions survived the cull and it was reinforced by two other battalions whose soldiers who met the Army's original height and fitness standards. As two-thirds of the battalions in the division were bantam units, the division was regarded by the Army as a bantam division.

The division remained at Aldershot until December, when it moved to Blackdown Barracks in Surrey to complete its training and equipment. Many of the men were allowed home to enjoy Christmas leave with their families. Conditions at their new barracks were far from perfect. The new camp at Blackdown was muddy in the winter and dusty in the warmer weather. Signalling and pioneer sections were formed in the New Year. Men were trained in bombing, and in the use of Lewis guns. A full transport section came into existence. Every man had a new rifle and was getting to know how to use it. In March, as the division assimilated its new recruits, rumours began to spread that it would be sent to Ireland to deal with the aftermath of the Easter Rising. It proved to be a false trail. The division continued to train in earnest.

Off to war

The division was inspected by the King on 25 May on Laffans Plain, a certain sign that orders to move overseas were imminent. Three days later an advanced party left Blackdown for France. On 2 June, the rest of the battalion, now under the command of Lieutenant-Colonel Ritchie, left in two trains from Frimley station to Southampton where they embarked on the SS *Clementine*. A smaller party came across the Channel in the SS *Huntsman*.

The battalion arrived at Le Havre at 6 am on 3 June. The men stayed the night at a rest camp in the dock area. The following day at 4.30 pm, the battalion minus C Company went by train to Lillers, fifteen kilometres north-west of Bethune. C Company, under Major Shipley, joined them two hours later. The journey took the best part of twenty-four hours to complete. The battalion marched into its first billets that afternoon. A and B Companies were camped at Lieres, C and D at Lespesses.

The first week was spent training. The men had lectures in the morning and route marches in the afternoon. The weather has hot and dry. In the morning of 11 June, the division was moved nearer to Bethune. The 11th King's Own moved into new billets at the Orphanage in Bethune. For the next four days, the battalion continued to immerse itself in the reality of its new situation. The battalion was attached to a number of units in 15th Division, a Scottish new army outfit, for its first direct experience in the trenches near Hulloch on the Loos front. A Company was attached to 9th Black Watch; B to 8th Seaforth Highlanders; C to 7th Cameronians and D to 10th Gordon Highlanders. For the first two days, each company was split up amongst their host battalion. For the last two days, each platoon formed its own trench garrison. The battalion had its first casualty on 12 June. Private W Garsden was killed instantly by gun fire when a shell landed directly in the trench he was holding. For much of this time, their positions came under sporadic enemy fire. They certainly fired their weapons in anger for the first time in the war.

After these defining four days, the battalion moved back to billets near Bethune where the men underwent four more days of lectures, training and drill. On 20 June they were back in the trenches at Hulloch. This time the companies manned sections of the trenches as whole units, although they were still under instruction from units of 44 Brigade. On 23 June they were relieved by the 13th East Surreys. The battalion moved into billets at Sailly les Bourses.

The battalion made a good impression on the commanding officer of the 10th Gordons. He wrote:

> In spite of the most adverse weather conditions, the men have kept up a remarkably cheerful spirit and have at all times done their work very well. They have been employed on patrol duty, wiring, digging, sentry duty, signalling, machine gun work and bombing and I trust they will benefit from the experience gained. They have seen two mines fired and have been shelled, trench mortared and rifle grenaded. I am glad to say they have only had one serious casualty. Four others have been slightly wounded.

On 24 June, the battalion moved to Bruay, where it continued to train and prepare for the time when it would take responsibility for a section of the line. On 4 July, the men moved to billets in the village of Petit Sains where it was acting as Brigade Reserve. On 11 July, the battalion moved into the front line at Maroc, relieving the 21st Middlesex of 119 Brigade, on the infamous Double Crassiere. This was an enormous slag heap formed from the pit spoil of the nearby coal mines. It projected into the British lines and was keenly contested by both sides because of the advantage of observation it conferred. In fact one end was held by the Germans and the other by the British. Underneath it tunnellers from both sides were busy laying mines. Two platoons of A Company were in the front line, with two in support. Another platoon from C Company joined them in the firing line. The rest of C Company formed a special bombing party to occupy the Crassiere itself. B and D Companies were in reserve.

This first tour of duty was a lively one, full of menace and violence. There would be no slow introduction for the bantams. The battalion came under sustained artillery fire on 13 July, with several direct hits collapsing the trenches in many places. Enemy trench mortars kept up a steady rate of fire too, as did the snipers and machine guns. At night the men were employed repairing the damage. Others were sent out into no man's land to erect more barbed wire. The 14th was quieter, but there was still intermittent shellfire throughout the day. In the evening, the battalion opened Lewis gun fire on a ruined house 800 yards away which was suspected to be housing several enemy snipers. The trenches came under much heavier fire again on the following day. Thirteen men became casualties before the battalion was relieved by the 14th Argyle and Sutherland Highlanders on 15 July. The men moved back to Petit Sains and into brigade reserve. At this time, seven new subalterns joined the battalion, Lieutenants Sternberg, Ashburner, Moon, Pepper, Ellis, Harris, Cook and Bradbury.

As brigade reserve, the battalion was required to provide working and carrying parties for the men in the front line. Every night, the men were busy. On 22 July they were back again in the front line this time in the Calonne sector further to the north, relieving the 12th South Wales Borderers (SWBs), another bantam battalion of 119 Brigade. Three companies manned the front line with one in reserve. This sector was not as active as Maroc. Eight men were listed as casualties over the next eight days in the firing line and the battalion was eventually relieved on 30 July by the 12th SWBs and marched back to Les Brebis in brigade reserve. The battalion remained there for the next four days and continued to train.

Their next spell in the front line began on 4 August, where they went back into the right sector on the Loos front, near the Double Crassiere, relieving the 13th Yorkshires. This time two companies were in the firing line, with a special party of bombers occupying the British end of the Crassiere. Here they would spend the next seven days. There was constant enemy activity for much of this time. German snipers and rifle grenadiers were particularly busy. The battalion suffered 39 casualties during this spell of duty: 11 men were killed and 28 wounded. This rate of loss had, by this stage of the war, become accepted as the standard 'wear and tear' of front-line duty, even in a sector like Loos, where the British trenches were deep and well constructed. The battalion was simply occupying its positions. It did not mount any offensive operations at all during in the week it spent on the Crassiere. The battalion marched back to Les Brebis and went into billets, ready to support the 21st Middlesex who had replaced them in the front line.

On 20 August the battalion was sent up the line again to Calonne, where it relieved the 18th Welch. This section of the front continued to be much quieter. One man was killed and six others wounded by shellfire before they were relieved on 24 August by the 14th Argyle and Sutherland Highlanders. Before the month was out, the battalion would serve one more period of duty in the front line at Calonne, where it sustained a further eleven casualties. German artillery fire was fairly consistent throughout this period, and the men were busy most nights repairing the damage to their trenches and dugouts. But the front line at Loos remained static, as the British and Germans continued to concentrate their resources on the long-drawn-out struggle on the Somme.

September was spent in a similar routine, in and out of the front line at Loos. When the men were not directly employed in front line duties they were billeted at Les Brebis, in either brigade or divisional reserve. The battalion's first offensive operation was mounted during the night of 18/19 September. One officer, Lieutenant Pritchard, and 36 men mounted a trench raid around the Maroc area of the front. The purpose of the raid was to capture some enemy soldiers and to inflict as much damage as possible on the enemy's positions in the process. Sadly, the war diary does not record the result of this historic mission, although it does state that 12 men became casualties during the period 12–19 September.

Another 'minor operation', as trench raids were frequently described, was mounted on 29 September. Under Lieutenant Moon, 24 men managed to enter the German trenches with a view to taking prisoners. The trench was blocked at one end and no Germans were discovered. The dugout was also found to be clear of the enemy. They returned empty-handed after 45 minutes without suffering any losses. September would turn out to be one of the quietest months the battalion would spend during its time in the front line. Three men were killed and fifteen wounded.

The battalion continued to serve at Loos until the end of October, when it began to move further south, eventually to take up positions at Hebuterne, at the northern end of the Somme front. October was very much like September. While the battalion occupied front trenches at Hulloch, it launched another trench raid on the Germans. This time, there was contact made. Lieutenant Cook and 11 men attacked the German lines on the night of 13/14 October. On getting halfway through the German wire, the party saw heads looking over the enemy parapet at them. Cook ordered his men to throw their grenades at the enemy and they rushed into the trench behind the exploding bombs. On entering the German trench, Cook found himself alone with four of the enemy. The remainder of his raiding party had entered the trench at a different point. He killed two of them with his revolver, shooting a third in the leg. The remaining German fled into a nearby dugout. Cook threw his last grenade into it, wounding the German soldier. Cook tried to carry the wounded soldier out of the trench but could not do so. The trench was 12 feet deep and the prisoner was simply too heavy for him to lift out on his own. Of his own men there was no sight. Cook had also been wounded in the head and knee. He gave up any thought of taking the man prisoner and managed to get back to his own lines by crawling from shell hole to shell hole. He was later awarded the MC for his action, the first to be given to an officer of the battalion. Lieutenant Sternberg was killed at Hulloch during October along with two other men.

On 27 October, the battalion marched south to billets at Bruay and on the following day to Ostreville. By 29 October they had arrived at Maisnil, where C and D Companies were billeted. A and B Companies found accommodation at nearby Neuville au Cornet. Here the men stayed until 2 November, when they began a forty-mile move south and into the front line at Hebuterne on the 14th. The men marched via Sericourt and Prouville, where they remained for a week and were issued with winter clothing. They continued their attack training. On 12 November they marched to Doullens and from there to Souastre, where they began their final preparations for front-line duties.

In the early hours of 14 November, the battalion relieved the 5th Yorks and Lancs of 49th Division in the front line. Battalion HQ was in the village itself, A, B and C Companies went into the firing line with D in support. Here they spent the next six days, in conditions that were extremely difficult. The weather was atrocious and the trenches themselves were wet and muddy. Active hostilities between the two front lines had, however, largely come to an end. There was occasional artillery fire, but no trench raids or infantry action. Six men were killed and twelve wounded over this period. Privates Walsh, Marshall and Grower were killed on 15 November when a single shell landed in their dugout.

On 20 November the battalion was relieved by the 10th East Yorks of 31st Division and moved back to billets at Coigneux. Two days later they were on the move again. On 23 November they moved to Ampliers and then the following day to Bonneville, via Doullens and Candas. On 24 November they arrived at their destination – Bussus: Busseul, between Amiens and Abbeville – where they were to remain for the next three weeks. The division had now passed to XV Corps of the Fourth Army. The battalion was being withdrawn well behind the front line to enable it to train intensively for the year ahead. It had been out for six months and had held generally the quieter sections of the front line for much of that time. It had learnt the art of trench warfare but it had not been entrusted with any role in the major campaign of 1916 – the Battle of the Somme. The other bantam division – the 35th – had taken part in the heavy fighting around Guillemont in July and August with mixed results. The issue of medical fitness of the bantams still seemed to loom large in the minds of the senior army commanders. Colonel Davidson, commanding one of the division's artillery brigades, claimed that:

> any undersized degenerate man was at this time considered to be a bantam and sent to the 35th Division, and this in the midst of the most appalling battle the world had known up to date and against the best troops in the German army.

Hardly a ringing endorsement. The division was eventually pulled out of the battle and sent to a quiet section of the Arras front to re-equip and retrain. In November an unfortunate incident took place which further added to the poor perception of the bantams. On 26 November the Germans mounted a series of raids against the trenches held by the 35th Division. It proved too much for some of the men of the 19th Durham Light Infantry. They abandoned their trenches in disarray. Twenty-four were court-martialled for a variety of offences arising from this notorious episode, including cowardice, quitting and desertion. Most were given long prison sentences; three were executed, including a sergeant and two of the lance-corporals. As a result, the staff of the division took drastic action to remedy its deficiencies. By the end of the year over 2,700 of its soldiers were returned to Britain, with their places being taken up largely from drafts drawn from dismounted cavalry regiments. The division began to lose its bantam status. Its rooster divisional emblem was replaced in the spring of 1917 by one depicting seven fives in a circle.

The 11th King's Own remained at Bussus until the middle of the month when it was ordered to move to the Somme front. The division moved partly by road and partly by rail. The battalion marched on 14 December to L'Etoile and on the following day went by train from Longpre to Morlancourt. It then marched into camp a mile north of Chippily. It remained here until Christmas Eve, continuing to train. The main priority seemed to be its living quarters. The camp was knee-deep in mud and new drains were dug as well as other improvements to the huts the men were billeted in. On Christmas Day the battalion moved to a new camp a mile north of Bray sur Somme. The following day the battalion relieved the 1st East Surreys of 33rd Division in the Bouchavesnes sector and became brigade reserve. It went into the trenches with 600 men. The division was starting a three-month tour of duty on the extreme right of the British line in France. Immediately on their right was the French 15th Division and on their left was the British 4th Division. The next few days were largely uneventful and the battalion was relieved on 31 December and moved to new billets in a camp 750 yards north of Suzanne. No casualties were reported for December.

The divisional history records the dismal state of this section of the front line.

> It consisted of a mass of shell holes; of a general sea of mud; of lesser lakes and lagoons of icy water. Trenches did not exist, except for short lengths on higher ground; of communication trenches there were none; men had to do the best they could to improve such shell holes. Looking back on those days, it is hard to realize how human beings could have existed in such conditions.

The battalions in the reserve lines had an extremely difficult time in bringing up supplies to the front. The churned-up, muddy ground was a nightmare to cross in the dark. It would take hours to cover the relatively short distances involved. The physical stamina of the men was sorely tested. Pack animals would often be left stranded in the mud and then shot to be put out of their misery. It was a depressing time for all concerned.

1917: the year of heavy fighting

On 4 January 1917, the battalion was once again in the front line, this time at Rancourt, on the northern banks of the Somme River, with two companies in the firing line, one in support and one in reserve. The shelling was considerable. It was a hazardous tour. The ground between the front-line posts needed constant patrolling as the trenches were still not continuous. The main focus of their work was on improving the conditions in the front line and in trying to keep the trenches dry in particular. Much of the work would easily be undone by an hour's rain. On 8 January the battalion was relieved by the 14th Argyles and moved to the brigade support lines behind the village of Rancourt. There would be no rest for the men. Each day they were working under the Royal Engineers, digging, carrying, and laying cables. On 12 January they were moved back to divisional reserve at Suzanne. The camp still needed major work. Trench boards were relaid and acres of mud cleared away.

The men stayed a week at Suzanne before rotating back to the front line, this time at Bouchavesnes. The trench strength now had been reduced to about 100 rifles per company, largely through ill health, especially from pneumonia. The enemy artillery was particularly active during this time, and many gas shells were fired on the battalion's new positions. On the night of 22/23 January the battalion was relieved by the 14th Argyles.

On 26 January the battalion was driven by lorries to a new camp near Albert. The next day they marched to new billets at Corbie, twelve miles to the south-west of Albert. Here the battalion was reorganized into smaller fighting units of platoon strength in preparation for its forthcoming new role in offensive operations designed to exert further pressure on the German forces in France and Flanders.

The battalion remained at Corbie until 10 February, when they moved back to the Rancourt sector. The division was replacing the 8th Division in the front line, becoming the left division of XV Corps. 119 Brigade held the front line while 120 Brigade was employed on corps fatigues. Once again, it did the labouring rather than the fighting for the division. The battalion was out day and night for the next fortnight without a break. At this time, Lieutenant-Colonel Ritchie returned home to England on sick leave. He would never serve with the battalion again. His place was taken by a regular army officer, Major Macdonald of the 2nd Royal Berkshires.

On 24 February the battalion was relieved by the 12th SWBs and moved to another wet, dilapidated campsite at Suzanne where it continued to develop its tactics and capabilities as a fighting unit. However, an outbreak of German measles amongst the men of B Company put a temporary brake on the battalion's training regime. They were to remain at Suzanne until 6 March.

Rumours were rife in the division that the Germans were about to withdraw from their positions on the Somme. They had started to dig a new defensive line – what was to become the Hindenburg Line – towards the end of October 1916. The new position would provide the Germans with a better defensive line which would be easier to hold than the positions they had been forced back to on the Somme. Towards the end of February, the Germans had started to withdraw slowly from their forward posts astride the Ancre River on the front held by the Fifth Army. At that time XV Corps, part of the Fourth Army, had been ordered to test the strength of the German defences on its front, but these were found to be strongly held. Captured prisoners revealed that a retirement to the Hindenburg Line would be made in the near future. Every unit in the Fourth Army was put on alert.

On 6 March, the battalion relieved 4th Suffolks of 33rd Division in support lines in Howitzer Wood near Rancourt. As the battalion came up the Clery–Maricourt road they came under German shell fire, causing casualties to the Lewis gun teams. On 7 March the battalion was in the front line at Rancourt. The trenches were in a very poor condition, but there was, as some compensation, very little hostile enemy activity to contend with. There was some sniping and some shelling, but it was desultory in nature and seemed designed simply to confirm the continued presence of the Germans rather than seriously inconvenience the British. It meant that the men could set about improving their own trenches without fear of losses. At night they sent out constant patrols to see if there was any sign of the expected enemy withdrawal. None could be found. In fact the biggest fear at this time was an outbreak of trench feet amongst the men.

On the night of 10/11 March they were relieved by the 14th Argyles and went into brigade reserve. The men were heavily employed on working and carrying parties. Two days later they were again in the front line. The Germans were still holding their front line in the early hours of 17 March, but the sniping stopped during the day. Patrols came under artillery fire until the late afternoon. At 4.45 pm, one officer and six men went forward and found the enemy front line abandoned. Patrols pushed out a mile or so to the Peronne–Bapaume road, finding no trace of the enemy. By 11.44 pm the whole battalion had moved forward, handing over its new positions that evening to the 14th Argyles and returned to their original front lines. The German withdrawal was slow and systematic, with strong resistance from rear guards. The British were content to follow the German withdrawal carefully and slowly rather than attempt to disrupt or interfere with it. There was no close-quarters contact between the 11th King's Own and the German forces. It was cat and mouse tactics on both sides.

Up to the middle of April, the battalion was employed on road improvement work in the area. The Germans had pursued a scorched-earth policy in withdrawing to the Hindenburg Line, denying the British the use of any of the natural or man-made resources of the territory they had given up. Roads had to be filled in, crossroads repaired, cables laid. This was the usual kind of work given to the men of the 40th Division, the work they had come to expect. They also worked on the roads behind the old British front line. For much of the rest of the month the battalion could be found working on the Vaux–Hem–Clery road on the banks of the Somme. Three men had been killed and twenty-one wounded in March, the first recorded casualties from hostile action since November.

On 16 April, the battalion left the banks of the River Somme and marched eight miles north-east to Equancourt, following on the heels of the German withdrawal. They left at 9.40 am and marched via Clery and Allaines where they stopped for their dinner for an hour at midday. They eventually arrived at Equancourt at 4.45 pm, having stopped for rests at Moislanes and Menancourt. All of these villages had been destroyed by the Germans in their March retreat. Equancourt was a smouldering ruin. The men's billets were in roofless shells of former village houses, exposed to the elements, with trench sheets their only protection from the elements. Drinking water was a scarce resource. The village wells had been poisoned and there was difficulty in carrying enough water up for the front-line troops on the congested and poorly surfaced roads.

The men had a great deal of heavy labour in front of them. The brigade front ran roughly along the eastern edge of Gouzecourt to the south-east corner of Havrincourt Wood, a distance of about three miles. The new line had to be consolidated and a main line of resistance established. An enormous amount of digging would have to be done and for the next three days the men set to it. On 20 April, they were ordered to take over from the 20th Middlesex who were in huts in Gouzecourt Wood. On the 22/23 April the battalion went into brigade reserve at Dessart Wood near Fins. The British were still pressing the German rear guards as they approached the main Hindenburg positions. The division had been tasked with taking the fortified villages of Gonnelieu, Villers Pluich and Beaucamp on 24 April. 119 Brigade would capture the ground around Gonnelieu while 120 Brigade would capture Beaucamp and Villers Pluich. The latter was the target of the 13th East Surreys while the 14th Argyles would take Beaucamp. The 11th King's Own would be in reserve.

At 2 am on 24 April the 13th East Surreys launched their attack against the village. They advanced under a heavy barrage and against heavy enemy machine gun fire. The village was reached by 5.30 am and patrols began to push out from its eastern edge. Corporal Foster won the Victoria Cross at this point in the battle when he and another soldier stormed a succession of German machine gun posts that were holding up the advance. A hundred prisoners were taken. The 14th HLI came up to support the attack and, despite a strong enemy counter-barrage, the village and a line 300 yards to the east of it remained in British hands for the rest of the day. The fighting for Beaucamp would prove to be more difficult. The attack started a little after 4 am and was met by very heavy artillery fire and a thick belt of enemy wire which the British barrage had not broken. The Highlanders entered the village at about 4.50 am. No resistance was encountered as the men moved through the village, but on emerging from the main street they came under a murderous machine gun fire from the direction of Bilhelm, a collection of farm buildings on higher ground to the north. It had not been attacked by any British troops and was able to check the advance of the Argyles. By 6.30 the position in the village had become serious. It was impossible to subdue the enemy fire from Bilhelm and a decision was made to withdraw through the village and to consolidate a couple of hundred yards further south.

Further attempts during the day to move back into the village were thwarted by strong enemy fire. It was clear that no progress could be made unless Bilhelm was successfully put out of action. That night, soldiers from the 12th KRRC of 60 Brigade, 20th Division, overcame German opposition in Bilhelm after bursting through an undefended gate into the complex, holding out the prospect for a successful attack on Beaucamp. At 1.30 am on the morning of 25 April, the 11th King's Own moved forward to the attack. Zero hour was 4.15 am, but the battalion, owing to the late arrival of its final orders, was late in getting into position.

At 5.15 am, A and C Companies pushed patrols into and beyond the village.

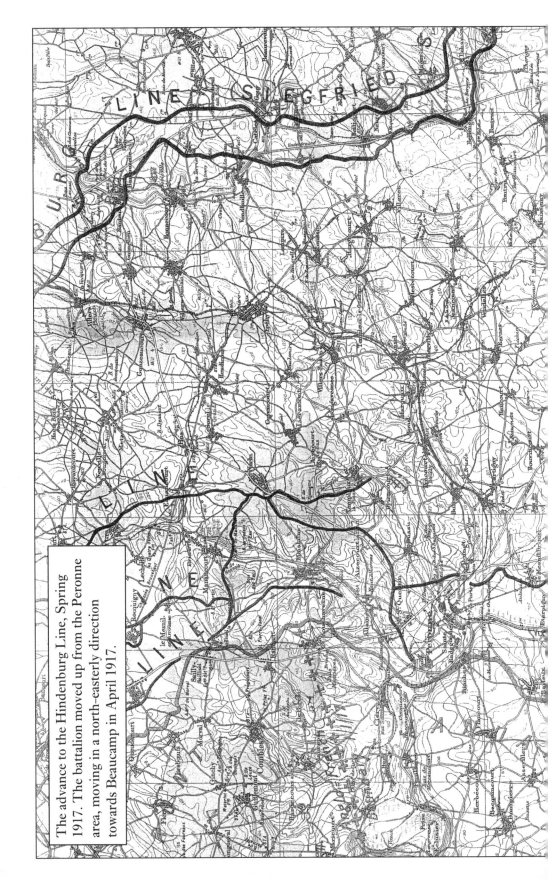

The advance to the Hindenburg Line, Spring 1917. The battalion moved up from the Peronne area, moving in a north-easterly direction towards Beaucamp in April 1917.

The village was unoccupied. The battalion moved up and through the village and began to dig in on its final objectives – an outpost line east of the village – at 05.30. Here they remained for the rest of the day until they were relieved by the 21st Middlesex at 4.50 am on 26 April. Two wounded officers of the Argyles were found sheltering amongst the ruins. They were patched up and sent to the casualty clearing station. The new positions were subjected to heavy artillery and trench mortar fire for most of the day and night. But the men held on. Private Walter Foley who had joined the battalion in Barrow but was originally from Derby was killed during the attack on Beaucamp, as was Private Edward Roberts. Edward came from Wrexham but he too had enlisted with the King's Own in Barrow. One of the casualties during this spell of fighting was Private Joseph Bradley of Barrow. He was 35 years old at the time of his death. He died from wounds sustained during the shelling of Beaucamp at Bray on 28 April. In truth, the Germans had no intention of attempting to retake the village by infantry assault. Their rear guards had done their job by inflicting as many casualties as possible on the British as they moved up against the Hindenburg Line. Having lost the village, their mission was to make its retention as expensive as possible.

After ten months in France, the 11th King's Own had taken part in its first major offensive operation. And they had done well. They had shown no intention of giving up their new front line. They had endured under heavy and persistent enemy fire. Six men died and sixteen were wounded. One officer, Lieutenant Beswick, was missing. He was never seen again.

The 40th Division continued to hold the positions around Beaucamp and Villers Pluich for the next few days, during it which it launched an unsuccessful attack on the last remaining hamlet on their divisional front that remained in German hands: La Vacquerie, east of Villers Pluich and just off the Cambrai road. The 11th King's Own was not involved in the fighting. The Germans eventually incorporated the hamlet into their main line of resistance.

On 1 May the battalion was back in the front line in trenches east of Beaucamp. The shelling was still heavy and continuous. On 2 May over 100 enemy shells exploded on the battalion's front. The enemy were no more than 500 yards away and the nights were spent patrolling no man's land and improving their dugouts and wire defences. On 5 May a fighting patrol of one officer, two Lewis gun teams and fifteen men were sent out to harass enemy working parties, but none were found. On 6 May the battalion was relieved by the 14th Argyles and went back to the support lines west of the village. The following day they too were relieved by the 14 HLI and in the evening retired to Equancourt and into brigade reserve.

The men stayed there until 12 May. They were allowed some rest and were able to visit the divisional baths at Etricourt. One company at a time went out on working parties each night. On the afternoon of 12 May, the battalion marched three miles along the St Quentin road to the south-east to Heudecourt where it came under the orders of 24 Brigade, the reserve brigade of the 8th Division, 40th Division's sister unit in XV Corps. During the evening of 13 May the battalion relieved the 2nd Middlesex on the left sector in front of Gonnelieu, a couple of miles to the south of Villers Pluich, on the other side of the Cambrai road. Two companies were in the front line, and two in support.

The next day was fairly quiet in comparison to the previous fortnight. There was no opportunity to patrol in no man's land because of the heavy British gun fire pounding away at the Hindenburg Line and the ground between it and the British front line. The weather was the men's main enemy. Heavy rain on 14 May caused most of the dugouts to collapse and flooded the trenches. The weather broke overnight and so the men spent the following day draining and repairing the trenches. The isolated outposts were joined up into a continuous line. Fire steps were built and dugouts reconstructed.

Frequent night-time patrols failed to establish any contact with the enemy. He was largely content to remain behind his new positions. Artillery on both sides kept up a constant fire, but casualties were light for this spell of duty. Three men were killed by enemy gas shells on 17 May. The battalion was relieved at midnight on 18 May and went into brigade support in nearby trenches. All through the next week the men were busily employed on endless working parties and fatigues. On 26 May the battalion returned to the front line at Gonnelieu. The next four days were exceptionally quiet. There was little enemy activity of any kind. Patrols reported the same thing night after night – there was no sign of the enemy in no man's land at all. On 31 May this was to change. A patrol under Lieutenant Pritchard had advanced about 200 yards when it spotted a German patrol about 30 yards away on the right. Pritchard and his men opened up with everything they had. The enemy patrol immediately retreated, leaving one man seriously wounded behind. He belonged to the 123rd Grenadier Regiment. There were no casualties amongst the King's Own men. The following night, the same officer was to lead another successful patrol, capturing a German captain of the same regiment. On 3 June the battalion was replaced in the front line by the 14th Argyles. The men moved to Sorrel le Grand, three miles to the rear near Fins, where they would stay for the next fortnight. The division passed into the command of III Corps at this time.

Thus ended the battalion's first full year in France. The men had certainly been worked hard. They had laboured on the roads and in the trenches. They had fought well but infrequently and had not been deployed in any of the main campaigns of the preceding twelve months. The total casualties for the past year reflected this fact. In total, 7 officers and 279 men were listed as dead, injured or missing during this time – a remarkably light toll, given the losses posted by the other battalions of the King's Own for the same period. The war diary records the strength of the battalion at this time as 11 officers and 815 men – a very high number for front-line battalions at this stage of the war.

On 19 June, the battalion was back in the front-line trenches at Villers Pluich. The next week was once again almost completely devoid of any hostile activity. There was no infantry contact between the two opposing sides. Patrols went out at night on a regular basis, but would always return without having made any contact with the enemy. The German guns kept up a steady and harassing rate of fire, but there were no heavy bombardments on the front or rear areas to deal with. The occasional sniper caused some nuisance. Pot shots would be taken at enemy aircraft flying overhead, but always without any result. On 27 June, they were relieved by the 13th East Surreys and went into brigade reserve in a sunken road about a mile behind the front line. The men lived in the dugouts built into the banks on eastern side of the road, facing the enemy front line. At night they laboured until dawn, when they would return to rest and eat. For the whole of June, the battalion only recorded two casualties.

The battalion remained in these dugouts along the road until 5 July, when they returned to the front line at Villers Pluich. In the early hours of 7 July, tragedy struck. Three officers of C Company were killed when a shell scored a direct hit on the shelter in which they were sleeping. One of these officers was from Barrow: Second Lieutenant Maurice Fairbairn. Maurice was 23 years old and the son of the late William Walker Fairbairn, a sculptor who lived in Rawlinson Street, Barrow. Maurice had joined the Army in 1916 and went out to France with the Artists Rifles as a private soldier. When he took a commission he joined the King's Own in early 1917. The last time he saw his family was in April, when he had been in Barrow for ten days leave. Prior to the war, he had worked in the local office of accountants W B Peat and Co. Lieutenant-Colonel Macdonald, in a letter to Maurice's mother, wrote:

> Maurice and two other officers were killed by a shell whilst in their dug out asleep about 2 am. I know how futile words are on these occasions. I can only express my deepest sympathy and that of others in your bereavement. Your son was a reliable and plucky lad.

The Germans continued to shell the battalion's trenches heavily over the next twenty-four hours.

In the morning of 12 July, the enemy shelling intensified again, wounding sixteen men. That night, a raid on the German lines failed to penetrate their trenches as the wire in front was simply too thick to cut through. The battalion was relieved on the night of 13 July and moved back to support position just off the Cambrai road just to the north of Gouzeaucourt. Here they would stay until 21 July. Once again, the battalion was worked hard every night, with two companies employed on rotation on carrying parties and fatigue duties. On the night of 21/22 July, they were back at Villers Pluich in the front line. This time there was little shelling of any kind. The men worked on their trenches at night, and during the day they were able to rest largely undisturbed by any hostile German activity. Patrols were sent out regularly at night, but had very little to report on when they returned. A patrol on the evening of 26 July disturbed some partridges and was fired on as a consequence by enemy machine guns and rifles.

The battalion was relieved by the 13th East Surreys on the 29th. July had been harder on the 11th King's Own. Eight men had been killed and thirty-eight wounded.

On 1 August, the battalion was in brigade reserve along the Gouzeaucourt–Trescault road, providing large working parties every night. Between 2 and 10 August the battalion had another generally quiet spell of duty in the front line at Beaucamp. The German guns occasionally opened up on the British positions, but the fire was not persistent or heavy. A patrol on the night of 5/6 August discovered two bags full of German stick grenades and a box of machine gum ammunition and brought them in. Another patrol on the night of 7 August ran into some Germans who opened fire. One officer and two men were wounded. The encounter took place amongst a dense growth of thistles 4–5 feet high and so the Lewis gun team protecting the patrol could not come into action for fear of hitting the men.

On 10 August the battalion was relieved by the East Surreys and went into brigade reserve at Gouzeaucourt Wood, where it would spend the next four days training. On 14 August it went back into the front line at Beaucamp. This tour of duty was even quieter than the last. The battalion moved back to Gouzeaucourt on 20 August for six days of training and fatigues. On 26 August it was back again at Beaucamp. No man was killed during that long, hot, quiet August. Eleven men were wounded.

Exactly the same pattern repeated itself in September, with the battalion rotating between front-line duty at Beaucamp and support and reserve duties behind the lines at either Dessart Wood or at Gouzeaucourt. On 22 September the battalion mounted a highly successful trench raid on the German lines opposite Beaucamp. A smoke cloud hid the advancing men from enemy observation as they crossed no man's land. The men entered the German trenches, destroyed a number of dugouts and took ten German soldiers prisoner. The enemy retaliated with a heavy artillery bombardment on the battalion's trenches, killing one man and wounding three others. On 24 August a new draft of 240 men arrived to join the battalion. The battalion was being strengthened for its forthcoming role at Cambrai. None of these men were bantams. The character of the battalion changed dramatically as a result.

The battalion remained on the Beaucamp sector of the front line for the first few days of October. On 5 October the division was replaced by the 20th Division and the men were moved back to huts at Heudecourt and into the Third Army Reserve after nine solid, if largely uneventful months in the line. On the next day, the battalion moved by bus at noon via Fins and Norlu to new billets in Peronne. It was being withdrawn from front-line duties in order to prepare for action at Cambrai, the last important campaign of 1917. On 8 October the men took advantage of the continuing hot summer weather and bathed in the river at Peronne. The following day the whole brigade paraded in the town square as the corps commander, Lieutenant-General W Pulteney, distributed medals to the men. On

9 October the battalion was on the move again, this time by train to Boisleux au Mont and then by route march to Simencourt, where they took up billets in newly erected Nissen huts. From 9 to 28 October, the battalion was engaged in intensive training in offensive operations. It wasn't all work however. Three afternoons a week were given over to sports and the men played soccer and rugby amongst themselves and with other battalions of the division. Towards the end of the month the division moved to the Lucheux area, twelve miles to the south-west. The battalion marched from Simencourt via Beaumetz and then along the main Doullens–Arras road, the modern-day N25. The march took over six hours. The battalion was now up to full strength with 44 officers and 973 men. The men were found billets around Halloy.

For the next two weeks the men were drilled night and day. The area lay in a junction of valleys, the slopes of which were heavily wooded. Here the men trained in wood fighting, which would be a feature of their engagement in Cambrai.

On 16 November they moved back to Simencourt, and then in the next few days to Beaulencourt, a small village a couple of miles to the south-east of Bapaume. On 21 November, the day after the start of the Battle of Cambrai, the battalion began moving closer to the front line. On 21 November, it moved up to Lebucquiere via Haplincourt, arriving in mid-afternoon. It rested the following day. On 23 November it moved into divisional reserve near Demicourt. The battalion was poised to join the battle and for its most significant engagement of the war.

The initial success on 20 November had been considerable. A large section of the Hindenburg Line had been breached under a heavy barrage. Six infantry divisions, supported by hundreds of tanks, had succeeded in punching a huge gap in the German lines. Despite determined German resistance at Flesquieres, on a front of over six miles an advance of between three and four miles had been made. Two strong trench systems, covered by an outpost line, had been captured in a little under four hours. Nothing like it had been achieved by the British in over three years of fighting on the Western Front. Not every objective had been taken however. Haig had planned to capture the Bourlon Ridge on the first day and this had not been secured. It had not even been attacked. Its capture was considered to be the key to any chance of exploiting the gap that had opened up in the German lines. It would have to be taken before German reinforcements could arrive. But the warning signs were obvious. The British attack had few reserves to call upon. The nearest reinforcements that could be brought into action were in fact the troops of the 40th Division, now part of Lieutenant-General Fanshawe's V Corps. These were still eight miles away from the point of the British advance.

The priority for 21 November was the capture of Bourlon Ridge. The Germans were determined to hold their ground. Their positions were strongly wired and consisted of a double line of trenches and numerous reinforced concrete machine gun posts. The attack, led by troops of IV Corps, failed to capture the Bourlon

Ridge. The enemy resistance was simply too strong. Haig faced the difficult choice of either continuing his attacks on Bourlon in the face of growing enemy resistance or withdrawing altogether from the forward positions his soldiers currently occupied, as they could not be easily defended, overlooked as they were by the high ground on the ridge. Haig decided to press on with the attack. To give any renewed attack a better prospect of succeeding, the British would need to bring up additional artillery as well as fresh troops, so the attack was delayed. Inevitably, this gave the Germans the time they needed to strengthen their defences even further.

The tanks had also sustained heavy losses. No new machines would be available on 22 November to renew operations, so the attack on Bourlon would have to wait until the 40th Division was ready to join the battle on 23 November. All through 22 November the Germans mounted a series of counter-attacks against the British line in front of Bourlon Ridge. The 40th Division was entering a veritable cauldron. It was to replace the battered 62nd Division which had been leading the fighting at Bourlon. The task given to the 40th Division was the hardest one on battlefield. Aided by tanks, it was to complete the capture of Bourlon Wood and village. The relief of the 62nd Division was carried out on the night of 22/23 November. It was an extremely difficult operation, largely because of the congested state of the roads. Part of divisional HQ took the best part of fifteen hours to cover nine miles.

119 Brigade, supported by sixteen tanks, had the job of clearing Bourlon Wood, while 121 Brigade with thirteen tanks would attack and seize the village and the eastern shoulder of the ridge. 120 Brigade would be in divisional reserve, ready to push up and support the two attacking brigades if needed. The troops of 40th Division had never trained with tanks, or even seen them in action, before the attack at Bourlon. Zero hour was set for 10.30 am. Twenty minutes before zero, an enormous artillery barrage descended on the German lines on the edge of the wood. At 10.30 am the tanks and men began to move forward. By 11.40 am, the 19th Royal Welch had reached the middle of the wood, along the Fontaine–Bourlon road. After a short pause in which to reorganize, the two battalions pressed on to the northern edge which was reached about an hour later. A line of outposts was then established on the northern edge of the wood, extending on the right as far as the Fontaine–Bourlon road, where two companies of the support battalion, the 17th Welch Regiment, came up to join them. Enemy fire intensified at this point and the posts had to be withdrawn 100 yards or so. The 12th SWBs met with even tougher resistance. Progress up the western slopes of the wood, although helped by two tanks, was extremely difficult in the face of concentrated machine gun fire. Losses were heavy. One of the companies got as far as the houses on the eastern edge of the village but was eventually driven back by a fierce counter-attack which had left their flanks in the air. The battalion ended up consolidating along the Fontaine–Bourlon road, leaving a gap between it and the Fusiliers on their right. About 3 pm, an even heavier counter-attack

developed against the 12th SWBs and the two companies of the 17th Welch Regiment which had come up to support them. It looked touch and go for these men. In the nick of time, the brigade reserve battalion, the 18th Welch Regiment, came up to lend support. The Germans began to waiver. As the light faded, the crest of the ridge was secured. Only the northern slope of the wood remained in German hands by nightfall. The fighting had been bitter. No quarter was given or received on either side.

120 Brigade now began to enter the battle. Two companies of the 14th Argyles arrived about 8 pm to reinforce the depleted ranks of 119 Brigade. Covered by patrols, a continuous line was established and improved so that when another German infantry counter-attack was launched against the men just before midnight, it was effectively repelled without any ground being lost.

The 121 Brigade had been given a final objective about 500 yards beyond the village. From the outset, the whole advance was fully exposed to German artillery and machine gun fire. The advance of the 13th Green Howards was soon halted. The 21st Middlesex, covering the left flank of the brigade, fared no better. The 20th Middlesex on the right was attacking the southern edge of the village. Three of the six tanks supporting this attack were soon knocked out by anti-gun fire. Eventually, seven tanks made their way into the village, where they came under heavy and effective fire from the German defenders. Many of them were quickly put out of action. Some of the 20th Middlesex got into the village on the southern side and a few small groups of the 12th Green Howards appeared as well. A period of chaotic and confused fighting took place, with no one quite sure who was firing on whom. The Germans were well dug in, and there seemed little chance of forcing them out of the village which was now a warren of rubble and brick. Reinforced by the 12th Suffolks, the troops began to dig and defend a line a little short of the village to the left boundary of the point where their attack had commenced. The division, although not entirely successful, had nonetheless made an impressive appearance in the Battle of Cambrai. They had taken the wood – something that had eluded the 62nd Division – and had fought hard to enter the village. So far, eight of the division's twelve battalions had been employed in the attack. Soon it would be the turn of the 11th King's Own.

So far, the battalion had remained at Demicourt. In the evening of 24 November the battalion began to move closer to the front line. During the fighting the forward lines held by 119 Brigade had been forced back by the middle of the afternoon to the middle of the wood by the ferocity of repeated German counter-attacks. Although they had been reinforced during the night of 23 November, this was not sufficient to stem the new onslaught. The fighting grew heavier and more deadly. Exhausted by thirty-six hours of non-stop fighting, the front line was in desperate need of relief and resupply. The British were by now facing considerably superior enemy forces, both infantry and artillery. It took extraordinary bravery and disciplined leadership to hold on to any part of the wood at all.

As a result of a breakdown in communications, a renewed attack by 121 Brigade on the village which was scheduled to take place at 3 pm went ahead, despite the orders for the attack being cancelled by the corps commander. Troops of the 14th HLI, supported by the 12th Suffolks passed right through the village and reached their objectives along the railway line east of the village, where they promptly started to dig in. But this was far from the victory it might at first glance have appeared. The village itself, owing to inadequate reserves, still contained significant numbers of Germans and the advanced troops were effectively cut off from their own lines.

It was time for the division's reserves to be committed. By midnight, two companies of the 11 King's Own under Captain Wilson and Lieutenant Rumsey, and the 2nd Scots Guards had come up to support the remnants of 119 Brigade in their new positions running through the centre of the wood. The King's Own men arrived in their support positions at 9.30 pm on 24 November. At 11 pm they were ordered further forward. Here they unexpectedly came across a German strong point. Their guides had taken the men too far. They were forced to retire to their original lines along the Fontaine–Bourlon road. At 8 am they were ordered to attack the enemy positions in front of them. They made four attempts to do so in the face of extremely heavy machine gun fire. Here they remained until 2 pm, when they were ordered to advance again and try and take the ridge. Very heavy fighting continued until 6 pm. The men were able to move forward slowly and they held off two heavy counter-attacks. They were eventually relieved by the 62nd Division at 10 pm and returned to their battalion. Both company COs were wounded in the fighting.

On learning what had happened, the divisional commander immediately placed under the command of 121 Brigade all that remained of his reserves: the 13th East Surreys and the two remaining companies of the 11th King's Own. These two companies began to move up at about 12.30 am on 25 November, arriving at the quarry just off the Cambrai road, south of the wood, at 3.15 am. Haig had still not given up the prospect of putting the cavalry through the gap in the German lines. But this could not be done unless both the wood and village were in British hands.

The priority for 121 Brigade was therefore to capture Bourlon village and join up with the isolated units holding the railway line to the north. This job was given to the 13th East Surreys, with the two King's Own companies acting in support. It was a grim scenario. There were no tanks available to support this attack and there could be no artillery barrage either, as the exact whereabouts of the 14th HLI was unknown. At 6.15 am the advance began but was immediately met by heavy machine gun fire from the wood. Platoons reached the village but could make no real progress in the close-quarter fighting. There seemed little chance of getting through to the railway and the Highlanders who were hanging on there. Unknown to the East Surreys, the Highlanders had been forced to surrender at about 9.30 am when the last of their ammunition ran out. The East Surreys held on to a few houses on the eastern outskirts of the village. Here the fighting continued as the men held on all day.

On their right, little progress was made in clearing the wood of the German defenders. The British line was still dangerously thin. An attack by the Guards designed to clear the wood coincided with a German counter-attack. The result was a stalemate. The line had moved a little further forward, but there neither side had delivered a decisive blow. The cavalry was stood down at noon. The 2nd Cavalry Division sent its horses back to Fins and its soldiers formed three dismounted infantry battalions which were placed under the orders of the 40th Division.

The two companies of the King's Own taking shelter in the quarry were not sent forward into Bourlon village to support the East Surreys. The men were heavily shelled from 10 am to 10 pm on 25 November. They began to be relieved by soldiers from the 62nd Division at 2 am on 26 November. Later that morning, the whole battalion, now reunited, marched to its new billets at Trescault via Havrincourt. The battalion had suffered heavily. Ninety-one men had become casualties over the preceding twenty-four hours. Seven were confirmed as dead and fourteen were missing. Four officers and sixty-six men were wounded.

The division had made an important but not decisive contribution to the Battle of Cambrai. In its first major engagement of the war, the division had pushed the British line forward in extremely difficult circumstances and had fought tenaciously in the face of heavy German resistance. It could be proud of what it had done.

On 27 November the battalion moved at 8.30 am via Metz to Ytres where it went by trains to Beaumetz. From there it marched to huts at Blaireville, arriving at 6.15 pm. the division was now transferred to the command of VI Corps. For the next five days the battalion would remain in its new billets and was allowed to rest and recuperate. At 8 am on 3 December it marched off to Hamlincourt, a few miles away, and became part of divisional reserve. The 40th Division had relieved the 16th Division in the front line at Bullecourt, north-east of Bapaume. Here it would spend the next week training and drilling. Lieutenant-Colonel Macdonald went home to England on 5 December and Major Bracey took over command of the battalion. On 10 December the battalion moved to Croiselles and into brigade support. D Company was attached to the 12th East Surreys.

On 11 December, a fresh draft of one officer and 167 men joined the battalion, bringing its trench strength to over 900. On 12 December the Germans attacked the 3rd Division on the right of the 40th Division. The front held by the 40th Division was shelled with gas. Sixteen men in the King's Own were wounded by these shells. On 14 December the battalion relieved the 13th East Surreys in the front line. Over the next four days, little enemy activity of any note seems to have taken place and on 18 December, the men were relieved by the 21st Middlesex and went into reserve at Boyelles. The relief was completed by 4 pm. Here the men would spend the next week in the usual routine of carrying and working parties. During the day the men underwent training in using Lewis guns and did map reading exercises. On 22 December the corps commander visited the battalion to present medals for the fighting at Bourlon Wood. The battalion had won ten Military Medals.

The next day was observed as the battalion's Christmas Day. Christmas dinners were served up for the men and they had a concert party in the evening. The following day they were back in the support trenches at Bullecourt, where they would spend the next three days and nights. On 27 December they marched to a new camp at Hamlincourt. On 29 December they relieved the 1st Royal Scots in the front line at Bullecourt, where they would remain until 2 January.

Between 30 and 31 December the enemy shelled the front line extensively. Two men were killed in the early hours of the 30th by shellfire.

1918: the end of the bantams

The enemy attempted to fraternize with the King's Own men on New Year's Day. These attempts were met with machine and Lewis gun fire. At night the men were sent out on regular wiring parties to strengthen their defences. A German counter-offensive was expected at any time. On 2 January the battalion moved back to brigade reserve lines at Mory. There was no attempt by the enemy to interfere with this relief and the whole front had settled down into a calm mood. The weather did not help matters. It was freezing.

At Mory, the battalion continued to be worked hard and relentlessly. It provided nightly working parties for the front line. The men did however enjoy hot baths at Ervillers on 4 January. On 5 January, the Germans launched a strong trench raid against 121 Brigade and succeeded in penetrating the British front line, reaching the support lines. The battalion was ordered to 'stand to' between 6.30 and 8 am, but was not called on to help eject the Germans. A counter-attack by the 12th Suffolks succeeded in restoring order. On 6 January the battalion was back in the front line at Noreuil. Major Jupe took over command of the battalion as Lieutenant-Colonel Macdonald was given command of the brigade.

The 8th was a busy day. A German attack in the morning had succeeded in getting into the front line. A counter-attack by the battalion bombers at noon, in the middle of a snow blizzard, drove them out again. The following day was quiet and uneventful and the battalion was relieved in the evening of 10 January by the East Surreys. A thaw set in on 10 January and the immediate effect on the trenches was dramatic. They began to fall in and fill with heavy mud.

January would prove to be fairly quiet for the battalion. It moved in and out of the front line at Noreuil, spending time when it was out of the line at Mory. Conditions in the front line continued to deteriorate. By the middle of the month, the front line had become a series of outposts. There was no longer a continuous line of trenches as they could not be properly maintained in the appalling weather conditions. One soldier was killed and nine wounded during January. The last time the battalion would hold a section of the British front line in the war took place between 30 January and 3 February. It was a completely uneventful time. Four men were slightly wounded by shellfire but, for most of the time, the Germans were quiet. The men occupied themselves with trying to improve their living conditions. On 3 February the men returned to Mory. On 5 February, at Mory, the 11th Battalion King's Own ceased to exist as a battalion in the British Army. Most of the men went to the 8th Battalion where they continued to serve with great distinction until the end of the war. Nearly 300 men and 11 officers went to join the 1st Battalion, one of the two regular army battalions of the regiment. The remainder went to serve with the 2/5th Battalion, a second line territorial unit of the regiment, raised in 1915.

The battalion had served less than twenty months in France. For most of that time, it was employed in quiet sections of the front, and in doing much of the hard labouring required to keep an army functioning. 120 Brigade was usually given the support or reserve role in offensive operations, but when the moment arrived and the battalion was pitched into heavy fighting at Cambrai, it behaved with bravery and courage.

Major-General Ponsonby, commanding the 40th Division in February 1918, sent this message of farewell to the battalions that were being disbanded:

> Although the battalions in which you have served so long in this country are to be broken up, the memory of their splendid achievements will never fade. The record of your past services, the fine fighting spirit you have invariably displayed and your constant determination to maintain the high traditions of your battalions, not only rebound to your credit and to that of the 40 Division, but will add still further to the glorious reputation of your regiments.

The 'little men' had acquitted themselves well.

Chapter 6

Shot at Dawn

During the course of the war, 3,080 British soldiers were sentenced to death by Field General Courts Martial, battlefield tribunals charged with the responsibility of enforcing military law. Of these cases, 346 men were executed by firing squad. The rest of the sentences were either commuted or quashed. There were forty-one such cases brought against men serving in the King's Own. This might, at first glance, seem to be a lot. But it is worth remembering that over 40,000 men in total served with battalions of the King's Own between 1914 and 1918. The death penalty was carried out in five of these cases and three involved men serving in the 4th, 7th and 8th Battalions. Controversy has raged ever since about the fairness and justice of these executions.

The vast majority of the convictions – 2,005 – were for the offence of desertion, of which 272 ended in the death sentence being carried out. The 1914 edition of the *Manual of Military Law*, published by the War Office, provided a clear explanation of the essential elements to this offence. 'The offence of desertion . . . implies an intention on the part of the offender not to return to His Majesty's service at all, or to escape some particularly important service.' In most of these cases, the intention to desert was established not by trying to determine the precise mental state of the offender, but from drawing inferences from the salient facts of each case. What clothes the offender was wearing at the time of his arrest, whether he was in possession of his rifle and equipment, whether or not he had been given permission for his absence, or where he was arrested, would often be crucial pointers in determining guilt.

The *Manual of Military Law* made this clear (p. 391):

> To establish desertion it is necessary to prove some circumstance justifying the inference that the accused intended not to return to military duty . . . or intended to avoid some important particular duty, such as active service . . .

The issue therefore for the court in all of these cases was the simple question whether or not the behaviour of the accused revealed an intention to avoid active service. His reasons for doing so were neither an excuse nor a defence. Even a temporary absence was enough to convict. The length of time a soldier had been away from his post would not, on its own, permit an acquittal on a change of desertion if it was nonetheless clear from all the other evidence that the soldier was not planning to return at all or was trying to avoid the particular duty to which he had been entrusted.

Establishing these facts in a court martial would be relatively straightforward. The man either had permission to be absent or not. He either performed the duty he had been ordered to perform or not. This was not complicated evidence requiring an audit trail of paper to confirm. The routine of trench warfare did not lend itself to such an attention to paperwork. Evidence to support such a conviction would come from confirming the orders that had been given to the accused, his subsequent behaviour and any supporting evidence from his comrades who observed his actions.

It is striking that in each of the three courts martial described here, the accused never cross-examined any of the key witnesses to dispute the evidence before the court. There is a grim fatality about the simple statements of fact produced by all of the prosecution witnesses in these trials. It almost defied cross-examination. The evidence did not lend itself to contradiction. It spoke for itself. Guilt was obvious and could be satisfactorily drawn from the clear and unambiguous evidence before the court.

There is an equal fatalism and hopelessness about the nature of the defence offered in all of the cases brought against the men of the King's Own. In essence, two of the soldiers simply claimed that they could not remember what had happened, and when their memory returned to them they were discovered and arrested before they could take steps to return to their battalion. Not surprisingly, this kind of argument would cut little ice with the Field General Courts Martial. In the third case, the prisoner claimed to have been medically unfit for duty. Unfortunately this was his own personal diagnosis rather than the view of the battalion medical officer. There was no independent evidence to back it up. It too was given pretty short shrift. In all of these three cases, the real issue was not, in truth, whether the men were guilty as charged. They were. The main issue is whether it was right for them to be executed.

Ever since the war, there has been a vigorous debate about the policy of executing soldiers for these and other military offence. Concerns have been expressed about both the standard of justice dispensed by these tribunals as well as the appropriateness of the sanction inflicted on the men who were convicted. It is very easy now, with the benefit of hindsight and the luxury of peacetime, to draw the conclusion that these convictions and sentences represented very rough justice indeed and that the system of courts martial in operation at the time was in fact a corruption of due process. To some extent, the harshness of the death sentences handed down was clearly mitigated by the commutation of most of them into a sentence of imprisonment, suggesting at least a proper process of higher scrutiny over the decision-making machinery, as well as some recognition of the fact that many of these men were probably not fully responsible for their actions.

But, for many, there still seemed to be insufficient allowance made for the sheer horror and brutality of the conditions these men were confronted with. Undoubtedly, these conditions could turn brave men who had served with gallantry and distinction for long periods in the trenches into 'deserters' or 'cowards'. Military law, however, provided no defence on the basis of previous good conduct, and it was, after all, military law that the Field General Courts Martial had to enforce. All of this looks harsh and clumsy to many people today.

It is much harder to judge the standards of behaviour of one generation by the standards we take for granted today. This was a time, after all, of unprecedented danger to the state. Its very existence was in immediate peril. The conditions on the battlefield were more extreme than in any previous military campaign fought by the British Army. To go 'over the top' in most circumstances meant either instant death or serious injury. Discipline in these horrendous conditions, many would argue, required strong enforcement of military laws. The consequences of disobeying orders had to be understood by all.

Applying the death penalty to these serious breaches of military law was not in itself an obviously disproportionate sentence, given the overall penal climate. In the early years of the twentieth century, the death penalty was widely used in criminal cases. During the period 1914–18, over fifty murderers were put to death in the UK by the criminal courts. The death penalty was therefore an integral part of the criminal justice system in the United Kingdom. It would have been odd, in fact, if this were not also to be found in the code of military law, where a high importance had always been attached to standards of discipline and obedience to orders.

The system of dispensing justice in the Army worked to a different rhythm than that of the civilian criminal courts. Most acts of indiscipline would have been dealt with either informally or by action taken by a soldier's commanding officer. In other words, it would have been kept within the battalion or regiment in order to avoid the public display of dirty washing. Sanctions would have been imposed with the minimum of fuss and procedural niceties. Instigating the procedure of a court martial was an altogether more serious step. But it too would usually also be accompanied by the sense that the prisoner was already guilty of the crime for which he was charged. Although he was entitled to a presumption of innocence, the fact that the overwhelming majority of cases resulted in a conviction confirms the sense that the process was largely formulaic.

Much of the criticism of the system of Field General Courts Martial (see the works listed in the short Further Reading section below) also misses the point that the Army itself was fully committed to military operations in the most extreme conditions imaginable. Front-line battalions could simply not afford to send officers away for extensive periods of time to try these cases at their leisure. Legal procedures had to be complied with. Court martial officers ensured that this happened. Courts martial that failed to ensure this happened would see their convictions quashed by the Judge Advocates General Department. But the

Army's mission was to kill as many Germans as possible and it was difficult to detach officers to perform what was clearly regarded as an unpleasant duty.

The traditional view has always been that good order and discipline in the army during war conditions depended on strict punishment for those who disobeyed orders, particularly when this might set a precedent and undermine the fighting spirit of a battalion, brigade or even a division. The death sentence was executed only in a minority of cases. Clearly, the military authorities felt that good discipline could be maintained without resorting to the death penalty in every case. For the vast majority of other cases, a stiff prison sentence would suffice.

The punishment regime was undoubtedly a harsh one, even for lesser offences. Field punishments for such offences could involve tying men to gun carriage wheels for lengthy periods of time. In the violent and brutal conditions prevailing in the front areas, so the argument goes, only a clear understanding of the serious consequences for failing to follow orders could guarantee the necessary authority of superior officers. And in the conditions prevailing, this argument could be seen by many as being fully legitimate.

The German Army took a very different approach. In an army nearly twice the size of the British, 150 men were condemned and only 48 executions took place. Few would argue that the fighting capacity of the Germans was seriously weaker than the British. This controversy has now been partly assuaged by the recent decision of the British government to grant a retrospective pardon to those who were convicted for these offences – offences ranging from cowardice and desertion to insubordination and striking a senior officer.

No regiment of the British Army was to emerge from the war without at least one of its soldiers being sentenced to death for such an offence. The forty-one convictions in the King's Own were split fairly evenly between the regular and service battalions. Of the five men executed, two were serving with the service battalions (the 7th and the 8th). One soldier serving with the 4th Battalion suffered a similar fate. This account of the war service of those from the Furness area who served with the King's Own could not be complete therefore without looking into these tragic casualties of war.

The first of these soldiers to face death by firing squad was Private John Sloane. John was the youngest of five children of John and Mary Sloane of 244 Ribbleton Lane, Preston. He was born in 1895. His family ran a grocery shop in the town. He had joined the battalion in France on 4 May 1916 when it was stationed in a section of the front line at Arras. He had only been with the battalion for fourteen days when the offence took place on 18 May. He was charged with desertion. He had been ordered to attend a bombing course at Riviere. He never arrived.

His trial took place on 29 June (see PRO WO71/482). Four officers would decide his fate. Major Bridgewater of the 5th Lancs Fusiliers presided, and sat with three junior officers, Captain Widdows of the 4th Loyal North Lancs, Captain Hall of the 5th Lancs Fusiliers and Second Lieutenant Cowthorpe of the 1st Battalion, Bedfordshire Regiment.

John Sloane pleaded not guilty. Such a plea was automatically entered in all cases where the death penalty could be carried out. The evidence against him was strong and obvious. Sergeant William Bell, who had won the Military Cross for bravery at Givenchy in June 1915, was the first to testify. Bell was B Company Sergeant-Major and John Sloane was serving in his company. Bell revealed that at 8.00 am on 18 May, the men were in support trenches at Wailly. He had detailed John Sloane to parade later that afternoon for the purpose of going to the brigade bombing school at Riviere. There were fifteen men in the party in total. Sloane marched off with the others. The party returned to the trenches at 17.15. Sloane was not amongst them. Bell searched the trenches for him but he could not be found. Bell next saw Sloane on 28 May, under arrest in the trenches on his return to the battalion.

Private John Hart also gave evidence. John Hart was to serve almost to the end of the war. He was killed in October 1918, as the battalion fought in the final advance to victory. He was one of the party detailed to take part in the bomb training course at Riviere. The group had come to a halt near to the school in order to get their final bearings and determine the exact location of the training area. Private Hart saw John Sloane fall out. He took off his equipment and walked away.

Sergeant Butcher, Sloane's platoon sergeant, had joined Sergeant Bell in the search for Sloane later that afternoon. He was nowhere to be found.

The evidence was clear. He had been ordered to attend the training course but had instead disappeared without permission and failed to return to his battalion with the others. Sloane was eventually found in the Rue de la Republique in Rouen four days later. He had no rifle or equipment on him. Lance-Corporal Ferrier, a military policeman, had asked Sloane if he was 'on a pass'. Sloane told him he was bound for England on leave and that all his papers were on the boat. When challenged further, he could not remember the name of the boat. He was immediately arrested and returned to his battalion under close escort.

Sloane's defence was completely unconvincing. He had fallen out from the bombing school party to go to the latrine. After this, he claimed he was waiting outside an estaminet which was full of men. He remembered nothing else until he was brought back to his battalion on 28 May. In his evidence, he said he had been suffering from a loss of memory for a while. He had, however, never reported this to the battalion medical officer.

Sloane had one character witness. Captain Brocklebank said that Sloane had done good work during his time with the battalion and had shown intelligence in his work.

The trial could not have lasted more than a couple of hours. The verdict of the court was unanimous. Sloane was found guilty of desertion as charged and sentenced to death by firing squad. After the verdict, the opinion of the battalion, brigade and divisional commanding officers as well as the Third Army commander were sought as to whether the sentence passed should be carried out or commuted. This was a requirement of military law. No death sentence in the field could be carried out without the consent of the commander in chief.

Major Swainson, commanding the 4th Battalion, saw no reason why the death penalty should not be imposed. He wrote:

> He was only with the battalion for 14 days. There was no particular fighting going on during the period he served. He was not an efficient sentry and did not appear to be either capable or willing to learn his duties. He was a very good and hard worker when under fatigues. In the opinion of his Company CO the crime was committed not so much as to avoid the particular duty as to get away. I have no knowledge of the man as such. The above remarks are of his Company CO who is now the second in command of the battalion.

Swainson himself was to die in action commanding his men six weeks later during the Battle of the Somme.

Major-General Jeudwine, GOC of the 55th Division took a similar view. In his opinion, Sloane's conduct 'showed he had no intention of returning'. There was nothing in these reports which pointed in the direction of any mitigating factor. It had been a blatant act of desertion. However, there was no evidence of poor discipline or lack of fighting enterprise in the battalion. Far from it: the 4th Battalion had an excellent track record as a combat-hardened unit.

On 13 July, Field-Marshall Haig confirmed the death penalty and it was duly carried out at 3.50 am on 16 July. John Sloane was buried in the Barly French Military Cemetery.

Lance-Corporal George Edward Hughes, of the 7th Battalion King's Own, was charged on 6 November 1916 with desertion at a Field General Court Martial held at Aveluy (see PRO WO71/521). Major Ruxton of the 9th Cheshires presided at the trial. His day in court was even more peremptory than John Sloane's.

On 21 July, the battalion had been serving in the trenches near Mametz Wood. They had been involved a lot of hard fighting at that time, as the battle for High Wood began to develop. The men had been under heavy shellfire for several days. The battalion war diary described this period as one of the most testing the men had experienced since they had landed in France just over a year before. Company Sergeant-Major James Corrigan had ordered Lance-Corporal Hughes to take charge of a water-carrying party. The men left the trenches and began walking down Death Valley, the principal communication route to and from the front-line positions in that area of the Somme battlefield. The Tommies had not christened it Death Valley for nothing. Any daylight movement there was likely to attract enemy attention. Sure enough, as soon as the men started along their journey, Death Valley came under German shellfire. Several rounds exploded near to the men and they had to take cover in one of the many shell holes that littered the area around them. The party eventually returned to the trenches with the water. Lance-Corporal Hughes was not amongst them and could not be found anywhere.

There was no evidence produced at the court martial from anyone who had been on the water-carrying party. No one testified as to the circumstances of Hughes's absence. No one had seen him leave the area. In fact he was reported as 'missing' on the return of the men to the trenches. It had been assumed that he had been killed by the shelling and that his body would not be found.

Hughes was eventually arrested at Etaples, the main British infantry depot in France, eighty-eight days later. A military policeman had seen him enter a tent on his own one evening and immediately became suspicious. He was arrested and returned to his battalion for court martial proceedings to begin. Hughes himself gave no proper account of the intervening period. In his statement to the court Hughes said,

> I was badly shaken up by shell fire at la Boiselle shortly before the date on which I was reported missing. I tried to report sick on the 20th July but was told by the Medical Officer to wait till the battalion came out of the line. The water party I was in charge of on the 21st July was heavily shelled going down the valley. I remember getting to the water carts and starting back but nothing further, until I found myself 7 kilometres from Etaples. I enquired where I was and went to look for my base depot. I went into a tent on a Saturday night, meaning to report next morning. The provost sergeant found me there and confined me in the guard tent.
>
> I have been out to France three times and have been invalided home twice, gassed.

The shelling referred to by Hughes had taken place two weeks before he deserted. Strangely, he made no reference to the shelling endured by the battalion on the Bazentin Ridge and around Mametz Wood. On this evidence, Hughes was found guilty of the charge of desertion and sentenced to death. None of the senior officers who were asked for their view on whether the sentence should be carried out had any doubt that it should.

Lieutenant-Colonel Tudor Fitzjohn, commanding the 7th Battalion at the time, did however provide an interesting insight.

> Hughes joined the battalion on 8 June 1916 and left it on 21st July. I knew very little about him. During this period he was detached for duty with the Brigade Carrying Party from about 24 June to 10 July. He only served with the battalion for a few days. Since his arrest and return to the battalion, he has done a few days duty in the trenches. His Company CO and CSM state that he is quite irresponsible for his actions when under fire. His nerves seemed to be shattered and quite out of control. Both the

Company CO and CSM are of the opinion that the mans nerves are broken and that he was not fit for active service and under the circumstances was not responsible for his actions. Even in ordinary conversation he was extremely nervous, his face and hands continually twitching.

His character, from the point of view of behaviour, was good. Out of the trenches he was always willing and even anxious to do his utmost. He stated that he had been gassed twice before coming to this battalion and possibly this may account for his behaviour.

These observations were written on 10 November. The following day, Fitzjohn confirmed that he saw no reason why the death penalty should not be carried out. It is impossible to infer however from these remarks whether the nervous condition that Hughes appeared to be suffering from in November was as acute in July, when the offence was alleged to have been committed. Hughes himself refers to being 'badly shaken up' after the action at La Boiselle. But he made no attempt to introduce any evidence to support this claim at his trial.

Brigadier-General Rowley, GOC of 56 Infantry Brigade, was of the same view.

In my opinion, Lance-Corporal Hughes displayed cowardice under fire. He was in charge of a water party and was the only one who failed to do his duty, although he, as commander, should have set an example to his men. He was absent for a period of 88 days and though eventually found in a camp at Etaples had made no effort to return to his battalion. Under the circumstances, I recommend that the sentence be carried out.

General Rowley was clearly confused as to the charge against Hughes. He was not being accused of cowardice. Reference to this charge seems completely inappropriate in the circumstances and was surely not a relevant consideration in deciding whether or not the sentence should be carried out. His rank as an NCO and the length of time he was absent seem to have been significant factors against Hughes. His fate was sealed.

In his final statement in mitigation, Hughes said: 'I am 23 years of age. I ask for one chance to redeem myself. I will stay with the battalion.' This final, pathetic appeal was to no avail. He had no voices to speak up for him. And no one was prepared to give him the benefit of any doubt. Maybe there was no doubt to express in this case.

General Gough, commanding Fifth Army, confirmed the sentence on 14 November without expressing any reasons. Field-Marshall Haig confirmed the death penalty on 18 November.

Hughes was executed at 6.25 am on 23 November 1916. His grave can be found in the Warloy–Baillon Communal Cemetery Extension. George was the second son of railway worker Thomas Hughes and came from south Manchester.

The final case of the death penalty being carried out against a soldier from the service battalions of the King's Own concerned Private Albert Holmes, who was born in Marsden Street, Kirkham, near Blackpool (see PRO WO71/646). The contrast between this case and the other two could not be stronger. The army records relating to Private Holmes reveals a totally different picture – that of a soldier who had become desperate to avoid front-line service, but only after being wounded twice since his arrival in France with the 8th Battalion in September 1915. He was initially injured in September 1915 and then again in October 1916. There was some suggestion that this second injury – a foot wound – had been self-inflicted, although no formal disciplinary action had been taken against him. It was after this second wounding that his problems began to become altogether more serious.

In early October 1916, he had been sentenced to ten days' field punishment for falling out of the line of a route march without permission. He was then sentenced in December 1916 to two years' penal servitude for being absent without leave. He was released from prison after one year and returned to his battalion for active service on 21 December 1917.

Shortly after returning to the battalion, on 24 December, he committed an act of desertion and was tried by Field General Court Martial in January 1918. There are no surviving details of this initial offence or trial. He was found guilty on 30 January and sentenced to death. This sentence was subsequently commuted to fifteen years in prison. On 21 February, however, this sentence too was set aside and he was returned to the 8th Battalion for duty in the trenches. Holmes had been given every opportunity to redeem himself, the last-minute plea of Lance-Corporal Hughes. He was not to take it. Maybe by now he was not in any fit state to do so. Having been sentenced to fifteen years in prison, Holmes must have thought, probably not unreasonably, that his trench duties were over for good, as the war would surely be finished by then. He was 'out of it' at last. It was not to be.

On the evening of 23 February Holmes found himself once again in the trenches. One can only imagine what would have been going through his mind. Under escort, he was handed over to the custody of Sergeant Jones. The battalion was then in the support trenches at Wancourt. Sergeant Jones immediately posted Holmes for duty in his platoon's Lewis gun teams. He was warned straight away that the battalion would be going into the front line the next day. This was unwelcome news for Holmes as he would undoubtedly be right back in the thick of things. Lewis gun teams provided essential fire support for their platoons. For these men there were no safe places, no quiet tours of duty. Holmes was still with his section the following morning. At 10.00 am, the roll call was taken. Holmes and the other men of the Lewis gun team were again put on notice that they would be going up the line that afternoon. At 16.15, when the roll was called again by Sergeant Jones, Holmes was nowhere to be found. A search of the trenches revealed no trace of him. He had gone missing again.

Both Sergeant Jones and Company Sergeant-Major Wood gave evidence to this effect at his court martial on 6 March. Sergeant Wood swore that he had given Holmes personal notice of the battalion's impending return to the front line.

Holmes pleaded not guilty. He told the court that after the morning parade on the 24 February, he had taken 'French leave' to get medical attention for his eyes which the battalion medical officer had refused him. He felt he was incapable of doing the duties given him by Sergeant Jones. He went first to nearby Achiet Le Grand to seek treatment. He saw a medical orderly who advised him to return to his battalion as he had no permission to be absent. Holmes testified that he decided not to go straight back to the battalion but go elsewhere for attention. He spent that night at a reinforcement camp. The following morning he started his search for another field ambulance. He got as far as Albert. By now he claimed to be tired and hungry and handed himself in when he saw a military policeman walking towards him in the street. He claimed that he had reported problems with his eyesight on 24 December, the last occasion when he had deserted from the battalion.

Captain Whitaker, his company commander, told the court that Holmes had had 'rather a rough time in his platoon and had been given all the dirty jobs to do'. Given Holmes's record, this would not have been surprising. It could not have made things easy for him although it is hard to see what else he could really have expected. His fellow soldiers almost certainly would not have felt comfortable in his presence nor would they feel he could be relied on to perform his duties properly. Lewis gun teams provided hugely important protective fire to the soldiers, both in offensive as well as defensive action. They needed him to stick at it. They suspected he would not, putting them at extra risk. It was a no-win situation for both Holmes and his comrades. Holmes, inevitably, was to come out as the loser in this conflict of interest.

He was found guilty and sentenced to death. The evidence was undoubtedly very clear indeed. He had not been given permission to seek medical care. He had been under clear orders to return to the front line and had also been charged with a specific duty to perform. All of the necessary ingredients to support a conviction for desertion were present.

On this occasion, however, there was, surprisingly, a disagreement amongst the senior officers concerned as to whether the death sentence should be carried out or not. On 7 March Brigadier-General Porter, commanding 76 Brigade, recommended that the death penalty should be commuted. There had been a series of administrative errors in how Holmes had been treated on his return to the battalion. The practice in the brigade involved the GOC interviewing each man after he had returned to the trenches following a conviction by a court martial so that he could be warned about his position. This had not happened in this case. Holmes had been allocated a front-line duty and deserted again before General Porter could interview him. The divisional commander, in his comments on the case, noted these failures and confirmed that he would be taking disciplinary action against those concerned.

General Porter's main argument was to do with the discipline within the 8th Battalion. He commented:

> The state of discipline within the battalion is high and it always fights with great gallantry. No example is required in the Brigade or battalion and I consider a death penalty in a battalion of high fighting efficiency always lowers the morale of the men. I recommend the sentence be commuted to life penal servitude and most strongly urge that the whole sentence be carried out. It would be useless to return this man to the ranks.

Major-General Deverell, commanding 3rd Division, disagreed.

> The desertion appears to me to have been deliberate to avoid service in the trenches with his battalion and the irregularities brought to notice do not justify me in recommending any leniency, taking into account the previous record of the prisoner and the character given him by his commanding officer.

The sentence was confirmed by both the army commander, General Byng and by Haig himself. Holmes was executed at the rifle range at Labeuvriere at 5.20 am on 22 April. His body is buried in the Chocques Military Cemetery.

Albert Holmes was clearly a troubled man and his service record was demonstrably poor in comparison to both John Sloane and George Hughes. Whether any of these three men deserved to die in the way they did will always be a matter of controversy and disagreement, where strong arguments on both sides can be made. In all of these three cases, however, it is clear that the pressures created by the prevailing conditions finally proved too much for each of them. But it wasn't always so. Hughes and Holmes had fought before and both had been wounded. It could not be argued that these two soldiers had not been prepared to put themselves at risk. They had. John Sloane's case was in this respect different. He spent only a few days at the front before his nerves deserted him. In fact he had never been in harm's way at all. He had never fired his weapon in anger.

Each of these cases reveal differences too in the way senior commanders viewed the death penalty and when it was necessary. It is surprising to see these disagreements emerge in the case of Albert Holmes – the most 'obvious' case of desertion. Yet the evidence of George Hughes's shattered nerves, revealed not in evidence at the trial, where it must have been evident from his demeanour that there was clearly something wrong, but in later written comments by his battalion commanding officer, was discounted. In each of these cases there are inconsistencies and contradictions. Should we surprised by this? Probably not. Do these inconsistencies in attitudes and approach undermine the entire process of administering military law? Again, probably not. It is reasonable to expect that senior officers might disagree occasionally about how an individual prisoner should be treated. That is normal in any appeal or oversight process. The final decision was the sole responsibility of the commander in chief, and he was entitled to take all of the available comments into account.

There is no reason to assume that these three cases were anything other than typical of the hundreds of others tried by Field General Courts Martial during the war. These tribunals were there to impose military law as it stood at the time in the circumstances that prevailed then. In all three of these cases, there was clear and unequivocal evidence that could be legitimately used to support a conviction of desertion. The real question is whether the sanction itself was appropriate in each of these cases. Here it is likely that the controversy will continue.

But one thing is at least clear and beyond dispute. These men were, in every sense of the word, victims of the war. We might all have different views about their behaviour. Some might be prepared to forgive, some might not. Some can equate their deaths with those who died in action, others cannot. Some will argue that, even though they had offended, they were not responsible for their actions. In two of the three cases – Sloane and Holmes – there was no fighting taking place in the area at the time the offences were committed. It is hard to argue that the actions of these two soldiers were therefore directly attributable to the shock and fear that exposure to gun fire could naturally generate. After all, Sloane had never undergone such an experience in the first place. He must, however, have dreaded the prospect of fighting. And preparations for the forthcoming Battle of the Somme would have been visible all around him. The 'Big Push' was about to start. It was something he could not bring himself to face.

In contrast, Holmes had already experienced the horrors and the reality of it all. He had clearly had enough. Hughes deserted at the height of the fighting on the Somme, when the sound and fury of the battle must have been ringing in his ears. Perhaps fear was the common denominator in all of these cases. And it is this same emotion that can both drive soldiers forward into action as well as propel them away from it.

In relation to the tribunals, there is no suggestion that anything other than the proper procedure was employed, both in relation to gathering evidence and in providing a proper opportunity for the accused to rebut the charges against him. So is there any real purpose in trying to apportion blame? Are we really in any position now to pass a moral judgement on either the behaviour of these men or on the system that resulted in them being shot at dawn, disgraced in the eyes of their comrades and country? On this fundamental question, nearly 100 years later, the jury is still out.

Further Reading

The following works cover issues surrounding the sentencing to death of soldiers at courts martial in the First World War.

Anthony Babington, *For the Sake of Example* (Leo Cooper, 1983)
Cathryn Corns and John Hughes-Wilson, *Blindfold and Alone* (Cassell, 2001)
William Moore, *The Thin Yellow Line* (Leo Cooper, 1974)
Gerard Oram, *Death Sentences Passed by Military Courts of the British Army, 1914–1924* (Francis Boutle Publishers, 2005)
Julian Putkowski and Julian Sykes, *Shot at Dawn* (Leo Cooper, 1989)

Index